Better Performance. The empirical insights on how purpose, social support, and virtue affect performance and engagement were well received. How do we know the ideas from *Better Human, Better Performance* created a resilient culture despite pressure and uncertainty? In addition to enriching the culture we built to recruit and retain nearly 1,200 people to the Cleveland Clinic London team, we were also proud to have achieved engagement scores that were among the highest in the clinic's system of 70,000 caregivers.

—Brian Donley, Chief Executive Officer, Cleveland Clinic London

A company's financial value is measured by the balance sheet. A company's true value is in its team members, its culture, and how well its people perform together every day. *Better Humans, Better Performance* is a great tool for building on that value and developing happier, fulfilled people who will dedicate themselves to better performance every day.

—Parker Chief Financial Officers Jon Marten, 2010 to 2017, Cathy Suever, 2018 to 2021, and Todd Leombruno, started 2021

Decades of work with elite performers across domains as diverse as sports, art, business, special military operations, nonprofits, divinity, medicine, and many others have taught us this: some of the most powerful performance determinants have to do with an individual's character as defined by virtue, regardless of pure talent. While people can succeed without practicing virtue, their performance is ultimately less than optimal. More importantly in team environments, their impact on others will detract rather than enhance a high-performing team culture. The research and tools detailed in this book unite people of every age, background, discipline, and identity through a shared passion to become better humans and better performers.

—Andy Walshe, PhD, Chief Executive Officer and founding member, Liminal Collective

As we build our teams and our organization, the San Antonio Spurs rely on values as our first filter for selecting players, coaches, and staff. Basketball is a global sport. Our program has engaged players, coaches, and staff from more than 20 countries around the world.

Shared values including character provide alignment to build elite teams. Through character and diversity, the Spurs compete by recognizing our obligations to each other as people, not just as performers. *Better Humans, Better Performance* makes clear through research and stories how performance starts with relationships—the order matters. We learn that virtue is the best relationship technology ever invented. Virtue is the language of excellence that cuts across time and borders. To create the high-performing organization of the future, it is powerful to look backward to this ancient wisdom. Character defined as virtue has a profound performance impact on culture, teamwork, resiliency, coaching, families, innovation, diversity, and more. *Better Humans, Better Performance* captures why the word *compete* means "strive together."

—R. C. Buford, Chief Executive Officer,
Spurs Sports and Entertainment

The world of professional sports revolves around individual, team, and organizational performance. In recent years, we have been charged with delivering performance in an increasingly complex environment exacerbated by a once-in-a-century pandemic and a once-in-a-generation labor disruption. In complex environments like this, it is impossible to plan our way forward and follow a predetermined script. Instead, we rely on guiding principles and values to chart our future. By spotlighting the classical virtues and clearly making the connection between better people and better performance, the authors have given us a time-tested and researched-based framework to rely upon in those moments when the path seems unclear and the choices seem impossible. I am grateful for the time and energy the authors devoted to such important work and their commitment to share their learned wisdom and knowledge with others as we seek to better ourselves and the performance we aspire to achieve. The ideas detailed in *Better Humans, Better Performance* made a strong culture founded on teamwork even stronger.

—Chris Antonetti, President of Baseball
Operations for the Cleveland Guardians

BETTER
HUMANS,
BETTER
PERFORMANCE

BETTER
HUMANS,
BETTER
PERFORMANCE

*Driving Leadership, Teamwork, and
Culture with **Intentionality***

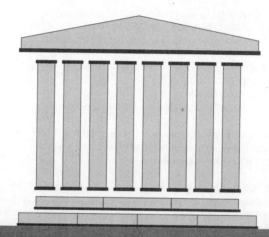

PETER REA, PhD
JAMES K. STOLLER, MD, MS • ALAN KOLP, PhD

NEW YORK CHICAGO SAN FRANCISCO ATHENS LONDON
MADRID MEXICO CITY MILAN NEW DELHI
SINGAPORE SYDNEY TORONTO

1 2 3 4 5 6 7 8 9   LCR   27 26 25 24 23 22

ISBN 978-1-264-27815-2
MHID   1-264-27815-2

e-ISBN 978-1-264-27816-9
e-MHID   1-264-27816-0

Library of Congress Cataloging-in-Publication Data

Names: Rea, PhD, Peter J., author. | Stoller, MD, MS, James K., author. | Kolp, PhD, Alan, author.
Title: Better humans, better performance : driving leadership, teamwork, and culture with intentionality / Peter Rea, PhD, James K. Stoller, MD, MS, Alan Kolp, PhD.
Description: New York : McGraw Hill, [2022] | Includes bibliographical references.
Identifiers: LCCN 2022030652 (print) | LCCN 2022030653 (ebook) | ISBN 9781264278152 (hardback) | ISBN 9781264278169 (ebook)
Subjects: LCSH: Corporate culture. | Virtue. | Organizational behavior. | Leadership. | Performance.
Classification: LCC HD58.7 .R3793 2022 (print) | LCC HD58.7 (ebook) | DDC 306.3—dc23/eng/20220805
LC record available at https://lccn.loc.gov/2022030652
LC ebook record available at https://lccn.loc.gov/2022030653

McGraw Hill books are available at special quantity discounts to use as premiums and sales promotions or for use in corporate training programs. To contact a representative, please visit the Contact Us pages at www.mhprofessional.com.

McGraw Hill is committed to making our products accessible to all learners. To learn more about the available support and accommodations we offer, please contact us at accessibility@mheducation.com. We also participate in the Access Text Network (www.accesstext.org), and ATN members may submit requests through ATN.

We dedicate this book to Tanya Malone,

the most creative CPA we have ever met.

As the manager of ethics and integrity at Parker,

her content expertise and artistic insights are unmatched.

Her skill helping leaders and teams practice virtue has

supported the success of others for years.

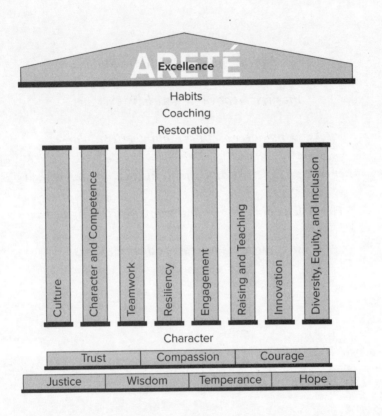

CONTENTS

PREFACE:
HOW DO WE GET GREAT PERFORMANCE?   ix

ACKNOWLEDGMENTS   xv

1   BETTER HUMANS, BETTER PERFORMANCE   1

2   THE SEVEN CLASSICAL VIRTUES   21

3   ORGANIZATIONAL CULTURE   47

4   HIRE FOR CHARACTER, TRAIN FOR COMPETENCE   59

5   TEAMWORK   75

6   RESILIENCE   103

7   ENGAGEMENT   125

8   RAISING AND TEACHING BETTER HUMANS,
BY JULIE REA   145

9   DRIVING INNOVATION   161

10   CREATING DIVERSITY, EQUITY, AND INCLUSION   185

11   RESTORING CULTURES   207

12   COACHING   217

13   FORMING GOOD HABITS   233

14   THE VALUE OF VIRTUE   251

EPILOGUE   265

NOTES   271

INDEX   287

PREFACE

HOW DO WE GET GREAT PERFORMANCE?

*Does the person of high competence and low character
get a pass? Does the person of high character with
threshold competence get a chance?*

How an organization's leaders answer those questions reveals
how they think great performance can be achieved.

The evidence that we will present in this book is that great
performance happens by getting better at "who we are" by practicing virtue to get better at "what we do." The concept is captured in the
book title—better humans, better performance. And how do we get
better at who we are? The time-honored solution to this question is
that we get better at who we are when we practice the seven classical
virtues: trust, compassion, courage, justice, wisdom, temperance, and
hope.

Throughout the book, whenever we use the word *virtue* or *virtues*, we mean these seven classical virtues. For the ancient Greeks,
the word *areté* translated as "virtue." *Areté* means "excellence" of any
kind, such as the fitness of an athlete, the skill of a soldier, the healing abilities of a physician, the teaching and research of a scholar, and
the design insights of an engineer, as well as the ability of anyone to be
wise, brave, and caring. Virtue is the act of living up to our potential,
thus enabling us to flourish.

When flourishing and living up to our potential are the goals, virtue is the name of the game. The hard part is practicing virtue when it is most needed, during periods of instability. In 1987, the term VUCA (*volatile, uncertain, complex, and ambiguous*) was coined by the US Army War College.[1] Interestingly, the phrase was created during a time of relative stability between the fall of the Berlin Wall and before the terrorist attacks on September 11.

For that reason, VUCA may misrepresent our time as more volatile than periods such as World War I, the Great Depression, World War II, or the Cuban Missile Crisis. That said, at the time this book was written there was no shortage of VUCA situations such as the world being besieged by the COVID-19 pandemic, social injustice issues, climate change, and the Russian assault on Ukraine. In whatever time we live, we would like to drive disruption down to zero even though the world doesn't offer that option. So, our best response to disruption is learning to normalize discomfort. When we do so, we better adapt to disruption, pressure, stress, and adversity. We contend that virtue helps vaccinate us to normalize discomfort so that we can perform well even during periods of disruption.

Virtue has guided high performance in humans during adverse conditions for 3,000 years at least, yet somehow virtue must be rediscovered in every age.

The wisdom of the ages makes clear that priority matters. Character defined by the seven classical virtues comes first. Performance follows. Performance is a collateral benefit of practicing virtue intentionally and wisely.

We readily acknowledge that practicing virtue in an uncertain world where some want to win at all costs and where narcissism sometimes runs amuck is anything but easy. Making lives better for others might feel sentimental when we are competing for our slice of the pie. Yet, the practice of virtue can be more serviceable to our self-interest than our skeptical minds might realize. At least in the long term, the pursuit of virtue is both strategically smart and a better way to live.

WHOM DOES THE BOOK HOPE TO SUPPORT?

Humans. Humans who want to become better people and better performers, like for-profit and nonprofit leaders, physicians, engineers, athletes, coaches, teachers, and soldiers—in short, everyone including families. Humans already strive to perform at a high level and recognize the importance of character. Yet too few understand that virtue is a performance amplifier. Too many lack insight into how the language and practice of virtue tighten the band of reliable performance, especially when things go sideways with VUCA events.

Our aspiration is to make this research accessible to any person interested in becoming better at who they are so that they can become better at what they do—in school, work, and life. The concepts in this book are relevant to the young and old alike, regardless of status, income, or education. The powerful impact of character on performance is generalizable across geography, race, and context—in business, academia, and healthcare and in families, teams, and organizations. Integrating human performance research with the practice of virtue is what we hope to democratize.

HOW CAN THIS BOOK BE READ?

The virtues undergird and lead to high performance, as depicted in Figure P.1.

Together the virtues make up character, which you can see is the floor to support all the pillars that are needed for performance. These pillars include culture; teamwork; coaching; habits; resiliency; diversity, equity and inclusion; and family. Each of these pillars will be developed in separate chapters, which can be read in any order. These various pillars are the key to the "better performance" part of the book title.

Because the virtues are underneath it all, people often don't know how character is formed nor how to enhance character development. While virtue is good in and of itself, virtue also offers four important performance benefits:

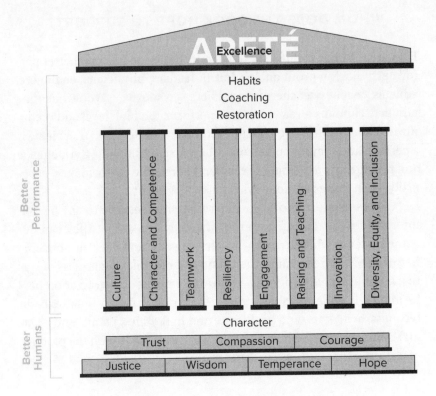

Figure P.1 The Virtues Undergird and Lead to High Performance

1. Virtue provides a common language for leaders, teams, and organizations to understand what it means to excel.
2. Virtue is a performance amplifier for competence.
3. Virtue is malleable, and it is available to everyone.
4. Virtue leads to more reliable performance under pressure.

This book is organized so that each of the chapters regarding applications to better performance (Chapters 3 onward) has a similar cadence. Each begins with stories or case studies exemplifying how the virtues inform leadership, teams, and cultures. Following the stories are discussions of the supportive evidence, coming from multiple sectors, including those in which the authors work—technology-manufacturing, healthcare, and academia. Lastly, tools are woven into the chapter or included at the end, along with key takeaways.

IS THIS A BOOK ABOUT SUCCESS
AND HUMAN PERFORMANCE?

Yes, but success is a by-product of getting better at "who we are" through the practice of virtue. For many of us, our ultimate concern is external achievement. There is nothing wrong with getting ahead. Still, be mindful that the pursuit of getting ahead can bring disorder to our priorities. This disorder is captured insightfully with what David Brooks called the "résumé virtues" and the "eulogy virtues."[2] Résumé virtues reflect the skills we bring to the marketplace. Eulogy virtues, such as compassion and courage, are what we hope people will say about us at our funeral. We know that eulogy virtues are more important than résumé virtues. However, most of us are more skilled in building an external career than in building an internal core of character.

Virtue-based leaders are best developed by the company they keep and by the culture in which they operate. When personal and professional relationships are defined by virtue, we feel safe. And when we feel safe, we are prepared to act with courage, to lead change, and to innovate. Ultimately, virtue is internally developed and requires practice. What we can't see leads to success that we can see. As Plutarch pointed out over 2,000 years ago, "What we achieve inwardly will change outer reality."[3]

ACKNOWLEDGMENTS

n 2019, the vision for this book happened at about 10,000 feet on the Wind River Reservation in Wyoming. During a National Outdoor Leadership School Expedition, a weeklong conversation about human performance and character created a friendship with our Aussie mate Andy Walshe. Andy has worked with elite performers from every conceivable sector including athletics, military, nonprofits, and business. His research and experience have demonstrated that when people become better at who they are, they get better at what they do. We agree, and so does Andy, that there is no better way to get better at who you are than to practice virtue.

We are indebted to three organizations that formed, piloted, and scaled the practice of virtue: Parker Hannifin, the Cleveland Clinic, and Baldwin Wallace University. Parker is a Fortune 250 Company, with sales of about $17 billion, composed of nearly 60,000 teammates located in 50 nations. Since 1917, Parker has practiced ethical leadership when its founder, Arthur Parker, built the company on the principle of "fair dealings." In 2012, Parker integrated the language and research of virtue into its continuous improvement culture. The company's financial team provides enterprisewide leadership for the practice of virtue. Chief Financial Officers Jon Marten (2010 to 2017), Cathy Suever (2018 to 2021), and Todd Leombruno, who became CFO in 2021, all concluded that the value investors see on financial statements is made possible by the value created by teammates who trust and care for each other. We are grateful for the ongoing support of Parker's Chief Executive Officer, Tom Williams, and Vice Chair and President, Lee Banks, who embody the ideas defined in this book. Every initiative depends on key leaders to pilot and scale ideas that drive results in the right way. Our key sponsors included Jenny Parmentier, Chief Operating Officer, and Andy Ross, Group President Connectors Group, as well as Kevin Ruffer and Stephen Shearon, Group Human Resource Executives. From the corner office to the production floor, thousands of Parker leaders have taught us how to practice virtue even against imposing headwinds.

The Cleveland Clinic provides a distinctive model of medicine that features a global presence, an extraordinary organizational culture, and deep clinical, scientific, and educational expertise. Dr. Brian Donley, Chief Executive Officer at the new Cleveland Clinic London, hired for character and trained for competence to withstand the pressures of Brexit, a global pandemic, and global supply chain disruptions.

The Baldwin Wallace University Center for Innovation and Growth represents the birthplace for *Better Humans, Better Performance*. Since 2006, students and faculty have worked with business and nonprofit leaders to address pressing innovation challenges by delivering growth projects guided by virtue. President Emeritus Dick Durst and President Robert Helmer supported coauthor Alan Kolp and Lacey Kogelnik, Director of Corporate and Organizational Engagement, to extend the practice of virtue to varsity athletic programs. "Sports teaches character" is more than a tagline for Baldwin Wallace athletes.

When it comes to athletics, we appreciate a special relationship with the Cleveland Guardians professional baseball team. We routinely share insights and best practices with Guardian leaders Chris Antonetti, Mike Chernoff, Jay Hennessey, and Josh Gibson. We have learned how character is a performance amplifier and competitive advantage. No one claims victory when it comes to the practice of virtue. Nevertheless, when we nudge a bit closer to this ideal, we become a bit more reliable when pressure inevitably rises.

We are grateful for McGraw Hill editing and publishing this book. McGraw Hill's editorial team led by Jonathan Sperling and Donya Dickerson have provided sound editorial guidance.

Our families have supported us despite our many faults, and they strengthened the content in these pages. Peter's wife, Julie, played a critical role in editing the book including writing a chapter on character applied to families. The conduct of Peter's sons, Scott and David, and daughters-in-law, Lisa and Hannah, provides loads of optimism for the next generation of leaders. Our grandson, Scottie, is in good hands with his parents, Scott and Lisa.

Jamie's best humans are his family and many dear friends, including Peter and Alan. They make him better. Terry, his wife, has heroically modeled the virtues in supporting him and his son, Jake; daughter-in-law, Abigail; and grandson, Willy, bring the virtues to life and anchor their importance for the world. They are the legacy of this work.

Alan's wife, Letitia, and daughters, Felicity and Christina, continue to be supportive of another writing project. And his four grandkids, Sienna, Logan, Eva, and Aiden, evidence the curiosity of young ones who are excited their names might appear in a real book! It is the hope for all the grandkids and young ones around the world that we offer a way to be a better human being.

We appreciate all that we have learned from elite performers such as soldiers, athletes, and astronauts. They have taught us that under pressure, we default to our training. We are impressed with senior leaders, physicians, engineers, financial experts, professors, and coaches who look out for the interests of others as if their interests were their own, often with limited training. We are in awe of production workers, administrative assistants, students, and truck drivers who handle adversity and pressure with grace and grit with no training.

We are so fortunate for the thousands of people who have shared their insights with us about character. We have learned that people want permission to practice virtue especially when things go sideways. We are grateful for all the people who taught us to become better at who we are by practicing virtue to become better at what we do. Imagine if more of us had training to do this by design rather than by chance.

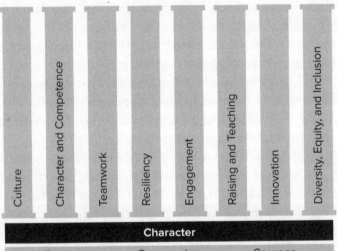

BETTER HUMANS,
BETTER PERFORMANCE

We can't always control what happens.
We can always control our response.

The ideas in this book were influenced by a dinner and a lunch. The dinner was with Anthony Ray Hinton, who was sentenced to the death penalty and was imprisoned for 30 years for a crime he did not commit. The lunch was with Edie Eger, a Holocaust survivor. Two stories of unimaginable cruelty that paradoxically inspire hope rather than despair. Two stories about becoming better humans and performing better that are relevant for any thoughtful leader, team, or family.

EDWINS, the name of the restaurant where Mr. Hinton shared his story,[1] is one of America's most successful social enterprises. And it's a place that illustrates the key ideas in this book. EDWINS (which stands for "Education Wins") gives formerly incarcerated adults culinary and hospitality skills while providing the necessary support to transition to civilian life successfully.[2] In 2007, EDWINS was founded as an expensive French restaurant. Since its founding, it has added a bakery, butcher shop, apartments, and basketball courts. During the pandemic, the restaurant pivoted within days to deliver takeout food for shut-in customers rather than close as many restaurants did.

EDWINS has achieved remarkable business success and growth by embracing people whom Bryan Stephenson calls, "the poor, the disfavored, the accused, the incarcerated and the condemned."[3] The mission of EDWINS is based on a simple principle: everyone deserves a second chance, including those who have served their time. This doesn't mean that EDWINS takes it easy on people. In fact, excellence in culinary skill, hospitality, and teamwork is expected. While people are held accountable for results, they also receive rent-free places to live, legal support, and healthcare to combat the challenges of a criminal record, poverty, and transportation instability.

EDWINS embodies the principle that what happens to people outside of work hugely affects how well they perform. So, EDWINS' business case is that investing in people to provide stability allows them to perform better in the workplace. Similarly, focusing on family and life issues is not just a nice thing to do. It is critical to achieving performance excellence in life and in the workplace. For most people, any anger or fear they feel at home and in their families will contribute to fractured teams at work and in society. All teams benefit from fewer fractures that are fueled by anger and fear, and they will benefit from more repair mended by goodwill and gratitude. The other business case for EDWINS, of course, is that by preventing recidivism of former convicts, the high costs to society of supporting the imprisoned are avoided.

EDWINS isn't a story about perfect people. It is a story about imperfect people becoming better humans and performing better, which is also what you need where you work. Customers win by receiving award-winning French cuisine. Graduates win by acquiring hospitality skills that are in high demand so they can change the trajectory of their lives. Society wins because EDWINS graduates pay taxes rather than costing taxpayers about $40,000 a year to be imprisoned.[4]

How successful is EDWINS in living up to its mission of giving people a second chance? About 95 percent have jobs waiting for them, and only 1 percent of their graduates return to prison compared to the 46 percent recidivism rate nationally.[5] The secret sauce isn't the chestnut fennel soup.[6] The key ingredient is helping people become better at who they are to become better at what they do.

This is a theme that reappears throughout this book. Better humans build the resilient muscles needed by all leaders, teams, and families to bounce back from setbacks. Mild setbacks don't do justice to the intentional cruelty experienced by Mr. Hinton and Edie. Thankfully, few of us face that level of injustice, and comparing our plight with their trauma isn't the point. The point is that no leader, team, or family goes through life unscathed. If we can avoid trouble, we should. However, when our backs are against the wall, Mr. Hinton and Edie offer lessons on how to handle painful events with more grace and grit.

We start with Mr. Hinton, whose only crime was being Black and lacking funds to afford legal representation to prevent prosecutors and police from hiding evidence that would have exonerated him. For 28 years, Mr. Hinton lived in a death row cell the size of a bathroom, which was 33 feet from where 53 men and 1 woman were electrocuted. After an inmate was electrocuted, the smell lingered in the air for several days.

For three years, Mr. Hinton refused to speak to guards or prisoners. He was self-absorbed with his innocence, holding tightly to the hope that the truth would finally set him free. One day, after an electrocution, a person who lived on the cell block near Mr. Hinton started to sob uncontrollably. Mr. Hinton hoped he would shut up since he was consumed by grief for not having been with his own sick mother. Overwhelmed, Mr. Hinton started crying. Empathy pulled him out of his grief and pushed him toward the scared prisoner whose name he didn't know. He asked his first question to a prisoner in three years: "Hey, you OK?" The question started a conversation. Mr. Hinton shared that his mother was the love of his life and that he had just learned she had died. The man responded that he was sorry. Then other unseen prisoners spoke up: "Sorry for your loss." For a brief moment, strangers replaced cruelty with kindness.

Mr. Hinton reflected on what his mother had taught him—treat everyone with respect—and she meant everyone. So, Mr. Hinton started a remarkable path to forgiveness. "I was on death row, but not by my choice. I had made the choice to spend the last three years thinking about killing McGregor [the prosecutor] and thinking about killing myself. Despair was a choice. Hatred was a choice. Anger was a choice. Hope was a choice. Faith was a choice. And more than anything else, love was a choice. Compassion also was a choice."

Mr. Hinton became the person to whom prisoners and guards went for advice. He made a family with the people who were in front of him—the innocent and the guilty; the harmless and the dangerous. He even taught a former KKK member how to discuss books with African Americans. Death row inmates learned that the more they got to know individuals' stories, the more they could forgive those individuals, at least a little bit, for what they had done. And they learned that forgiveness offered a new future.

In 2014, the US Supreme Court unanimously overturned Mr. Hinton's conviction on appeal. This outcome would not have happened without the competent and determined representation of Bryan Stephenson, founder of the Equal Justice Initiative. The Supreme Court ruled that Mr. Hinton's original defense lawyer was "constitutionally deficient." This led the state of Alabama to drop all charges against Mr. Hinton. As Mr. Hinton walked away after three decades of injustice, a guard told him, "You will be back." Mr. Hinton knew the comment was a lie, just like his conviction. He told the guard, "Watch and see."

The most incredible part of Mr. Hinton's story is how he transcended cruelty with compassion: "What I learned about forgiveness is that it's not about the other person. It's about me. I didn't forgive those people who did this to me because they asked me to or because they called me or wrote me. I didn't forgive them so that they could sleep good at night. I forgave them, so *I* could sleep good at night." Astonishingly, Mr. Hinton isn't bitter despite being treated with cruel injustice. He says, "Bitterness kills the soul. I've seen hate at its worst. How would hate benefit me?"[7]

Now for the lunch with Edie.[8] A retired Navy SEAL had read the book *The Choice*, and he learned that the author lived in San Diego.[9] He arranged for a small group to have lunch with the author, a Holocaust survivor named Dr. Edith Eger. She asked us to call her Edie.

In 1944, Edie and her mother and sister, Magda, were forced into a cattle car destined for the killing camp of Auschwitz where 1.3

million people were enslaved and 1.1 million were murdered.[10] Facing the three women as they exited the train was a cynical lie that had been posted to reassure the weary: *"Arbeit macht frei"* ("Work sets you free") hung over the entrance of the camp. Hungry, exhausted, and scared, the mother and daughters were herded into a stockyard to be inspected by the sadistic Nazi physician Joseph Mengele. He asked Edie whether the eldest of the three women was her mother. Edie said yes. Mengele then wagged his finger toward the gas chamber for the mother. He wagged his finger to the sign "Work sets you free" for the two sisters, with no mention that beatings, hard labor, and malnutrition came next. The following day, the younger daughter asked a guard where her mother was. The guard pointed to ash pouring out of a chimney, saying, "That's your mother."

At our lunch, Edie told us that the Nazis made clear that she was subhuman and a cancer on society. They told her that the only good that could come of her was to leave as a corpse. After telling us this, she punched the air to make clear what she thought of Nazi inhumanity: "Even at Auschwitz, I refused to be a victim!" Edie made a distinction between victimhood and victimization. Victimhood occurs when a terrible mistreatment or misfortune happens to us. Victimization occurs when we internalize that event and become a victim. Edie's point was that, while we cannot control our fate, we can always control our response, even in a Nazi death factory.

A couple of years after her release, Edie had recovered physically from the wounds inflicted by the concentration camp. However, she said the worst prison was not the one the Nazis put her in. It was the one she built for herself. Her point was that we can be psychologically chained to our past without realizing that the key is in our pocket. Viktor Frankl, who also survived a Nazi death camp and wrote poignantly about the experience, helped liberate her mentally. Frankl wrote *Man's Search for Meaning*, which chronicled his experiences at the hands of the Nazis and went on to say that true freedom is achieved in how we respond to our circumstances since we often cannot control those circumstances. Edie said, "Viktor Frankl gave me permission not to hide anymore. He helped me find words for my experience. He helped me to cope with my pain."[11] Edie credited Frankl for helping her find a purpose for her suffering.

Edie earned a PhD in psychotherapy so she could liberate others from victimhood. She concluded our lunch by encouraging us to foster strong relationships in which we give and receive support, to live by our highest moral standards, to view adversity as an opportunity to develop wisdom, and to replace victimhood with taking responsibility for our own growth. She taught us how courage, hope, and the other virtues lead to resilience.[12]

Hearing Mr. Hinton's and Edie's stories may make all of our troubles seem small by comparison, although Edie would be the first to say that there is no contest when it comes to trauma. When treated with intentional cruelty, we expect people to respond with fear, anger, doubt, and the desire to curl up in on themselves. That makes sense. What is harder to wrap our head around is how Mr. Hinton and Edie became better instead of bitter. Slowly, very slowly over years, they both became better humans, and then both began to perform better as authors, speakers, and humans. Mr. Hinton and Edie learned to normalize discomfort. Their resilience was strengthened by people who cared about them. Most importantly, their experiences taught them that character is a skill that, like any skill, can be learned.

BETTER HUMANS

The premise of this book, which is borne out by robust evidence from diverse sectors around the globe, is that we get great performance when we are better humans. A metaphor comes to mind here. The seven classical virtues are like the roots of a tree. When a tree has strong roots—as when cultures are grounded in the virtues—the tree and the leader, team, organization, and family are firmly grounded and will thrive, even in the face of gale-force winds, drought, or trauma. But the roots of the tree are below the surface. They are hidden while their effect—a healthy tree—is in full view. In a similar vein, the virtues are hidden while their effects on a person's behavior are in full view.

Fortunately, evidence-based habits to practice virtue are backed by academic and field research with businesses as well as organizations in sectors like healthcare, academia, professional and college sports,

NASA, and the military. This research has shown that leaders defined by high competence and low character cannot deliver sustainable results. They might deliver results when the market is in their favor, but this success won't be lasting, and the reputational risk to the organization isn't worth it. Likewise, leaders with high character and low competence cannot deliver sustainable results. The well-intentioned incompetent can do plenty of damage. However, part of being a person of character is not being satisfied until a reasonable degree of competence is achieved.

Despite the evidence that character increases performance, most leadership models focus on competence, ignoring character or limiting its impact to signage on the hallway walls. In contrast, leadership models at organizations like the US military service academies view virtue as the key to developing the competence and commitment necessary to build and lead resilient teams that can succeed under any conditions.

To be clear, virtue isn't a self-improvement plan. It is a way to live.

Virtue is also aspirational. No individual or culture is completely virtuous, nor is any individual or culture completely devoid of virtue. We all flunk practicing virtue perfectly, making it wise to practice virtue with humility. An unpretentious approach enables us to create a culture where we learn from mistakes rather than gain skill assigning blame.

Character-based leaders do want to win, just not at all costs. They protect their organization's reputation and financial strength by bringing value to the people they serve. They learn to view pressure as a privilege, an opportunity to make life better for others.

Twenty-five hundred years ago, Aristotle defined a "first principle" as the first basis by which a thing is known. The first principle is to improve the lives of others, which in turn improves our life. Applied to our professional life, when we cultivate virtue in ourselves and others, we not only flourish as a leader, physician, athlete, educator, engineer, or soldier, we also flourish as a human. Applied to organizations and teams, when we cultivate virtue, engagement goes up. Applied to our personal life, when we cultivate virtue, we deepen and strengthen relationships in our family and among our friends.

However, the benefits of flourishing, engaging, and caring relationships come with the price of struggle and blunders. The ancient Greeks were clear that excellence is not solely affected by the hand that is dealt but by how that hand is played. In fact, a life of relative struggle and tension helps us live up to our potential far more than an untested life full of comfort and pleasure. The affluent and the disadvantaged can both miss this essential insight, albeit for different reasons. The affluent might be insulated from adversity, which reduces their ability to excel in uncertain or difficult circumstances. Affluence can create a sense of superiority that can make people feel entitled and be self-absorbed. On the other hand, the disadvantaged face no end of adversity, with little support to help turn obstacles into character-enhancing triumphs.

Feeling either entitled if you are affluent or aggrieved if you are disadvantaged can lead to fragility in a world that demands resilience.

Since we are all susceptible to feeling entitled or aggrieved, what do we do? When we select a well-worn path to practice virtue, we will know how to respond to prosperity—of those to whom much has been given, much is expected. When injustice is directed at us or others, we move toward the kind of trouble former Congress member and civil rights leader John Lewis advocated: "Ordinary people with extraordinary vision can redeem the soul of America by getting in what I call good trouble, necessary trouble."[13]

It's curious to think that we need research to prove that a life governed by trust, compassion, courage, wisdom, and hope would be vastly superior to a life defined by their absence—distrust, callousness, cowardice, foolishness, and despair. That said, if you remain skeptical, data show that virtue significantly increases engagement. For example, at Parker, a Fortune 250 company, leaders completed seminars on the virtues and were then coached for three months afterward to integrate those virtues into their operations. At each facility, 9 to 12 months after the seminars, engagement scores increased by 10 to 20 percent. Additional research on engagement will be presented in Chapter 7.

Lastly, these seven virtues cross social, religious, and cultural divides. The research for this book spans multiple continents. Despite obvious cultural differences, North American, European, Middle Eastern, Asian, and African leaders with whom we have worked all know that virtue consistently unites rather than divides people.

The challenge is creating a culture where the practice of virtue becomes a norm, although we know we won't be perfectly virtuous. When we even tilt toward virtue a bit more, engagement increases. But there is a catch. We don't offer quick fixes. Creating a culture of excellence takes time and focused intention.

JACKASS ATTACHED TO ANGEL WINGS

Rumi, a thirteenth-century poet, gives us an image that affirms an insight offered by Mr. Hinton: "Nobody lives life perfectly." Rumi said, "Each one of us is a jackass, with wings of angels tacked on."[14] Rumi's point is that people are a complex blend of unwise—the jackass—and wise—the angel. He advises us to avoid being an ass and/or to stop being a stubborn mule. When we are governed by our lower mule impulses, we crawl. When we are governed by our higher angelic nature, we soar.

Let's be clear that virtue is not about a purity code that no one can actually live up to. Virtue is not about being self-righteous. Few have earned the right to measure others with their moral yardstick. Jigoro Kano, the founder of Judo, said, "It's not important to be better than someone else, but to be better than you were yesterday."[15] We are all unfinished business, continually making and remaking ourselves.

The theologian Reinhold Niebuhr captured our dilemma: "Man is his own vexing problem."[16] Niebuhr had hope that the human race could choose service over self. He also cautioned that virtue can easily become vice when we fixate on the shortcomings of others and yet are remarkably forgiving about our own failings. Similarly, physicist Richard Feynman said, "The first principle is that you must not fool yourself and you are the easiest person to fool."[17] In other words, narcissism is an impregnable shield against self-awareness.

Without these insights, we see the jackass in others, and we are blind to the jackass in ourselves.

This is fertile soil for hypocrisy and its close cousin, cynicism. Calling out others for hypocrisy is good sport. In addition, we can be cynical without having to lift a finger to enact any positive change. In a cynical office, the following sign could be placed next to the fitness center: "This department requires no physical fitness program. Everyone gets enough exercise jumping to conclusions, flying off the handle, running down the boss, knifing friends in the back, dodging responsibility, and pushing their luck."

Since cynics have no shortage of examples of when people fall short of virtue, it's not without reason that leaders shy away from calling for the practice of virtue or values. So, when cynicism inevitably kicks in, what do we do? Start by calling out the reality that we are all jackasses attached to angel wings. Invert the discussion from practicing virtue perfectly to how do we help a jackass soar? No one is perfect. Consequently, we have only one option: help people succeed despite their limitations and weaknesses. The only way to practice virtue is humbly. As former heavyweight boxing champion Mike Tyson said, "If you're not humble in this world, then the world will throw humbleness upon you."[18]

BETTER PERFORMANCE

In our age, disruption is around every corner. Globally connected economies, endless technology inventions, pandemics, and war constantly fuel volatility. Most people are not trained to handle the magnitude of change and volatility coming at us. We need to increase the number of people who know how to recover, persist, and even thrive in the face of rapid change. We need wisdom with a capital W.

For insights on how to perform despite volatility, let's consider how Navy SEALs, astronauts, and physicians are trained. Jonny Kim is uniquely qualified to speak about all three experiences because he trained as a SEAL and then went on to become a Harvard-educated physician and then trained to become an astronaut. He believes that over the long run, resilient people outperform the most talented. Excellent performers adapt their behaviors to the needs of others, and teamwork is strengthened under conditions of adversity. In fact, Kim states that adversity is the best way to test a teammate's character to determine whether you want that person on your team.

One of the most critical insights that cut across Kim's experiences as a SEAL, a physician, and an astronaut is a core idea detailed in this book. Pro-social collaborative relationships, defined by trust and care, make up the most important aspect of leadership, teamwork, and performance. The SEALs strive for this outcome by emphasizing suffering, which taught Kim that he could handle more adversity than he ever thought possible.

NASA relies on loads of testing and interviewing, though Kim believes that NASA's best test for collaborative behavior is the National Outdoor Leadership School (NOLS). The goal of NOLS is similar to SEAL training, though its program is far less rigorous and demanding. People have to work together in a wilderness environment to get through challenges together. In a hospital setting, working 80-hour weeks saving people's lives separates those who are other-focused and those who are not. Kim's point is that when you strip people of comfort and see them at their worst, then you learn about their capabilities, character, and willingness to support the team.[19]

While overcoming adversity is admirable, we all don't need to learn how to hold our breath under water for five minutes as SEALs do; or figure out how much g-force we can sustain before we pass out as astronauts do; or care for patients until we are bone-tired as physicians do. However, research backs up Kim's contention that noncognitive skills have a disproportionate impact on performance for all of us.

In 2000, James Heckman won a Nobel Prize in economics by demonstrating that noncognitive skills related to character were better predictors of personal, academic, and professional success than cognitive skills measured by standardized tests. His research refuted the belief that test scores predict life outcomes. Ironically, noncognitive factors contribute to cognitive achievement. Cognitive skills matter, but factors such as motivation, ability to work with others, and self-control matter more. How much more is captured by the "25/75 rule" coined by Mike Matthews, professor of engineering psychology at West Point. Matthews concluded that 100 years of psychological research showed that about 25 percent of the variance in academic and job achievement is explained by cognitive factors. The remaining 75 percent of human performance is explained by noncognitive factors defined by 3Cs: character, challenge, and commitment.

Performance then becomes a by-product of people strengthening their noncognitive skills. These skills have different names in different settings—for example, *soft skills* in business, *social-emotional skills* in education, *character* in the military, *mental toughness* in sports psychology, and *emotional intelligence* in medicine. How motivated we are to learn also influences the impact of noncognitive skills on performance. An interesting study was conducted by Mihaly Csikszentmihalyi, whose focus was on peak performance. He followed a group of gifted high school students from ninth grade to see how many remained gifted through twelfth grade. The kids who persisted in fulfilling their talents enjoyed what they were doing day to day; they had an intrinsic satisfaction in their work. They were motivated to learn. In contrast, the kids who were not intrinsically motivated to excel in school fell short of their potential.[20]

Being motivated to learn is a must-have during conditions of rapid change.

What happens to experts when the rate of change exceeds the rate of learning? They cease being experts.[21]

We can't steer around storms like a global pandemic or recession. We need to plow through storms by building better boats based on noncognitive skills that normalize discomfort, increase cooperation, and commit us to continual learning.

Learning from disruption is so important that those who learn the fastest win on the athletic field, on the battlefield, in business, and in school.

Winning is certainly more fun than losing, though paradoxically, we can learn more from losing than we can learn from achieving what we want. While we cannot control victory or ensure perfection, we can "get better at who we are." Case in point: the San Antonio Spurs basketball team won five championships over a 15-year period. Throughout this period, the Spurs were a talented basketball team, though talent alone doesn't win a championship never mind five championships. Their coach, Greg Popovich, focused on making sure that everyone felt like they belonged, and he focused on excellence rather than winning. In 2022, six of the eight coaches in the NBA basketball playoffs had either played or coached with Popovich.[22] These coaches and former players had learned from their San Antonio Spurs experience that winning becomes a by-product of focusing on relationships.

There is both a remarkable opportunity here as well as an incredible miss. Despite clear evidence that relationships and noncognitive factors affect performance and our ability to thrive during periods of rapid change, most academic and professional development programs still focus solely on developing cognitive abilities. Think about it. Where in academic or professional development programs are noncognitive skills such as virtue practiced under pressure and rapid change? The opportunity is the most powerful noncognitive skill of all, virtue, is available to us all.

COLLAPSING INTO COMFORT

Learning to normalize discomfort is interesting, though not as alluring as leaning into comfort. A life of wealth that comes with a nice home, car, and job acts as a buffer against life's blows. Money certainly matters if you can't afford basic needs, you are loaded down with debt, and/or you lack adequate emergency funds, never mind savings. In that case, you bet money matters.

Yet, after one achieves a certain degree of security and/or material wealth, if we aren't careful, what we own starts to own us. The trappings of comfort can dull the urgency to be courageous, to sacrifice, and to connect with others in pursuit of a common purpose. Comfort can insulate us from struggle and danger, so we no longer need to prove our worthiness or band together to overcome hardship. Comfort can blunt the need to come to grips with who we are and how we want to live. Sebastian Junger stated, "The beauty and the tragedy of the modern world is that it eliminates many situations that require people to demonstrate commitment to the collective good."[23]

Virtue doesn't just focus on avoiding harm. It also asks, what good did we fail to do?

There is a paradox in our lives today. We live in a century when people's material wealth far exceeds what most would have dreamed of 100 years ago. In 1900, most people didn't live past 55. In 2000, most people lived to about 80. Despite material gain and longevity, depression and suicide rates, especially among teenagers, have risen significantly. In 2020, Vivek Murthy was in his second term as the US Surgeon General. He concluded that the greatest health threat facing Americans wasn't heart disease or diabetes. It was loneliness.

Dorothy Day, social advocate for the poor, proposed that loneliness can be resolved only by thinking less about our needs and more about the needs of others. She cautioned that this effort will always come with disappointments and discomfort, "such as life will never be easy or tidy; the work is endless and will always stretch on before us."[24] Yet, when we strengthen untidy relationships, we strengthen performance. And if performance is our aim, then leaning into discomfort will be our means.

PRESSURE: LEANING INTO DISCOMFORT

The New Zealand All Blacks are arguably the best rugby team in the world. They win 77 percent of their games, and they are the only men's team to have won more matches than they have lost against every opponent. Even more remarkably, the team draws players from New Zealand's modest population of 4.6 million. The name of the team refers to the color of the uniforms that are worn with the pride that comes with intense pressure to perform at a world standard. In New Zealand, the All Blacks are expected to win.

You don't have to be a world-class rugby player to feel pressure to perform at school and at work. But what exactly is pressure? Until we can define pressure, we can't improve our performance when we feel it. According to Ceri Evans, a forensic psychiatrist and mental coach for the All Blacks, pressure is defined by high stakes, uncertainty, rapid change, small margins for error, and judgment. Pressure is further increased by the fact that performance comes with expectations and is scrutinized. And, if you fail, there will be consequences. All this obviously leads to discomfort. Some may think that performance increases when we are comfortable. In fact, the opposite is true.[25]

In 1908, Robert Yerkes and John Dodson discovered that performance improved up to the level of "optimal pressure." The relationship between anxiety and performance is graphically displayed as an inverted U-shaped curve (Figure 1.1).[26]

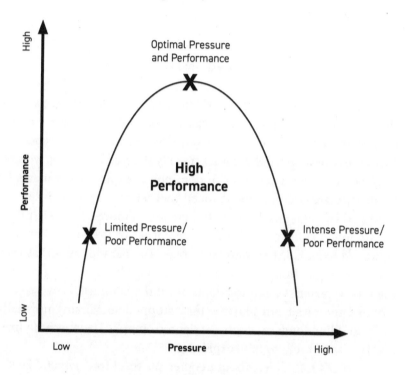

Figure 1.1 The Yerkes-Dodson Law: Inverted-U Model
Source: Adapted from Collins Kariuki, "Retitling Stress: A Look at the Yerkes-Dodson Law," *Biological Sciences News*, February 7, 2021.

The good news is that performance isn't fixed. The more we lean into discomfort, the more pressure we can handle.

At the same time, there is a point where the level of discomfort is too high, causing performance to decline. As an aside, the opposite of anxiety isn't excitement. It's boredom. While we don't have to seek excitement by leaning into discomfort every waking moment, when we are ready to improve our performance, we need to start leaning.

Our stress is low when plans work out. What separates good from great performance is what happens when plans blow up. When pressure and uncertainty soar, performance is compromised. However, we can learn to handle increased pressure and perform at a higher level. Let's repeat this point: improving performance under pressure is learned!

STRESS: LEANING INTO DISCOMFORT

Stress is a close cousin of pressure. In 1936, Hans Selye borrowed the term "stress" from physics to describe the notion that force makes steel stronger and force can make people stronger too, especially when they are supported. He intentionally stressed rats to see whether they would cower in a corner or continue to explore their maze. He found that stressed out rats bounced back when they were licked and groomed by their mothers. Rats that were ignored by their mothers stopped exploring and hid in the corner of the maze. Rats also squeaked to signal they wanted to play. The paradox was that their play was rough, though the rats didn't hurt each other. Play prepared the rats to take risks and to adapt. But if the laboratory investigator stopped the rats from playing, they stopped socializing normally. They could no longer recognize friend from foe. They became fixed and rigid, and they stopped exploring.

So, that's rats. What about people? We react to stress and lack of play more like rats than you might think. The Center on the Developing Child at Harvard University defines three types of stress: positive, tolerable, and toxic. All three types apply to children and to adults:

1. *Positive stress* happens when a kid wants to do well the first day in school or a big kid wants to present well to a board of directors. Positive stress signals to us, "Hey, this is important, so bring your best effort."

2. *Tolerable stress* involves a job loss, a serious health risk, or the loss of a loved one for which we receive the human version of licking and grooming.

3. *Toxic stress* is attached to the same events as tolerable stress. The difference is that the stress becomes toxic because we are neglected when we need support.

Our best buffer against tolerable stress and our best aid to bounce back from toxic stress takes us back to the best pro-social behavior of all: virtue. By "pro-social," we mean behaviors that include the cultivation of trust and compassion. The really important point to make is that even toxic stress can be used to make us better rather than break us when pro-social behavior defined by virtue is present. Tough circumstances do not doom us to a life of misery. Of course, this isn't to suggest that bouncing back from tolerable or toxic risk is easy. It is anything but easy.

Here is the opportunity. We have the science, knowledge, skill, and tools to understand what it takes to flourish and to excel under pressure during periods of volatility, pressure, stress, and adversity.

Here is the challenge. At school, work, and home, too few people are getting the character-building knowledge, skill, and tools that cultivate excellence.

TOOLKIT

How can we learn to best respond to pressure? That question doesn't have a single answer because different levels of pressure are needed under different conditions for different people. An ultra-athlete who jumps off mountains needs extreme stress to improve performance. The rest of us would be glad to improve performance without putting our lives at risk. That said, anyone can learn to reframe a threat through some basic, intentional practices:

1. Get better at who you are to get better at what you do.
   - Practicing virtue makes us more resilient in the face of pressure and uncertainty. Remember, *virtue*, or *areté*, means "excellence."

2. Perceive the problem as a challenge rather than a threat.
   - Learn to face fear through deliberate practice and coaching. This isn't about taking crazy risk. The sweet spot is risk that you perceive as high, though the actual risk is low.
3. Assess rather than assume.
   - We can learn to mitigate the impact of our primitive brain by intentionally kicking into gear our executive function— by pausing, breathing, and thinking before we act.
4. Respond rather than react.
   - Can we remain curious for 120 seconds about why someone is upset so that we can get clear how we want to respond? We don't need to become a Navy SEAL to remain calm under pressure. We can practice responding rather than reacting when someone cuts us off in traffic or when a family member acts grumpy toward us. Though we may still fly off the handle, with practice we can learn to fly off the handle less often.

It is our character that moves us in the direction to improve performance when, not if, our best-laid plans get derailed. When we put these core tools into practice, we get the best out of people despite the pressure they face.[27]

KEY TAKEAWAYS

Mr. Hinton's and Edie's stories illustrate that trauma is often in the eye of the beholder. Other key insights from their stories can be used by the rest of us by design, not chance:

People change people. Mr. Hinton credits his survival to his mother who provided him with clear convictions on how to treat people. Lester, a lifelong friend, and his lawyer, Bryan Stephenson, both stuck by his side when he was in prison and after his release. Edie's sister was the key to her surviving the Nazi death camp. Viktor Frankl was the key to her thriving by teaching her how to replace fear and anger with meaning.

Most people are resilient. Research shows that many of us possess a resilience blind spot in that we misunderstand how humans respond to trauma. Many have heard of post-traumatic stress disorder (PTSD). Thankfully, we have made progress in reducing the stigma associated with seeking PTSD treatment to reduce the impact of its symptoms. At the same time, too few people know about *post-traumatic growth* (PTG). When we focus on only the adverse impacts of trauma, we miss the fact that most people bounce back from setbacks and some even experience PTG. This isn't to deny that PTSD is quite real. It is to say that PTG is quite real too.

People can accept and normalize discomfort. The research on resilience is clear: we are best served to accept and normalize discomfort associated with stress, anxiety, and fear. Stress is our response to an external event; it is not the event itself. This is why there is huge variability in how people handle stress. This is also why there is a huge opportunity to learn how to cope better and even thrive under conditions of stress. Once again, trusting and caring relationships are the best buffers against stress.

Character matters. Character defined as virtue is the most *pro-social* technology ever invented by humans. Being pro-social means we are not solely ego driven. Pro-social behavior is embodied by virtue that acts as a buffer against stress and that strengthens our resilience to bounce back from setbacks. Perhaps the most surprising science about virtue is that virtue is a more powerful performance amplifier than cognitive ability. Once we understand that the word *virtue* means "excellence," we might not be so surprised.

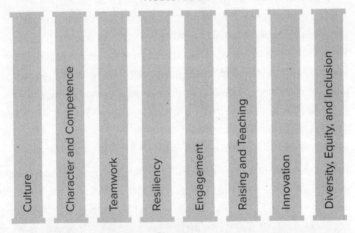

THE SEVEN
CLASSICAL VIRTUES

Virtues are not the stuff of saints and heroes.
They are tools for the art of living.[1]
—KRISTA TIPPETT

HIDDEN IN FULL VIEW:
NEUROLOGY CATCHES UP TO
EVOLUTION AND ARISTOTLE

For 10,000 years, it has been only humans who have learned to thrive in diverse climates that range from the Artic to the Amazon even though we aren't faster and stronger than other species. Physician, sociologist, and Yale professor Nicholas Christakis has asserted that human progress results from cultures defined by components of the "social suite": friendship, cooperation, and social learning. Christakis's research on shipwrecks between 1552 and 1855 illustrates this point. When virtues such as compassion and trust were present among those stranded and their leaders, shipwrecked crews tended to survive. When virtue was absent among the shipwrecked crews, the shipwrecked sailors died.[2]

Our negativity bias can blind us to the point that it is pro-social behavior such as collaboration and teamwork that makes human progress possible. This isn't to suggest that human nature's dark side of tribalism, cruelty, and violence has been eradicated. With the wrong conditions, evolution takes us where we do not want to go.[3] The best that humans can do, no matter how dire or desperate our circumstances, is to practice virtue. In Greek mythology, Areté, the goddess of virtue, embodied what it meant to live right. At a cross-roads, Areté appeared as a young maiden to Heracles. She offered Heracles a choice: glory earned from a life struggling against evil or comfort and pleasure made possible by wealth. Heracles chose struggle over comfort by achieving the moral agility of a hero to move quickly and easily to excel.

In the West about 2,500 years ago, this moral agility was achieved, according to Aristotle, by our habits: "We are what we repeatedly do. Excellence, then, is not an act, but a habit." In the East also about 2,500 years ago, Confucius said, "All people are the same; only their habits differ." That said, it is incredibly demanding to create a habit of virtue in the face of pressure, uncertainty, and injustice.

Fast-forward 23 centuries. In the late nineteenth century, philosopher William James was one of the founders of psychology. This quote from James makes it clear that virtue preceded psychology, not the other way around: "We are spinning our own fates, good or evil, and never to be undone. Every smallest stroke of virtue or of vice leaves its ever so little scar. . . . Nothing we ever do is, in strict scientific literalness, wiped out."[4]

In the twentieth century, psychology focused primarily on mental disorders. Emphasizing ill-being has helped millions to cope with mental health challenges. At the same time, it has become clear that the absence of ill-being does not ensure well-being, any more than the absence of illness ensures fitness. In contrast, Abraham Maslow stressed focusing on positive qualities in people, rather than treating them as a "bag of symptoms." Maslow suggested that the healthiest societies are those in which "virtue pays." He thought that this could start with early education that rewarded kindness and learning for learning's sake, rather than focusing on doing well on external metrics like standardized test results.

In the 1960s, behaviorism ruled the day. The environment was emphasized as the primary cause of our behavior with no attention given to the brain or biology. Then, the pendulum swung to emphasize genetics, which suggested there wasn't much we could do about behavior. In 2004, virtue made a comeback with positive psychology when Martin Seligman and Christopher Peterson comprehensively showed that virtues are considered a positive good by the vast majority of cultures. The essence of positive psychology is that it is the scientific study of life worth living.[5] Once again, we fall forward toward the ancient Greeks.

At the end of the twentieth century, neuroscience caught up to Aristotle, revealing that we become what we practice—again, excellence is not an act, but a habit. Thanks to several decades of research using functional magnetic resonance imaging (fMRI), we now know that the brain is highly malleable. *Neuroplasticity* means that the brain has the ability to change constantly, grow, and remap itself over the course of our life. Neuroplasticity is the brain's ability to modify its connections or rewire itself, which is important for learning, memory, and motor skill coordination. Each time you learn something new and practice it, your brain changes the structure of its neurons or increases the number of synapses between your neurons.

Once upon a time, we thought that one part of the brain was for emotions and the other for reason. Neuroscientist Iain McGilchrist makes clear that this is not true. The difference between the right and left hemispheres is attention. The right side of the brain pays attention to whether someone is friend or foe. It sacrifices accuracy for quickness. The left side pays attention to clarity of thought. It sacrifices quickness for clear thinking.

Once upon a time, we debated the issue of nature versus nurture. We now know that this debate is an outdated choice. The field of *epigenetics* makes clear that our behavior influences our genes and, conversely, our genes influence our behavior. In other words, the relationship between genes and behavior is fluid, not fixed.[6]

Virtue also isn't fixed. Virtue is fluid and can be learned. And virtue is best learned through guided self-discovery. This highlights the brilliance of the Socratic method. Questions uncover insights about virtue and excellence that individuals and teams already know to be true. Virtue as a common language works because the concepts, like compassion, trust, and hope, are deeply engrained in all of us. Sheer ignorance is rarely our moral problem. More likely, our moral challenge is to act in concert with the knowledge that we already have. Our conscience faces an uphill battle against self-deception, immediate gratification, and fear. This is why the practice of virtue requires intentionality, skill, and support. No matter our age, every thought and action changes us ever so slightly in a direction that either elevates us or degrades us. While we can seek good with every action, we are equally capable of cultivating a habit for being self-centered through a series of callous or cruel acts that debase who we are and who we become.

This chapter presents the seven classical virtues that have stood the test of time for as much as three millennia or longer. As the name "classical" would suggest, these virtues are universal, and, therefore, can be applied in any part of the world. This critical benefit means the virtues are our moorings to navigate changing markets and political forces. The virtues were the foundation of a 2,500-year-old leadership model known as Plato's Academy. The mission of Plato's Academy was to develop leaders of character, who would create a "good" society. You were not permitted to graduate from Plato's Academy until you were 50! The conclusion was clear: society dare not put someone in a responsible leadership role before they had had sufficient time to "know thyself" and to demonstrate their ability to put virtue into action.

In real life, we usually do not explicitly unpack how individual virtues inform any human action. But in order to get a sense of each virtue and how it manifests itself in our lives and work, we will break them down and look at each one individually. Having this in mind should make the basic premise of the book understandable— that when we get better at who we are (that is, we practice virtue), we will get better at what we do (that is, we will achieve better performance).

TRUST: TRUST IS EFFICIENT

The best way to find out if you can trust somebody is to trust them.[7]
—ERNEST HEMINGWAY

For each of us, virtue operates along a spectrum. Virtue in general and trust in particular are far more complicated than thinking you have them or you don't. So, the answer to the question of whether you are virtuous or not is yes.

So, what makes up trust? We use the words *trust* and *faith* as synonyms. They are rooted in the Latin words *fides* and *fiducia*, which means "faith." Thus the root of the legal word *fiduciary* is *faith*. *Fiduciary* is also a moral word that means that leaders look out for the interests of others as if their interests were their own. Leaders who fulfill their legal and moral fiduciary commitment earn people's trust. This is trust in action.

At an organizational level, trust makes us efficient, fast, and nimble. Trust is the basis of high-performing teams. We all have been on teams of bright, but egotistical people who can't get out of their own way. We all have been on teams where people trust each other. Distrustful teams move slowly and cost a lot of money. Trusting teams move fast and save a lot of money. We can lead change more easily when trust is high. Trust can bind diverse teams to a common good.

Here's a bit of evidence that trust is the foundation of high performance. Alex Edmans, finance professor at the London School of Economics, completed a four-year study on the 100 Best Companies to Work for in America. His research revealed that high trust cultures had delivered stock returns superior to peers by 2 to 3 percent a year over a 26-year period. In addition, turnover rates were 50 percent lower than competitors, and innovation, customer and patient satisfaction, employee engagement, and organizational agility were higher. In brief, Edmans found that the greater the trust, the greater the performance.[8]

These findings make clear that leaders who cultivate trust will thrive despite pressure and uncertainty. If you are looking for insights on how to do this, here is a good example that will surprise you. In 2018,

Lesley McKenzie was selected to coach the Japanese women's rugby team. She had played on the Canadian 2006 and 2010 women's rugby World Cup teams. She had coached rugby in New Zealand. So, how did a westerner earn the trust of young Japanese women to compete against teams that were often bigger and stronger? She put the interest of her players first and led from the back. She led from a position of vulnerability, and she asked questions and focused on their learning. She asked players to describe in their own words the rugby skills and teamwork they were learning. She asked players to describe how they could strengthen their performance. Most important of all, she took a personal interest in them as people.[9]

McKenzie's story illustrates how leading from the rear involves vulnerability because trust comes with no guarantees. Vulnerability means that someone could get hurt here—me! Vulnerability comes with a trust tax, and like any tax, we have to pay. We don't get to opt out of paying the trust tax. We do get to decide how much we trust others along the naïve-to-wary continuum. Sometimes we get burned for trusting when we shouldn't. Other times, we lose opportunities when we should have trusted but didn't.

When we make it clear that we don't trust others, others pick up on it and don't trust us. If we never trust anyone, then we guarantee that we never will have strong, deep, meaningful relationships. We will get stuck on our own little island of individual solitude. The trust tax is often higher for losing opportunities because we distrusted others than it would have been if we had paid the tax for getting burned. This isn't an argument for naïveté. It is to suggest that where we come down on how much we trust others defines our relationships and our character.

What doesn't ensure trust is a fancy job title. In fact, it is a voluntary act for each teammate to decide whether they trust a leader. The only outcome that the leader controls is whether they are trustworthy. In other words, trust is a by-product of being trustworthy. Trustworthiness depends on past experience with the person or organization. Trust can be limited to a formal agreement or contract. Trust can be based on giving someone a chance and then waiting to see what that person does with that chance. When trust is high, we are more understanding about mistakes. Unconditional trust happens when people rely on each other's word without question. Restoring trust is especially impressive since it depends on forgiveness, righting our wrongs, and putting aside our pride.

Lastly, what we place our trust in or how we perceive the world is a more powerful predictor of performance and life satisfaction than our circumstances. We only derive 10 percent of our happiness from our circumstances. So, the world we create is disappointing when we trust that happiness is "out there" in external events but just beyond our reach. This means that the odds are low that receiving a raise or buying a new car or home will bring enduring happiness. A better bet is trusting in how we develop our character. As our character develops, we will see the world in a new way. The important point is this: how we perceive the world is more important than what happens to us.

There are five enduring elements to creating a world in which we want to live:

1. Trust in practicing virtues and relying on our strengths
2. Trust in gratitude for what we have rather than focusing on what we don't have
3. Trust in reflection by slowing down and paying attention to our life
4. Trust in being engaged by enjoying the process of getting better
5. Trust in creating a meaningful life, which almost always means serving others[10]

COMPASSION: SERVICE BEFORE SELF

Cure sometimes, treat often, comfort always.[11]
—HIPPOCRATES

Again, we all operate along a compassionate-indifferent continuum. When we do practice compassion, we are more likely to have good health, better employment options, and stronger families. This is why it is in our self-interest to be compassionate since altruistic people receive more favors from others. When you give often, you receive often.

But don't just take our word for it. Research in neuroscience has proven that compassion has benefits. When we give, the area of our brain associated with positive feelings activates, lighting up on an MRI scan. Acts of compassion encourage a more positive perspective, reduce stress, and increase satisfaction. When we're out to get one another, our stress soars and relationships cannot flourish. When we look out for each other, the stress of extreme competitiveness dissolves, and we can better work together.

In Greek, love or passion is *eros*, which means energy, drive, and all that gets us moving forward. Compassion means that I have *eros*—energy and concern—for someone else. In brief, I care.

A leadership team at a factory in Tijuana, Mexico, asked employees what could be done to improve their lives. The workers' surprising request was not that the leaders focus on them but rather, that they help their neighbors who were living in dire poverty. The factory workers, who were paid well and lived middle-class lives, daily drove past poverty-stricken neighborhoods, and they wanted to improve their neighbors' quality of life. As a result, engineers started tutoring students in math and teaching school administrators about sustainability practices that saved the school money. Teammates purchased supplies for teachers and students.

It is a nice warm and fuzzy story, but what does it have to do with business? The Tijuana facility is part of Parker Hannifin, and this location was listed among the best places to work in all of Mexico. At the time of this compassionate community outreach, the Tijuana location had among the highest engagement scores and financial results in a company with operations in 50 countries. While increased profitability cannot be absolutely attributed to practicing virtue, there is a statistically significant ($p < 0.05$) relationship between virtue and engagement. A virtuous culture alone won't succeed when leaders are unable to craft and execute a competitive strategy. That said, strategy without virtue fails when leaders try to execute competitive advantages inside a dysfunctional culture.[12]

Compassion might seem like a loaded word, but Bishop Desmond Tutu argued that in order to be compassionate, you simply must act. This is exactly what medical students in Cleveland and, separately, in Minneapolis did during the early days of the COVID-19 pandemic. They developed a Google Docs signup sheet to volunteer for tasks that would help interns, residents, and fellows who were on the front line of COVID-19 care. Students signed up for grocery shopping, childcare, and organizing teaching syllabi as their institutions prepared to take on the surge.

Highly engaged teams are led by compassionate leaders—people who think less about themselves and more about others.

This theme was present in Parker's Tijuana story and the medical student story. Highly engaged teams are led by people who advocate for the teams' development and success. Highly engaged teams are led by people who reframe their jobs to foster engagement, satisfaction, and resilience. This is the kind of leadership that helps teammates feel like they belong, matter, and can make a difference. Those feelings increase commitment to the leader, to the team, and to the organization, and they help drive high performance.

COURAGE: DO THE HARD RIGHT
RATHER THAN THE EASY WRONG

Success is not final; failure is not fatal.
It is the courage to continue that counts.[13]
—WINSTON CHURCHILL

Like all the virtues, courage is not some absolute characteristic that either we have or we don't. We are human, so achieving virtue waxes and wanes, ebbs and flows. Indeed, our pursuit of virtue is iterative, borrowing from the Latin word for journey: *iter*. Sometimes, we are closer to achieving virtue by pushing through our fear to do what we know is right. Or, at the other end of the continuum, we don't admit or address our shortcomings.

Virtues must meet two conditions. They must be acted upon, and they must aim at the good. So, while skydiving might be gutsy, dangerous, and an exhilarating action to take, minus a moral quality, it is not courageous. In addition to confusing danger with virtue, we can limit our view of courage to heroism. We are impressed with the courage of a hero such as Mother Teresa or Abraham Lincoln. Heroes inspire, but a big remarkable life that lives beyond time and crosses national borders is out of reach for us mere mortals. Courage does not have to be a life-threatening or heroic act. Rather than limit our notion of courage to extraordinary acts of bravery in the face of danger, we can expand our understanding of courage to something that fits all of us—for example, to resolve a conflict effectively or take an intelligent risk.

Courage could stand at the headwaters of all the virtues. *Courage* is rooted in the French *coeur*, which means "heart." To have courage means taking heart and jumping in. Often it means to try something that we are not sure we can do. Courage usually feels risky.

There is a perfectly good neurological explanation for why we invest more in fear than hope: our primitive brain. Early humans were constantly threatened by wild animals or other tribes. Our primitive brain is an automatic response to physical danger that allows us to react quickly without thinking to avoid being skinned alive. The primitive brain is also known by its less interesting neurological term: the *amygdala*. This is the part of the brain that processes strong emotions like fear.

The trouble is that our primitive brain does a lousy job distinguishing between a meeting when our ego took a beating in front of our peers and real life-and-death situations. Hurt feelings generate the same emotion as physical danger, even though the threat is very different. An activated amygdala can lead to loads of regret—such as the time in a public meeting when we said our boss was a moron. When the amygdala disables our ability to reason, irrational overreaction follows.

Two hormones give an activated amygdala its power: *cortisol* and *adrenaline*. These powerful hormones do things that you may not notice:

- Relax your airways to take in more oxygen
- Increase blood flow to your muscles to increase speed and strength
- Increase blood sugar for more energy
- Dilate pupils to improve vision

The executive function of the brain can override the amygdala when a threat is moderate, but when a threat is strong, the amygdala can hijack our brain and overpower our executive functions. While you cannot eliminate an activated amygdala, you can learn to manage it by kicking your prefrontal cortex into overdrive. We will return to exploring this neurological backdrop throughout the book.

Here is the important insight about courage. It does not involve the absence of fear. Courage is pushing through our fears to do the hard right rather than the easy wrong. This is why courage is a fundamental measure of character. To act with courage means that we have chosen a greater benefit than individual comfort and achievement. Courage also means doing what is right even when pressured by others to do the wrong thing. Courage can involve overcoming self-pity or feelings of having been victimized. Courage is needed to overcome our shortcomings. All of these qualities of courage are why all cultures lift up courage as noble. Can you imagine a culture idolizing cowardice?

Let's turn to a story from medicine to illustrate courage as virtue. A three-year-old with a low platelet count and risk of bleeding was admitted to a children's hospital. The child was fussing and complaining of a headache. The doctor provided a cursory exam and reassured the mother, Mrs. Tom, that everything was all right. No tests were ordered or performed. Less than an hour later, the child had a seizure and developed a fatal brain herniation, the obvious result of bleeding in the brain.

The quality officer of the children's hospital, Dr. Ireland, was on call that night, and she became aware of the tragic events. Dr. Ireland visited the weeping mother, and she explained that by failing to order a CT scan of the head, the hospital had made an egregious mistake. Though Dr. Ireland was not involved in the child's care, she owned the error, and she explained to Mrs. Tom what could have been done that might have saved her child. Dr. Ireland courageously risked the wrath of a parent who had just experienced the inconsolable loss of a child. She risked feeding a lawsuit. She risked making an unpopular decision that could have negatively affected relationships with her colleagues.

Three months later, the hospital asked the mother if she would help prevent similar occurrences and invited her to make a videotape about what had happened. Mrs. Tom could have been enraged and refused the invitation. Instead, she made an impassioned video about speaking up and working with caregivers, so that this would never happen to another child. The video was posted on the hospital's website, and it has been viewed by hundreds of thousands of people. As an aside, no lawsuit was filed. One way to learn from Dr. Ireland's courage is to ask the question:

"What would I do if I weren't afraid?"

We conclude this section on courage with a word that is not often considered related to courage: *vulnerability*. Consider for a moment whether you have observed an act of courage that didn't involve vulnerability. Once we understand that courage is about taking prudent and intelligent risks, it makes sense that vulnerability is a part of that. The word *vulnerable* comes from the Latin *vulnerabilis*, meaning "to wound." Vulnerability means that we might get hurt. *Cowardice*, on the other hand, means "to cover up," or "to turn" or "back away." Vulnerability equals risk, uncertainty, and exposure. That is why vulnerability is not an act of weakness; rather, it is an act of strength.

Vulnerability is especially important when it comes to innovation. In fact, creativity is an act of courage precisely because we must put our neck out to try something new. It isn't exactly life-threatening to have our ideas or work rejected. Yet, brain scans show that experiencing rejection activates the same regions of the brain associated with physical pain.

How can you innovate without fear? You can't. Innovators who persevere understand that success often follows in the wake of painful mistakes.

When we fear failure more than we desire innovation, we play it safe—and thus the boldest and best ideas may never surface. Our fear of

THE SEVEN CLASSICAL VIRTUES

failure is outweighed by our distaste for not trying. Credit goes to those who are inside the arena trying, even if they fail. Ernest Hemingway put it this way: "Courage is grace under pressure."[14] Pressure is almost always found at the junction requiring courage. When life is easy and decisions are no-brainers, courage is not needed. Where there is pressure, we must take heart because the next virtue, justice, is often a real challenge.

JUSTICE: LIVE BY CONVICTION, NOT CIRCUMSTANCE

If you are neutral in situations of injustice,
you have chosen the side of the oppressor.
If an elephant has its foot on the tail of a mouse
and you say that you are neutral, the
mouse will not appreciate your neutrality.[15]
—DESMOND TUTU

What if we inspired trust by operating a marketplace based on a commitment to virtue rather than rules, while recognizing that the rule of law can't be ignored?

One of the main goals of justice is to treat everyone with respect, regardless of how they treat us. This is far from easy, requiring strength and practice. Character can seem quaint when we are threatened or disrespected. Indignation and rage can easily take over. Bloated egos cause us to take things personally. And when things get personal, our judgment gets fuzzy. Slaying our ego is difficult to do, but it is essential if we hope to treat others—all others—with respect and dignity. Doing so is just.

Justice involves the rule of law and virtue embodied in the iconic figure Lady Justice. She stands as a moral force in our judicial system. She instills trust by relying on a blindfold, a balance, her foot, and a sword. The blindfold signifies impartiality, and the balance weighs evidence objectively. Her right foot holds down a snake, embodying triumph over corruption, bias, and intimidation.

The sword is doubled-edged, suggesting reason can be used for good and ill. One edge of the sword makes clear that no one is above the law. If we were all angels, we wouldn't need rules. This is why rules have a place in society. In fact, the rule of law is the foundation of a civilized society. Compliance can be an effective way to enforce rules when our goal is to restrict choices and decisions related to medical records, money management, or driving practices that put truckers, as well as the drivers around them, in danger.

The other edge cautions against swinging the sword of compliance too broadly. Doing so can discourage what we want to encourage—moral will and skill. When rules are excessive, filling out paperwork comes at the expense of teaching students, caring for patients, and coaching teammates. When rules are excessive, creativity and innovation are reduced because by its very nature, innovation requires that rules are loose, not tight. Rules are often designed for a stable world. But much of our world today is dynamic and changing.

In 1996, Marines Jack Hoban and Robert Humphrey formed the Ethical Protectors program to teach Marines to use their powers to protect people by deescalating rather than escalating a conflict. This program combines the martial arts with character training to teach both Marines and police officers what it means to be an "ethical protector"—that is, a person who protects life, self, and others, all others, including the enemy.

Hoban started with the Marines' core values of honor, courage, and commitment. While these values are noble in purpose, without care, honor can become conceit, courage can become martyrdom, and commitment can become zealotry. The difference between Marines and the enemy, then, is a universal commitment to protect life. This protection extends to the enemy (all others) as long as they have stopped taking life.

Hoban's first hurdle was to redefine a warrior as a person who kills only to protect others. The second hurdle was to demonstrate that protectors are far more ferocious than killers. A mother lion protecting a warthog dinner from a pack of hyenas will fight up to a point. However, a mother lion protecting her cubs will fight to the death. The third hurdle was to stop the practice of dehumanizing the enemy by calling them "trash" or using racial slurs. Hoban wanted to be clear that killing people just because they disagree with our beliefs is indefensible.

Some Marines struggled to accept Hoban's thinking. They reminded him that they were facing a ruthless enemy that terrorized civilians and beheaded soldiers. Being soft against a callous adversary would get innocent people killed. In response, Hoban argued that treating people with respect and dignity is not going to make a Marine less capable of doing what needs to be done.

Everyone deserves to be treated with respect and dignity, even the enemy. This is justice embodied. Law follows society's vision of justice, not the other way around. This means that we decide what is just and then pass a law. However, what is legal and what is ethical can be quite different. The rule of law ensures that contracts are binding, ensuring supposedly just business practices. But those same laws have allowed executives to walk away with millions, even when customers were deceived, wealth was destroyed, and employees lost jobs. So, the distinction between law as rule and ethics as an exception to the rule is important to understand. Law is what we have to do. Ethics is what we should do.

The University of California at Berkeley Psychology Department used cookies to distinguish between what leaders have to do and should do. Students were organized into teams of three, one team member randomly selected to lead the group. The team was then asked to brainstorm solutions to problems, such as cheating and binge drinking. After 30 minutes, researchers brought each team a plate of four cookies, one more than the number of team members. In each case, the randomly selected leader quickly ate the fourth cookie and without any discussion. The leader was neither more virtuous nor more valuable to the team. The person simply believed that rank had its privileges.

Author and former investment banker Michael Lewis thought that this simple experiment captured what he observed on Wall Street. Leaders who were lucky to receive extra cookies believed that they deserved them, grabbing excessive compensation and leaving crumbs for shareholders, employees, and taxpayers. Lewis concluded that their morality was corrupted by the power of their position.

Let's consider one more point that implicates all human beings, namely, how we sometimes react when we are treated unjustly. There is an alternative to being ticked off. Epictetus notes, "If you do not wish to be prone to anger, do not feed the habit; give it nothing which may tend to its increase."[16] We know that people who learn to grow from injustice have less stress, less depression, better health, and better relationships with others. This is because exercising forgiveness helps them to repair their relationships—especially if the offender has also apologized and tried to make amends. Research shows that forgiveness helps coworkers rebuild positive relationships following conflict. Forgiveness reduces the desire for revenge, which is a major cause of negative behaviors in the workplace.

If we are not careful, power can replace compassion with inattention to the concerns of others and in the process, undermine justice. This is why we immediately follow justice with a look at wisdom. And when it comes to wisdom, we give the last word on justice to Mahatma Gandhi: "The weak can never forgive. Forgiveness is the attribute of the strong."[17]

WISDOM: STRIVE TO UNDERSTAND RATHER THAN TO BE UNDERSTOOD

The chief task in life is simply this: to identify and separate matters so that I can say clearly to myself which are externals not under my control, and which have to do with the choices I actually control. Where then do I look for good and evil? Not to uncontrollable externals, but within myself to the choices that are my own.[18]
—EPICTETUS

Edie, the remarkable holocaust survivor described in Chapter 1, has achieved hard-won wisdom. For example, she greets people by telling them she misses them and how good it is to see them rather than asking them how their day was. She suggested that we not fight with someone who disagrees with us. Instead ask, "How can I be useful to you? Let me know if you are interested in my perspective."

The kind of wisdom that Edie embodies is sorely lacking despite living in a world that can access so much knowledge so easily. The mere tap of a phone or computer keyboard gives us more knowledge than we can ever consume. Yet, knowledge alone does not teach us to act wisely by doing the right thing, in the right way, for the right reasons.

Being wise allows us to navigate complicated workplaces and situations. Being wise includes knowledge, but it is more than that. Wisdom adds the dimension of practical skill to knowledge and information. Wise people like Edie become more pragmatic rather than idealistic or self-righteous. With wisdom, we clarify who we want to be, train our emotions, and engage in a journey of self-cultivation.

Like all virtues, wisdom is learned. First, we make our habits, then our habits make us. By training our emotions and focusing on habits and behavior, we can make a lasting change. Wisdom is not a matter of high IQ or formal education. Sometimes, in fact, people with common sense lack a formal education, while well-educated people may have little or no common sense. Because wisdom requires experience, age is often associated with being wise. As people age and realize that they are vulnerable and that life can be swept away in a heartbeat, they are better able to see what is important and what is not.

However, young people can acquire a wise perspective too. Those exposed to life-altering events, such as the terrorist attacks on September 11 in the United States or the SARS outbreak in Asia, demonstrated a similar reordering of priorities as older folks. Living through a serious illness or crisis puts life into focus, revealing new insights.

Wisdom is critical to effective leaders. A wise leader listens, is not defensive, and is quick to recognize the contribution of others. A wise leader seeks mentors and mentors others. When it comes to increasing engagement, wise leaders are well aware that money alone isn't the only way to go. A good, competitive wage matters, but money is not sufficient to cultivate a passionate staff. Wise leaders start with the fully engaged people to understand what is going well and then figure out ways to do more of that with others. Wisdom starts with what is right, rather than what is wrong.

We are constantly changing as we reach different phases of life. The issue isn't *whether* we can change, but rather *how* we will change. Character is learned, practiced, and cultivated. Virtue is developed best when we feel responsible for our own growth. We are more motivated and perform best when we leverage our strengths and manage our weaknesses. This is wisdom—realizing that there is always room for growth.

Wisdom is a means rather than an end. Wise people like Edie cultivate inner strength through disciplined reflection. The reflection that we can't see cultivates acts of compassion and justice that we can see. Growing in wisdom is a wonderful way to get better. And when we get better at who we are (for example, we practice wisdom), we get better at what we do.

TEMPERANCE: CALM IS CONTAGIOUS

Calm is contagious.[19]
—ROARK DENVER, RETIRED NAVY SEAL

In a chaotic environment, the role of the leader is to lower anxiety. "Calm is contagious" is something you have to train for. Under pressure, people default to their training. Training alters our default setting. NASA trains its astronauts so thoroughly that what is learned becomes a default habit. Even the bravest of astronauts become terrorized when completing a spacewalk. Astronauts have reported that a spacewalk gives the sensation of experiencing a crushing free fall tumbling back to earth. Training does not eliminate this fear, but it can teach astronauts to cope. Habitual change is achieved by practicing until the trainees no longer need to think about the new habit. Under pressure, they will remain calm and default to the standard of their training.

Let's apply to ethics the idea that under pressure, we default to our training. Compliance training presents ethics as "What should we do?" and "Why should we do it?" The harder question is this: "What does it take to make us virtuous, given all the distractions, temptations, and complexities that lie in our wake?" If ethics were as simple as compliance training suggests, then acting with justice and compassion would be easy. But it isn't. Ethics is not simply knowledge. It is how we act, especially under pressure.

The compliance model of ethics is limited because it overlooks the fact that when rules collide with habits, habits win in a knockout.

To overcome our habits, we have to practice. Just as bridge builders improve by building more bridges and surgeons provide higher surgical quality and better outcomes by performing more surgeries, we become more just by doing just acts.

When threats, either real or perceived, are triggered, the amygdala can shut down the thinking brain. When the brain is focusing on the threat, it's difficult to change. After the amygdala is activated, it takes about 20 minutes for the thinking part of the brain to kick in. One simple technique to reset the brain is to pause and plan. This means that when adrenaline starts to flow, you take deep breaths for 60 seconds. Sit up straight in your chair, close your eyes, and rest your hands in your lap. As you calm your brain, you can think more clearly; make better, more rational decisions; and act with more self-control.

When it comes to work, people juggle multiple tasks at once, trying to get more done in less and less time. According to Clifford Nass, psychology professor at Stanford University, nonstop multitasking actually wastes more time than it saves. Multitaskers experience a 40 percent drop in productivity, take 50 percent longer to complete a single task, and have a 50 percent higher error rate.

To get the best out of technology, we have to practice temperance. This is why some organizations ban emails on the weekends. When it comes to resolving conflict or issues that are complex, technology is the wrong tool for the task at hand. Instead, consider this hierarchy:

1. **Whenever possible, talk face-to-face.**
2. **If face-to-face or Zoom isn't possible, then talk by phone.**
3. **When a phone call isn't possible, text requesting time to talk face-to-face. A limited number of characters forces you to get straight to the point. Relationships are improved when we develop a habit to talk or phone first, and text and email last for issues that involve conflict or are complex.**

We can practice temperance by making a concentrated effort to create new habits (see Chapter 13). We have to practice deliberately, devoting our full concentration and effort toward our goals. Learning to change our habits isn't easy though. Habitual change takes time and effort. To practice temperance, start with a compelling purpose governed by intrinsic, rather than extrinsic, motivation. Next, seek feedback from a trusted source and reflect often.

Our knowledge will not save us from ourselves. Like eating right, exercising regularly, and getting adequate sleep, temperance is less what we know and more how we live.

HOPE: BETTER, NOT BITTER

We must accept finite disappointment,
but never lose infinite hope.[20]
—**MARTIN LUTHER KING, JR.**

You don't need to be a famous athlete, astronaut, or national leader like Martin Luther King, Jr., to make a difference. Interestingly, one way to make a difference is to focus on how we are the same. The virtues give us hope by focusing on what we share in common, rather than what divides us. As Maya Angelou wrote, "I note the obvious differences between each sort and type, but we are more alike, my friends, than we are unalike."[21]

Having hope means viewing an adverse experience as an opportunity for growth. You can become better, not bitter, by letting go of a victim mentality and instead choosing to view yourself as a survivor.

In 1945, Rita (not her real name) was born to a Black father and a white mother in Cape Town, South Africa. Her story is about someone who replaced victimhood with growth. District 6, the neighborhood she lived in, was a multiracial, multireligious community. That is, it was until 1966, when the apartheid government, whose goal was to separate and segregate its citizens by race, declared the neighborhood white and then proceeded to bulldoze the homes of more than 60,000 residents.

Rita's father died in the early 1960s, a death that was ultimately a blessing to a family living in the cruel world of apartheid. A mixed-race marriage violated apartheid immorality laws, and her family would have been forcibly separated had he lived. During the campaign to bulldoze District 6, Rita's mother stood strong against those who would force her from her home. But in 1981, Rita's mother was told the house would be bulldozed, whether or not she was inside. The very day after she moved, Rita's mother died, another casualty to apartheid.

After all that she had suffered under the apartheid regime, losing both of her parents and her home, Rita was consumed by a hate so strong that she wanted to strangle her oppressors. Over the span of decades, Rita learned to let go of the hatred that gripped her. As she learned to forgive, Rita felt the dark emotional burden lift. It took years, but Rita put herself on the path to becoming better, not bitter, transforming all she had experienced into an opportunity to grow. One way to understand how Rita managed this is to understand that in spite of it all, she was realistically optimistic. Her form of optimism wasn't Disneyland.

In the 1960s and 1970s, Martin Seligman wanted to find out whether optimism and pessimism are genetic traits. In his research, Seligman found that people who had learned to be helpless viewed negative events as personal, permanent, and pervasive. They held these views even against evidence to the contrary. If they flunked a math test, they told themselves they had never been good at math and never would be and that this was the kind of failure that always happened to them. A single, negative experience became a general negative viewpoint that led to pervasive helplessness.

While the pessimist views failure as permanent, the optimist sees events as impersonal, temporary, and challenging. For example, optimists who have not been able to grow an organization are deeply disappointed, but they learn from mistakes, so they can improve performance next year. They understand that past failure does not preclude future success and that economic downturns happen to everyone. The good news is that realistic optimism can be learned, just as helplessness is learned. Thoughts are malleable, which means that hope can be taught, especially realistic optimism that involves boundaries and agency. Boundary conditions include events that we cannot change, such as economic downturns, global pandemics, and political polarization. Within the boundary conditions rests optimism. We have agency to respond to situations in our control, or at least we can control how we choose to respond to circumstances beyond our control.

In addition to realistic optimism, we can also learn to be grateful. We know from research that gratitude is a key ingredient in the virtue of hope. The root word of *gratitude* is *grace*, or a gift that we didn't necessarily earn. We can learn to appreciate people and experiences that make our life better and worthwhile. Gratitude involves humility. So, it is at odds with the idea of building a "personal brand," which is often touted as the basis for a successful life, and that makes practicing gratitude challenging. By practicing gratitude, you can learn to be humble rather than prideful. You can avoid the arrogance that can be so damaging to team relationships as well as homelife. *Gratitude* isn't a weak word. Research makes clear that *gratitude* is a muscular word. Research finds that practicing gratitude improves health, increases energy levels, and encourages optimism and empathy.

Hope is animated by courage and acknowledges that possible solutions exist. William Lynch, a *New York Times* reporter who became a priest, wrote how hope and courage are linked by "the fundamental knowledge and feeling that there is a way out of difficulty, that things can work out, that we as humans can somehow handle and manage internal and external reality, that there are 'solutions.'"[22]

Few people have lived by this statement more than Viktor Frankl, the Nazi death camp survivor mentioned in the previous chapter. In his book *Man's Search for Meaning*, Frankl described the horrific treatment of prisoners. Faced with humiliation, torture, and death, many prisoners became selfish and self-serving, but a small number of prisoners gave up food and blankets to those in need, even as they themselves suffered. Frankl wondered at the difference between the prisoners who gave and those who took. He concluded that neither wealth nor status, education nor any one religious tradition made the difference. The commonality among those who sacrificed was that they had a deep sense of purpose. They believed that even when they couldn't control their circumstances, they could always control their response. Knowing their fate might be sealed, these prisoners accepted their reality with integrity. Paradoxically, these were the individuals most likely to survive the death camps. According to Frankl, hope is a decision, a response to a choice, as is despair. Frankl asserted that the most powerful motivator sought by humans is meaning:

Everything can be taken from a man but one thing: the last of the human freedoms—to choose one's attitude in any given set of circumstances.[23]

KEY TAKEAWAYS

Can we become better performers without virtue? There certainly is no shortage of people or organizations that have done just that—fame and fortune achieved with limited or no thought given to virtue. So, consider life both with or without the seven classical virtues, described below.

TRUST: TRUST IS EFFICIENT

Trust is more than a feel-good exercise since trustworthiness is efficient, saves money, and increases agility. When we look out for the interests of others as if their interests were our own, we build healthy human relations.

Without *trust*, customer, colleague, and business partner relationships deteriorate. Mistrust slows down decisions and decreases quality.

A personal life absent trust lacks the social safety net that we all need to function and flourish.

COMPASSION: SERVICE BEFORE SELF

It sounds better to be pro-compassion than pro-ruthlessness. That's the easy part. The hard part is putting service before self when we are busy and preoccupied with our own priorities.

Without *compassion*, we fail to relate to others, gain insights from other people's perspective, or consider how our decisions affect others. We alienate people. Self-serving conduct results in narrow goals.

A personal life without compassion is empty and incomplete.

COURAGE: DO THE HARD RIGHT RATHER THAN THE EASY WRONG

Rather than limit courage to extraordinary acts of bravery, we expand courage to mean something that fits all of us: lead change, resolve conflict, be vulnerable. To act with courage means that we choose a greater benefit than individual comfort and achievement.

Without *courage*, we will not stand up to poor decisions. We back down in the face of adversity. We choose the easy wrong rather than the hard right. We lack the persistence needed to work through difficult issues. It takes courage to swim upstream against a current of cynicism.

Without courage, life is frozen by fear.

JUSTICE: LIVE BY CONVICTION, NOT CIRCUMSTANCE

We see treating people with respect and dignity as integral to who we are. We strive to right public wrongs with family, friends, teammates, and the community, though this is often complex since there are no objective standards for justice.

Without *justice*, we fail to make a difference. We do not benefit from diverse expertise, experience, insights, and skills, so the quality of our decisions and the speed of our execution suffer.

Without justice, our relationships deteriorate, and commitments decline when people feel they are treated unfairly.

WISDOM: STRIVE TO UNDERSTAND RATHER
THAN TO BE UNDERSTOOD

Wisdom means foresight, practical judgment, and common sense. Wisdom cultivates meaning and purpose.

Without *wisdom*, we make flawed decisions. We fail to empower and engage a higher percentage of people.

Without wisdom, we blame others for poor performance and create a culture of fear and disengagement. People stop caring. As apathy goes up, so does risk.

TEMPERANCE: CALM IS CONTAGIOUS

Temperance involves moderation, balance, and self-control. The root word of *temperance* is *tempus*, or "time," which raises the question, "What are we living for?"

Without *temperance*, we rush to judge, fail to gather relevant facts, fall short of our convictions, and lose credibility.

Without the temperance of self-control, discipline, and moderation, we lack the ability to be responsible.

HOPE: BETTER, NOT BITTER

Hope is about the future not yet realized. Hope involves what is possible and realistic, as opposed to fantasy. When hope links with courage, there is knowledge that possible solutions exist.

Without *hope*, we cannot be open-minded or consider the views of others. We cannot learn from others or reflect critically on our failures, so we don't improve.

Without hope, despair, cynicism, and fragility define who we become.

———

Virtue is a skill, and like any skill, it can be learned and practiced. We become the best versions of ourselves by intentionally practicing virtue and by leaning into discomfort.

Questions are an effective tool for self-discovery, especially during periods of adversity. A good question can start a journey to become a more skilled virtue practitioner:

1. At your best, how do you practice virtue with family and friends?
2. How can virtue make you a better teammate?
3. How do you use virtue to respond to stress, pressure, and trauma?

ARETÉ
Excellence

Habits
Coaching
Restoration

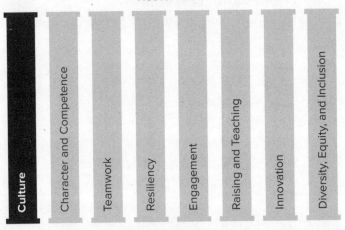

Culture

Character and Competence

Teamwork

Resiliency

Engagement

Raising and Teaching

Innovation

Diversity, Equity, and Inclusion

Character

Trust   Compassion   Courage

Justice   Wisdom   Temperance   Hope

ORGANIZATIONAL CULTURE

Growing a culture requires a good storyteller.
Changing a culture requires a persuasive editor.[1]
—RYAN LILLY

POWER OVER STRATEGY, PROCESS, TEAMWORK, AND STRUCTURE

Culture eats strategy for breakfast, process for lunch, teamwork for an appetizer, and structure for dinner. Clearly, this doesn't diminish the importance of strategy, process, teamwork, and structure. However, more than any strategy, metric, or asset, it's an organization's culture that will act as an accelerator that stimulates action or will act as a break that restrains performance.

While metrics are concrete and specific, a culture is abstract and general. This is why it is far easier for leaders to manage strategy and metrics than cultures and stories. We can't manage what we can't define. So, here is an exercise to convert the abstract into something specific. How would you diagram a culture? Ask your team to do the same. The diagrams are good for a laugh. The exercise also usually makes it painfully obvious that not only can most people not diagram an excellent culture but they also have difficulty describing one. However, recognizing that virtue means excellence, when we frame the question as diagramming a culture that is based on virtue, the picture becomes much clearer. Figure 3.1 is an image of an excellent culture: a pediment of excellence rests upon the pillars of the seven virtues.

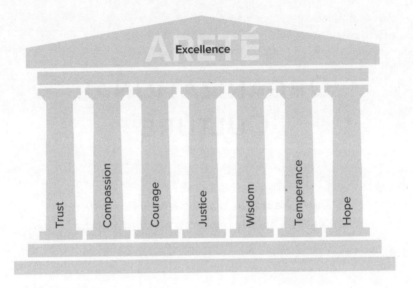

Figure 3.1 A Pediment of Excellence Rests upon the Pillars of the Seven Virtues

The virtues provide a common vocabulary. Adopting virtue as a shared language of excellence gives us ideals to live up to and a way to talk about it. Additionally, a common language provides an appreciation for what matters most to us. Aspiring to a set of ideals can deepen trust, contribute to a shared identity, and create a culture where people care about each other even when practiced imperfectly. Clearly, greater insights about each virtue can be useful. The key takeaway is that much of the shared language of virtue is already in us.

CULTURES, LEADERS, AND TECHNOLOGY

Cultures evolve whether or not leaders pay attention. So, why not be intentional with your most powerful asset since culture happens one way or another? The word *culture* is derived from the Latin word *colere*, which means "to plant" or "to cultivate." It's easy to think of a culture being like a garden that will grow whether or not it is tended. The principal gardener is the leader. Unkempt gardens, like cultures that grow without leadership intention or skill, are full of weeds. But gardens and cultures that are manicured are beautiful. The question is whether the leader understands how to envision the culture and has the skill to cultivate a garden that will flourish.

Culture is like the soil, which affects how we grow or fail to grow. Virtues are like the roots, hidden though foundational to growth. Each virtue is like a nutrient. Trust is a key nutrient to a healthy culture. Based on Edelman's 2021 Trust Barometer, we have work to do. For nearly 30 years, Edelman's Trust Barometer has surveyed over 33,000 people in 28 countries. People want leaders to have the courage to talk straight using reliable facts combined with empathy to address people's fears. What increases rather than reduces fear is technology, which is a source of distrust according to the 2021 Trust Barometer.

Technology advancements powered by the atom, the chip, and the gene are moving faster than our moral abilities can keep up, according to author Walter Isaacson.

Isaacson points out that physics led to nuclear power. But physics also created atom bombs. Binary digits birthed social media with the promise to bring us together. It also put a megaphone in the hands of those who breed hate. Jennifer Doudna won a Nobel Prize for helping to create CRISPR, the technology that edits genes that can treat Huntington's disease and some cancers. After creating CRISPR, Doudna had a nightmarish dream walking into a room where someone wanted to understand her technology. The person in her nightmare was Adolf Hitler.[2]

USING VIRTUE TO LEAD CULTURE CHANGE

For thousands of years, virtue has underpinned human progress. This is why a virtue-based culture is a must-have, not a nice-to-have. A virtue-based culture is a transferable set of beliefs and behaviors that enable any group to survive and hopefully thrive. Aristotle proposed that possession of virtue was not so much related to being knowledge-able as to it was to developing habits of virtuous practice. Virtue is action, not simply an idea.

So, how do we cultivate virtuous habits? With humility, since motivating another person to change, or for that matter, changing ourselves and our own behavior, is stunningly difficult. Once we accept this reality, we become less judgmental of others and more empathic. Besides, being judgmental simply doesn't motivate others or ourselves.

When it comes to motivating change, Nobel Prize winner Daniel Kahneman stated that the insights of Kurt Lewin on "restraining forces" is psychology's greatest contribution to humankind. In the 1940s, Lewin viewed organizations as being in a state of equilibrium created by driving and restraining forces working against each other. Figure 3.2 shows a diagram of Lewin's *force field analysis model*.

Figure 3.2 Kurt Lewin's Force Field Analysis Model
Source: Adapted from Creating Positive Change with Mark Connelly,
https://www.change-management-coach.com/.

According to Lewin, driving forces have a positive impact on change. Restraining forces are obstacles to change. Whether a force is positive or a restraint depends on the person or the culture. So, the key insight is asking the right question rather than assuming we already have an answer to why people don't change. Once people define their restraints or obstacles to change, then the task is to weaken those obstacles rather than to increase forces that drive change.[3] In other words, rely more on a pull strategy to help people pursue where they already want to go rather than a push strategy to force them to move in a particular direction.

Here's an example of how the idea of restraining forces can be applied to a sales team. Start by asking, what would be the obstacles for a sales team to practice virtue? The answer may not be the same for everyone on the team, so it's the question that puts us on the right track. Perhaps many report they feel pressure to hit their sales numbers at all costs. When they miss their sales targets, they won't earn a bonus, which they rely on to cover their living expenses; or worse, they're at risk for being fired. Leaders can reduce this restraining force by making clear that we want to win, but we want to win the right way. Of course, results matter. However, we will be forgiving if virtue is practiced but targets are missed. What we won't forgive is when targets are met at the expense of practicing virtue.

Another key restraining force might be that we push people to change without first having established a relationship. Good luck getting people to accept the brutal facts for the need to change without a foundation of trust and compassion. Here is a fun example to illustrate this point.

A general manager (GM) struggled to get a curmudgeon union leader to accept changes that were needed for the business to thrive. The GM invested time to get to know his cranky colleague. He learned that the union leader was hacked off that the canteen didn't have mayonnaise. The GM got the point and made sure that never again would a sandwich be without mayo. And ensuring his generosity wasn't lost on his grumpy colleague and others, he created a simple way to share that he did what he said he would do. He called it, "You Said, We Did." He included on his list of "You Said, We Did" accomplishments that you wanted mayo, so we bought mayo. Once the union leader had mayo on his sandwich, and, importantly, felt heard, he became more open to business change.

Mayo diplomacy might not be rational, but we know that sometimes facts don't change a person's perceptions. Being heard does. What restrained the union leader from change was past experience with leaders who didn't listen to his concerns. The GM weakened this restraint by demonstrating and documenting that he did listen to his concerns with the tool "You Said, We Did."

Let's discuss how virtue can be a useful tool for culture change at the organizational level. Here's a case study of applying restraining forces to a large global company.

CASE STUDY: PRACTICING VIRTUE

This company's commitment to ethical conduct embodied by virtue was on full display when the global pandemic slammed into North America. In March 2020, leaders quickly took steps to reconfigure factories to ensure physical distancing and to make masks and hand sanitizers readily available. These changes dealt with immediate health concerns, but a pending global recession put revenue at risk for many companies.

To prepare for economic decline, the CEO took a 50 percent pay cut. Senior leaders took a 20 percent pay cut. All salaried leaders took a 10 percent pay cut. Travel was canceled to keep people safe, which resulted in considerable savings. All of these measures were used by some organizations, though this company was particularly quick to implement and announce these across the company. But here's the really differentiating twist. Production teammates who were still making and shipping products received a 15 percent pay increase. Keep this thought in mind. Production teammates protected salaried teammates' jobs. Accordingly, the courage to care for their health with safety protocols and the wisdom to compensate them for their efforts was justice in action.

The long-term question was, could tens of thousands of teammates be trusted to accomplish from home what had always been done in an office? The key word was *trust*. Sissela Bok said, "Whatever matters to human beings, trust is the atmosphere in which it thrives." The performance benefit of trust is that people mobilize quickly and follow through on plans.[4]

So, how did the company's prepandemic (March 2020) performance compare to its postpandemic performance (March 2021)? Net income reached an all-time quarterly record in 2021, an increase of 28 percent. Cash flow from operations and earnings per share hit all-time quarterly records. The stock price hit an all-time high in March 2021. These metrics demonstrate how a healthy culture mobilized thousands of people to respond to an external stressor, the pandemic. Strong culture first. Performance second.

How Did This Commitment to a
Virtue-Based Culture Start?

In 2012, the company's leaders adopted the virtues to protect the balance sheet by preserving the culture. The goal was to help people perform at a high level despite pressure and uncertainty. The business impact was increased engagement, enhanced teamwork, and leadership development, all contributing to enhanced organizational performance.

To get started, more than a hundred *voice of the customer* (VOC) interviews were conducted with North American, European, Asian, and South American leaders. These leaders readily understood the need to protect the culture and reputation. They also appreciated learning that virtues were universally admired. The open question was, how could virtue be practiced and measured?

To answer the "how" question, the company learned a great deal about practicing virtue by connecting with a broad range of business leaders, professional athletes, and military leaders, in addition to connecting with academics in positive psychology and related fields. The leaders visited each of the US service academies (West Point, Air Force, and Navy), as well as organizations like NASA, to learn how cadet and astronaut selection and development integrated character. Here is what they learned.

Early in these conversations, the central question asked during these visits was, how will success be measured? The initial metric was simple. Did leaders call to schedule sessions that introduced the virtues with the intention of creating a common language to strengthen performance? Busy profit-and-loss leaders are not going to invest time and money attending virtue sessions if they don't see value. So, was the metric achieved? The phone rang so much that demand for virtue sessions exceeded supply to deliver those sessions.

A key takeaway: method was as important as the content. This takes us back to restraining forces. The leaders learned that virtue didn't need to be pushed or mandated. Teams quickly identified stories when virtues such as trust and compassion had a favorable impact on performance. The restraint or the obstacle was answering the question, how can we practice virtue better? To that end, teams came to seminars with their business strategies. The point was to connect the virtues to existing business priorities. The process arbitrarily assigned teams to present one virtue by sharing answers to three questions, which in this case was applied to the virtue of trust:

1. What is trust?
2. Why is trust relevant and useful to our current and future business priorities?
3. How can we increase trust?

These questions led to discussions about what it meant to practice virtue in a business setting that expected high performance.[5] This was achieved by considering how virtue would help achieve existing metrics. As a result, teammates were able to uncover how the presence or absence of virtue affected learning, collaboration, and ultimately, performance. Virtue wasn't one more thing to put on the plate. It was the plate.

The discussions were energizing, which led teams to ask for more, specifically for "rollout" plans. However, we said that well-intended rollout plans would be misguided because they often turn into push, rather than pull, strategies. In addition, a business already had a culture. Teammates who didn't attend the seminar would look cross-eyed at those who announced the launch of a new culture.

The wiser approach was to empower individuals and teams to apply ideas that were meaningful to them. Some might have wanted to practice virtue at home with their kids before they felt ready to do so with teammates. Some might have wanted to focus on their own leadership first. Others were ready to practice virtue as a team right away.

In general, where people start and evolve is a function of their motivations and abilities to "cultivate" virtue. An early sign that the culture is being shaped is when the language of virtue becomes part of the culture. Catchphrases help. People can't remember paragraphs, but they can remember simple phrases such as these:

- **Trust:** Trust is efficient.
- **Compassion:** Service before self.
- **Courage:** Do the hard right rather than the easy wrong.
- **Justice:** Live by convictions, not by circumstances.
- **Wisdom:** Strive to understand rather than to be understood.
- **Temperance:** Calm is contagious.
- **Hope:** Be better, not bitter.

HOW DOES VIRTUE AFFECT ENGAGEMENT?

In 2018, to answer this critical question, an experimental study was led independently by two academic investigators. Two facilities of identical size were sampled. Both locations completed engagement surveys at the same time. The experimental location completed training, and the control location didn't. Surveys were conducted 5 months and then 12 months following the sessions. In addition, to conducting pre- and postsurvey results, a total of 52 teammates were interviewed from both locations.

The quantitative findings revealed that the presence of compassion and trust in particular had a statistically significant positive impact on engagement and on resilience. Conversely, the absence of compassion, trust, and resilience was statistically significantly associated with a negative impact on engagement. These findings were independent of a person's tenure, length of time with supervisor, or shift.

Switch to qualitative results. Interviews with 52 teammates showed that every person cared about the company, its products, and its customers. Stated differently, no one expressed apathy. All 52 teammates wanted to be treated with respect and dignity, and they all wanted to have the opportunity to make a difference.

Two important conclusions emerged: First, the virtues of trust and compassion were key drivers of engagement. Second, the statistically significant impact on engagement wasn't a quick fix since the full impact took about 12 months to be realized.

In 2022, another experimental study was conducted comparing two different facilities. The treatment group received a half day of training on the virtues and six one-hour sessions on habitual change over two months. Again, the training resulted in a statistically significant difference. In this case, all seven virtues, as well as belonging, mattering, and making a difference, were strengthened at a statistically significant level of $p < 0.05$.

Did Nationality Influence the Practice of Virtue?

The short answer is no. Whether someone practiced virtue was not associated with over 30 nationalities. This finding was consistent with the premise that "classical" virtues are universal.

So, if nationality didn't influence the practice of virtue, what did? *Intrinsic motivation* (people practiced virtue because they wanted to, not because they had to); *growth mindset* (virtue is a skill that can be learned); and *deliberate practice* (intentional action). In addition, over a hundred teams reported making progress on their business goals three to four months after the sessions, and the coaches assigned to the teams agreed that progress on goals was achieved.

KEY TAKEAWAYS

Based on experiences with multiple organizations, Figure 3.3 gives a road map and a toolkit for cultivating virtue to amplify performance.

Road Map

- Adopt virtue as a common language to define excellence.
- Focus on people belonging, mattering, and making a difference to the organization.
- Integrate the practice of virtue into daily operations.

Toolkit

- Pull rather than push because the practice of virtue is an attractor, not a mandate.
- Rely on intrinsic, not extrinsic, motivation.
- Virtue is formed more by habits, coaching, and practice than by information.
- Apply a strength-based approach.
- Rely on evidence-based virtue tools and deliberate practice.

Figure 3.3 A Road Map and a Toolkit for Cultivating Virtue to Amplify Performance

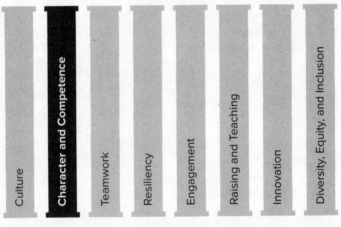

ARETÉ
Excellence

Habits
Coaching
Restoration

Culture

Character and Competence

Teamwork

Resiliency

Engagement

Raising and Teaching

Innovation

Diversity, Equity, and Inclusion

Character

Trust   Compassion   Courage

Justice   Wisdom   Temperance   Hope

HIRE FOR CHARACTER, TRAIN FOR COMPETENCE

*No matter what the job is, its description focuses on
two things: what the employee needs to know, and what the
employee needs to do. Knowledge and skill are essential
qualities in any employee. But are they enough?
Isn't there another aspect of a job candidate's profile
that is at least as important as knowledge and skill—
namely, that person's character?*[1]
—BRUCE WEINSTEIN

Hiring an impressive résumé seems like a good bet. We give the benefit-of-the-doubt status to those who have completed exclusive educations and who have worked for name brand organizations. Credentials and competencies are certainly important considerations when someone is being hired or promoted. So is character, which is why it is useful to understand how a candidate responds to a difficult teammate, customer, partner, patient, or student. It would be revealing to learn how someone performed when no one was looking. It is relevant to learn how someone performed doing work that was hard and important. In other words, there is the person we say we are when the sea is calm, and there is the person we really are during a storm.

Besides, consider the amount of wasted energy caused when character is missing in action. Despite the disproportionate impact of low character on performance, we might overlook this limitation for people with high competence. Examples: the very productive salesman who harasses people around him; the skilled, productive surgeon who has outbursts and throws scalpels in the operating room. Our admonition is to resist this temptation. Hire for character and train for competence.

Arguably, the most powerful way to build a culture of better humans and better performers is through rigorous assessment of who comes through the front door (new hires); who gets to sit in the corner office (promotions); and who is shown the door (separations). Where do you start? "Who Before What." That is a phrase that Jim Collins coined to describe the first necessary stage to building a great company.[2] *Who we are* defines our character. *What we do* defines our competence (Figure 4.1).

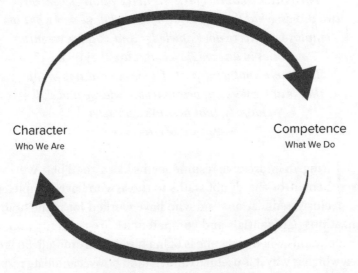

Character
Who We Are

Competence
What We Do

Figure 4.1 "Who Before What"

Character and competence can't be defined as either you have it or you don't. Certainly no one can claim they are completely virtuous. And even the most dismal among us have some redeeming character qualities. Similarly, no one can claim they are completely competent as a physician, engineer, carpenter, or student. Figure 4.2 demonstrates when it comes to character and competence, we need to be more nuanced than either/or thinking. We can think of both qualities existing along a sliding scale that when both character and competence are strong, the result is sustainable high performance. In contrast, when competence and/or character are inadequate, then high performance isn't sustainable.

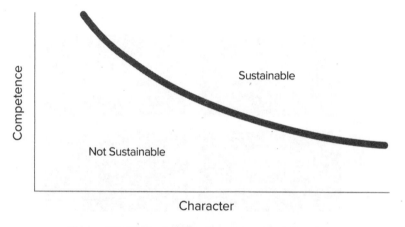

Figure 4.2 Sliding Scale for Competence and Character

Hiring for character and training for competence certainly doesn't mean ignoring incompetence. Perhaps evaluating whether the person has the educational background, professional experience, and knowledge and skills to do the job is the place to start. After all, a well-intentioned incompetent can cause plenty of grief no matter how high their character.

At the same time, there are important performance reasons to give significant weight to character. Character is a performance amplifier of competence. Character is malleable and can be developed. Character enables people to deliver sustainable performance during periods of uncertainty, adversity, and pressure. High-character people by definition are committed to grow and develop continually.

Despite the performance reasons for considering character, often competence is given more weight. This isn't because character is viewed as unimportant. It is because those making hiring decisions are unaware of the performance benefits of character or how character can be evaluated.

Figure 4.3 presents four quadrants that can be used to evaluate teammates on the character and competence continua. The easy decisions relate to *keepers of the culture* and *poor performers*. You are glad to have one on your team, and you plan to remove the other. The real test of what truly defines the culture is how we treat *potentials* and *culture killers*:

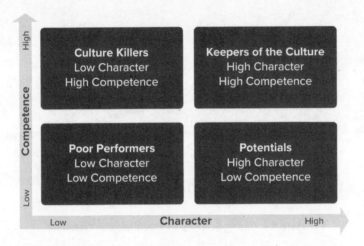

Figure 4.3 Character and Competence as Determinants of Performance

Keepers of the culture: Teammates who are high in competence and character define the culture at its best. They achieve the right results, the right way, for the right reasons. They seek advice and feedback about how to get even better. These are people you should drive to work each day! Ask them what they need and support them.

Poor performers: Someone who is low in character and competence reflects a selection error. People certainly can change, though no organization wants to see anyone in this quadrant. How one offboards these individuals also speaks to the culture. This should be done with grace and consideration, while maintaining rigor about the need for performance and character. Offboarding should in no way be a demeaning process but rather simply a recognition of poor fit with the organization's culture and goals.

Potentials: Employees in this quadrant have high levels of character but lower levels of competence. Clearly, some threshold of competency is necessary, though few candidates tick every professional and educational box deemed essential to succeed at the next level. Potentials are usually good bets because people of character by definition are motivated to become more competent.

Culture killers: Leaders in this quadrant are an organization's worst nightmare. They achieve results through fear and blame rather than engagement and teamwork. They may not break laws, but they surely break trust, increase cynicism, and decrease engagement. When people lack character, you'd prefer they were dumb and lazy, so at least you could see it coming. Being cunning, clever, and competent is a deadly combination to an organization. While it is tempting to put up with toxic leaders who pay the bills or surgeons who are surgically brilliant but who throw scalpels, doing so has tremendous adverse consequences for the organization. Retaining "culture killers" teaches everyone that while integrity may be good, financial results are better. Rather, culture killers need attention and prompt organizational action including separation if there is no commitment to improve.

PERFORMANCE VIRTUES

Nobel Prize–winning economist James Heckman demonstrated that noncognitive factors such as social skills, motivation, and persistence have a bigger payoff in the labor market and in school than achievement tests. Heckman reviewed numerous studies that demonstrate that high IQ people fail to achieve for noncognitive reasons.

Consider the adage, "People are hired on their competencies and fired on their character." Similarly, lower IQ people can succeed for noncognitive reasons. While cognitive abilities are largely formed early in life, noncognitive skills continue to develop throughout our life.[3] So, if you are convinced that hiring for character is an especially sound strategy for strengthening a culture, but don't know what to look for in candidates, consider the performance virtues that we call the 4Gs: *giving, gratitude, growth mindset*, and *grit*.

Giving and How to Spot It

Every day, people make decisions whether to act like givers, matchers, or takers, which author Adam Grant defines in this way:

> **Givers:** Help others unconditionally. They prefer to give more than they get.
>
> **Matchers:** Help conditionally. I'll scratch your back if you scratch mine. Most people are matchers.
>
> **Takers:** Will help only if they get something out of it. They are more interested in getting credit than helping.[4]

When it comes to performance, whom would you bet on: the givers, the matchers, or the takers? For example, if you have a team of salespeople, who sells more? If you have surgeons, who has the fewest medical errors? The answer: in the short term, taking works. The problem is that once people catch on to your taking, at best they stop helping and at worst, they sabotage your efforts. It's the givers who are both the best performers and the worst performers. For givers to succeed and be the best performers, they must avoid being doormats, especially when they go up against takers. That said, takers are the culture killers that have a disproportionate negative impact on performance. One taker can drag the matchers down to takers and the givers down to matchers.[5] If takers don't change, then—as with culture killers—what we tolerate is what we get. Sometimes we need to say to a taker—as we say to a culture killer—"We love you, but you need to leave now."

Look for individuals who share knowledge and help and who contribute to others without seeking anything in return. While takers tend to use "I," "me," and "my" pronouns and take personal credit, givers are more likely to use "we," "our," and "us" pronouns and share achievement. Takers can describe their own achievements. Takers struggle with how they contributed to other people's achievements. When takers talk about mistakes, they usually blame others, whereas givers own their mistakes and share what they learned. Givers help others achieve their goals, which lies at the heart of effective collaboration, innovation, quality improvement, and service excellence. Giving and generosity have one thing in common: being *other focused.*

Gratitude and How to Spot It

Gratitude gives us or others hope. Cicero said, "Gratitude is not only the greatest of the virtues, but the parent of all the others."[6] A few decades ago, science caught up to this ancient wisdom by running an experiment. One group wrote down three things that ticked them off for 21 consecutive days; the other group wrote down three things for which they were grateful for 21 consecutive days, and the third group did nothing. The results of the study were as you would expect. The miserable group was more miserable on day 22 than on day 1. The grateful group was more grateful on day 22 than on day 1. And the control group experienced no difference.

Appreciation or gratitude inspires engagement more than higher pay, promotions, empowerment, or training.

When people receive thanks for their generosity, they are more likely to continue giving, helping, cooperating, and collaborating. People who experience gratitude in their work are less likely to experience burnout and more likely to experience satisfaction in their work.[7]

Grateful people are humble, self-aware, and wise. They know that success is seldom achieved solely by one's own effort. For this reason, they share achievement rather than take credit. They live a reflective, intentional, and self-disciplined life, seeking the positives in all situations.

Grateful people value ethics and honesty. They want to do business in a way that promotes healthy work relationships and that also promotes the quality and safety of the products and services they create. Grateful people are more resilient, flexible, and better team players than people who lack gratitude. Look for evidence of a "Pay it forward" or "We're all in this together" mentality.[8]

Growth Mindset and How to Spot It

As Carol Dweck's research demonstrates, people with a "growth mindset" believe you can get better, smarter, and more collaborative. People with a growth mindset seek out challenges so they can grow. "Fixed mindset" people believe that you either have ability or you don't, so they avoid challenges.

Dweck offers some myth busters through her research. First, being flexible, being open-minded, and having a positive outlook are all laudable, but absent behaviors that lead to actual improvement, this is what she calls a "false growth mindset." In reality, we all are a mixed bag of fixed and growth mindsets because no person or species has a "pure growth mindset." Second, praising and rewarding effort are only a part of developing a growth mindset. Results matter. Adopting a "not-yet strategy" means that we haven't yet achieved results. "Not yet" means that we will keep trying, keep learning, and keep seeking feedback in order to ultimately achieve the desired results. Having a persistent not-yet mindset will lead to better results.[9]

It is incredibly challenging to acquire a growth mindset because we all exhibit both the insecurity and defensiveness that can shut down a growth mindset. When competition is a zero-sum game, sharing, collaborating, seeking feedback, and admitting mistakes can come to a screeching halt. When we activate our fixed mindset, defined as becoming defensive or scared, that is the time we most need to kick a growth mindset into gear.[10]

Here's an example of a growth mindset. Dweck was retained to help a professional sports team develop interview screening questions for prospective draft choices. Her suggestion was simple. Ask the candidates: "What do you expect at the next level of competition, and how do you prepare to improve?" Years of research have shown that we are not good at predicting future success on the basis of current talent assessments. Why? Because current assessments do not reveal people's future growth potential and how they might perform with the right support, commitment, effort, and training. In fact, research shows that people's level of support, commitment, effort, and continued training is what eventually separates the most successful people from their equally talented, but less successful peers.[11]

Grit and How to Spot It

Author and University of Pennsylvania Professor Angela Duckworth has defined *grit* as "perseverance and passion for long-term goals."[12] In fact, grit involves working hard for years to achieve a goal. Yet things get in our way. For example, as an automatic response to perceived or real danger, we tend to invest more in fear than hope. Yet, the primordial part of our brain does a lousy job distinguishing between small stuff and really big stuff, like the difference between getting our feelings bruised in a meeting because our idea wasn't accepted versus experiencing a serious physical threat.

The Giraffe Heroes Project provides an interesting way to cultivate grit. This international organization identifies largely unknown compassionate risk-takers who stick their necks out for the common good. For example, Joe Medalia uses his business to train dozens of youngsters with disabilities despite the time and cost of correcting errors. Medalia actively pushes other business owners to do the same. The Giraffe organization's strategy involves participants' listening and reading stories about others who have exhibited courage and then the participants' telling their own stories about courageous people they know.

We learn to "stick our neck out" by taking on problems that are sitting under our nose. For example, strive to be courageous by identifying a need in your community and contribute to solutions.[13]

HOW TO COMBAT BIAS

Anyone who has been involved in hiring decisions should be humbled by how poorly interviews predict future performance. What would organizations discover if a year after hiring decisions were made, they evaluated how many teammates were disappointments or diamonds in the rough? We filter information and make quick hiring decisions based more on confirmation bias than we may realize. Research has revealed that who gets hired has more to do with the interviewer than with the interviewee. We tend to hire people who are more like us rather than what the team or business needs. To make matters worse, it is easy to evaluate what matters least (education, grades, or age) but not what matters most (the 4Gs). There are two important ways to mitigate these hiring risks: conducting structured interviews and having multiple assessors.

First, put together a diverse hiring team, and make sure to compare evaluations. That simple step helps overcome bias. Second, structure the interviews because doing so increases the chances of making good hiring decisions. Using structured interviews means that all evaluators will be looking for the same evidence-based performance virtues—giving, gratitude, growth mindset, and grit—and asking the same questions. Then all evaluators can share notes with each other, so that everyone can assess the candidates from multiple perspectives using the same criteria. Here are sample questions to help create structured interviews:

- Tell us about a time your behavior had a positive impact on your team. (Follow-ups: What was your primary goal and why? How did your teammates respond? How do you see yourself contributing to teamwork if you join our organization?)
- Tell us about a time when you effectively managed your team to achieve a goal. What did your approach look like? (Follow-ups: What were your targets, and how did you meet them as an individual and as a team? How did you adapt your leadership approach to different individuals? What was the key takeaway from that specific situation?)
- Tell us about a time you had difficulty working with someone (can be a coworker, classmate, or client). What made this person difficult to work with for you? (Follow-ups: What steps did you take to resolve the problem? What was the outcome? What could you have done differently?)

- Tell us about a time when you faced personal or professional adversity. (Follow-ups: How did you respond? What did you learn from the experience? How did you grow?)
- Tell us about a person who had a significant positive impact on you. (Follow-ups: What did that person teach you? How did they help you grow?)

Structured interviews conducted by a diverse hiring team are more fair than unstructured interviews conducted by a homogenous team. As a result, candidates report a better interviewing experience. However, the cautionary note is that the 4Gs are easier to observe when we see how someone responds to stress, failure, and working in teams and harder to predict during an interview. With that caution in mind, let's shift from how to select people to how to develop people.

THE IMPORTANCE OF INTERIOR DEVELOPMENT

External development can be seen—impressive job titles, big house, nice car, and expensive vacations—while internal development is often "hidden in full view." When it comes to internal development, we learn to give, to develop grit, to develop a growth mindset, and to be grateful. And we also learn to take, to quit, to have a fixed mindset, and to be ungrateful. A freshly minted college graduate put it this way: "I have always been goal directed with the aim to build my engineering credentials. After attending a session on the importance of practicing virtues, I want to pay more attention to the kind of person I want to be." The virtues and the 4Gs offered her an operating model to do just that.

Given the personal and professional importance of the 4Gs, how do people seek feedback about their strengths and where they can improve? Most people want feedback. Too few know how to seek feedback. Too many wait passively to receive it.

One of the reasons seeking feedback is a challenge is that it sits between our drive to learn and our desire to belong.

There are ways to both learn and cultivate our sense of belonging. One way is to start a "50 cups of coffee" learning tour by identifying 50 people a year whom you want to learn from. Request 20 to 30 minutes from each of them to learn something specific. If they have observed your performance, perhaps you will ask for feedback about a project they watched you lead. Or you might ask them questions about building strong teams, how they prepare for presentations, or insights about their career path. The Honor Foundation proposes this goal to military special operatives who are transitioning into civilian life. However, a 50 cups of coffee tour doesn't have to be limited to making a career transition. It can be an ongoing way to make connections and learn.

KEY TAKEAWAYS

We will end this chapter with a 4Gs scorecard (Table 4.1). Its purpose is to provide a guide for internal development. The 4Gs scorecard is a tool to compare how you see yourself and how others see you when it comes to giving, gratitude, growth mindset, and grit. Identify people you know, like, and trust to complete the 4Gs scorecard so you can compare your self-assessment with their evaluation. It is worth repeating that it is hard to know our strengths without feedback from others.

4GS SCORECARD: GIVING, GRATITUDE, GROWTH MINDSET, AND GRIT SELF-ASSESSMENT

Directions: Mark the criteria of the 4Gs and habits using the following scale: 1, almost never; 2, rarely; 3, sometimes; 4, often; and 5, almost always.

Table 4.1 **4Gs Scorecard**

	How I See Myself	How Others See Me
Giving: I practice serving others.		
I spend time with people who bring out the best in me.		
I demonstrate respect toward customers and colleagues regardless of how others treat me.		
I am committed to developing my virtues to positively affect the team and the business.		
I help other people succeed.		
Growth mindset: I learn and improve, with a focus on effort and process.		
I focus on the process of improving, rather than accept that my talent is fixed.		
I am willing to take risks and innovate as ways to get better.		
I look at challenges as opportunities, not obstacles.		

	How I See Myself	How Others See Me
I deal with frustration and setbacks in a positive, action-oriented way.		
Grit: I persevere with passion to achieve my long-term goals and aspirations.		
I have a passion for my work. What I do is very important to me.		
I am highly engaged to follow through on goals and plans, even if it takes sacrifice and hard work.		
I try very hard, especially after experiencing failure.		
I practice in a deliberate and disciplined way to leverage strengths and manage weaknesses.		
Gratitude: I appreciate the support and opportunities I have been given.		
I appreciate having a purpose to be part of something bigger than myself.		
I understand where I am, where I want to go, and how I will get there.		
I actively practice gratitude.		
I constantly assess progress on my plan, and I appreciate the support of coaches and teammates to help me adjust.		
Practice character habits: Wisdom and temperance.		
I am disciplined in reflecting on ways to get better than I used to be.		
I intentionally practice compassion and justice.		
I strive to do the "hard right rather than the easy wrong."		
I actively work to learn from mistakes.		

The higher the cumulative score, the more you demonstrate giving, gratitude, growth mindset, and grit, and the more you practice character habits according to your own and others' ratings. The greater alignment between the "self" and "others" scores, the higher the level of self-awareness. Clearly, a person might be high in one of the 4Gs and less so in another of the 4Gs. For example, they are high in giving and gratitude though not as high in growth mindset and grit, at least according to their self and others' ratings.

The findings from this evaluation might reveal unknown strengths. Once identified, a strengths-based approach focuses on what you do well and how you can do more of that. In some cases, the evaluation might reveal a fatal flaw defined by a limitation that regularly has a negative impact on relationships and performance. Whether results are favorable or unfavorable, the developmental question is, how can insights from the 4Gs scorecard be used to strengthen performance?

ARETÉ

Excellence

Habits

Coaching

Restoration

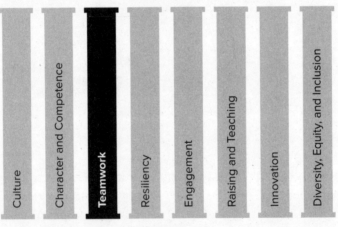

Culture

Character and Competence

Teamwork

Resiliency

Engagement

Raising and Teaching

Innovation

Diversity, Equity, and Inclusion

Character

Trust   Compassion   Courage

Justice   Wisdom   Temperance   Hope

TEAMWORK

*It is the long history of humankind
(and animal kind, too) that those who
learned to collaborate and improvise
most effectively have prevailed.*[1]
—CHARLES DARWIN

This is a story about teamwork that involves two really different types of leaders, both of whom were devoted to high-performing teamwork: Navy SEAL instructors and professional baseball coaches. Between deployments, SEAL instructors train SEAL cadets. Professional baseball coaches have played the game at a high level and now coach minor and major league baseball players. In 2020, both teams came to the Cleveland Major League Baseball spring training in Goodyear, Arizona, to share insights on performing at a high level under conditions of extreme pressure.

The acronym SEAL stands for Sea, Air and Land, the three theaters of special forces operations. For example, SEALs might be tasked with the mission to control a perimeter around a building held by terrorists. SEALs give time for "friendlies," or someone who is a supporter, to clear the building. Those who remain are assumed to have bad intent until proven otherwise. SEALs enter the building facing agonizing "shoot or don't shoot" decisions. A 10-year-old boy might be tied to a suicide vest, or a wife might be held against her will. Don't shoot, and SEALs die. Shoot, but there's a victim with no gun, and you are brought up on charges and have to leave the country. A CNN story about killing an innocent person damages military strategy more than anything the enemy can inflict. On a personal level, a solider suffers a lifelong moral injury sentence for killing an innocent civilian.

Professional baseball players do not face life-or-death decisions, though they do share the SEALs' mandate to perform under intense pressure. Baseball is a game of failure, and when a player screws up, their mistakes are seen by thousands of fans in the stands and millions on TV. The game of baseball demands that players get better by learning from, rather than fearing, failure.

The SEALs and coaches traded places to learn again what it felt like to be a beginner. For example, a SEAL sprinted with impressive closing speed to catch a fly ball; however, the closer he got to the ball, the clearer it became that he played like a beginner. In a batting cage, a SEAL swung violently, but again the probability of ball contact was low. Then, the coaches talked smack to the SEAL and then quickly diagnosed and corrected the flaws in his swing. Soon, he started hitting the ball.

Then, it was time to trade places. The SEALs taught the baseball coaches how to clear a room, including making split-second, friend-or-foe decisions. The SEALs cleared a room with precision and speed. Every movement was carefully choreographed. When it was the coaches' turn, the coaches were slow and clumsy. They shot when they shouldn't have, killing an imaginary child. They didn't shoot when they should have, which simulated a coach getting killed. The SEALs talked smack to the coaches. They quickly corrected the flaws in the coaches' footwork. While the coaches were not going to become honorary SEALs anytime soon, their speed increased and they better distinguished between people of goodwill and ill will.

So, what lessons on teamwork did each group learn from the other? Baseball coaches learned that the military has long held the view that bonding and trust are essential to performance. SEALs train by holding up logs or 300-pound boats to reveal who literally doesn't pull their weight. The rest of us aren't interested experiencing that kind of punishment. And we don't need to be ultra-fit to know which of our teammates metaphorically carry their weight. We all have experienced hardship that on a good team cultivates the kind of trust necessary for sacrifice and selflessness. When teams achieve the "I have your back" culture, they perceive stress as a challenge instead of a threat.

SEALs don't see themselves as super soldiers. They do see themselves as being part of super teams. SEALs never want to let their teammates down and never want to be average. It is not just about being tough, smart, and skilled. To be elite, you have to excel in helping your teammates. Each SEAL literally puts their life in the hands of their teammates, so that trust, not just military tactical skill, makes teams tough to beat.

The SEALs learned that the Cleveland baseball team won the most regular season games over a half dozen seasons, even though they had fewer resources than other teams. They carefully invested in areas, such as technology, that could efficiently improve player performance. For example, a small device attached to a bat calculated the hitter's bat speed and launch angle. A small device inserted into the back of a player's uniform tracked effort, heart rate, and where the player ran. But player performance depends on more than technology. A wise coach doesn't talk baseball when they first meet a player. They read a player's bio and ask, "Hey, I see that you grew up in a small town in Texas. What was it like to live there?"

In trading places, the SEALs and coaches learned about the "curse of knowledge." What is that? Once we know something, we are not able to imagine not knowing it, which acts like a blind spot. More often than not, experts forget what it is like to be a beginner. The more we know, the harder it is to put ourselves in the shoes of those unfamiliar with our area of expertise.

Experts in special operations and baseball cannot unlearn what they know, and typically they don't imagine what it is like to be a beginner. The SEALs were incredibly competent in clearing and taking control of a room. However, based on the curse of knowledge, some offered too much advice. But one SEAL instructor was particularly effective. Why? He was empathic toward beginners and economic in his language, and he offered a single cue to improve footwork. He could put himself in the shoes of the beginner, and he taught patiently.

It is interesting to peek into the worlds of special operations and professional baseball and see how they intersect on the common theme of developing high performance in teams, despite pressure and uncertainty. However, this is not a story about being a solider or an athlete. Few of us have the skill, never mind the interest to do either. It's a story about developing high-performing teams.

Here's the real challenge for all teams. Whether we know too much or know too little, the hard part is coming to grips with our shared plight to avoid looking stupid or inept, or to stand out against the team.

Imagine a team that does not expect perfect teammates. They trust each other because they know their teammates will get back up after they fall. Imagine teammates that understand that learning is best achieved by helping another person succeed, even above their own individual success. Imagine being part of a team like that. Now that would be an awesome place to work.

When we unpack the elements of high-performing teams, five common themes jump out as actions that just might make a place to work occasionally awesome (see also Figure 5.1):

1. **Build relationships.** Teams whose members enjoy strong relationships defined by virtue, even if not perfect, create the psychological safety necessary for learning under conditions of pressure and uncertainty. Trust and compassion are foundational to the work of the team.
2. **Leverage strengths.** Teams that perform well offset one teammate's weaknesses with another member's strengths. It is easier to build on a strength than it is to overcome a weakness.
3. **Create clarity.** Great teams ask: "What does good look like?" They start by getting clear about their goals and what success would look like.
4. **Define purpose.** Great teams are really clear about the purpose of their work together. They are clear about whom they serve.
5. **Drive results.** Great teams ask and are clear about the desired outcomes of their work. They recognize the differences between tangible outcomes, which may not always be in

their control, and the intangible results, which usually regard the process of their teamwork and the culture that they do control. Again, when we get good at who we are, we get better at what we do.

Figure 5.1 Five Actions to Make the Workplace Awesome

These five steps are sequential, though they may not be linear. Let's start with the first step: building relationships.

1. BUILD RELATIONSHIPS

When your team fears they will be ignored, humiliated, or blamed for making suggestions to improve or mitigate risk, they will underperform. Teammates need to feel safe and trust one another. Lack of trust is a major source of team dysfunction. Evidence that these ideas are generalizable comes from Brandeis University Professor Jody Gittell's work on relationships and high performance.[2] She initially studied the then high performer among airlines: Southwest Airlines. She identified three elements that composed the "secret sauce" of Southwest's performance that differentiated the company from other airlines:

1. An environment that emphasized shared goals, shared knowledge, and mutual respect.
2. Robust communication techniques that made communication frequent, timely, and focused on problem solving.

3. Having an inventory of organizational practices that built relationships between managers and frontline employees. These included hiring and training for relationship excellence and using conflict to build relationships.[3]

Professor Gittell concluded that Southwest's leaders "see these relationships—with their employees, among their employees, and with outside parties—as the foundation of their competitive advantage, through good times and bad. They see the quality of these relationships not as a success factor but as the most essential success factor."

OK, you say. Works in the airline industry. Anywhere else? Does the power of relationships to achieve high performance extend beyond airlines? Yes! Professor Gittell went on to study the complex world of healthcare.

In a landmark study of surgical outcomes in nine hospitals around the United States, she framed the concept of *relational coordination* to summarize how coworkers work together. Relational coordination "comprises frequent, timely, accurate communication, as well as problem-solving, shared goals, shared knowledge, and mutual respect among health care providers." No surprise: measures of relational coordination showed tight correlations with improved surgical outcomes in all hospitals. The more we value people and the better they work together, the better the outcomes of our work.

Let's consider another example of relational coordination in one of the most complicated places in a hospital: the intensive care unit (ICU). Good outcomes there are literally life or death, and they depend critically on the fluid interaction of lots of healthcare providers. The ICU team in the Shock Trauma ICU (STRICU) of the Latter Day Saints Hospital in Utah cares for the sickest of the sick—patients with medical illnesses that threaten life, like overwhelming infection and literally body-crushing trauma. A STRICU team consists of caregivers such as physicians, nurses, respiratory therapists, technicians, nutritionists, pharmacists, ethicists, and unit administrators. All are committed to improving patient outcomes by embracing five principles to enhance teamwork. These five principles were informed by Nobel Laureate behavioral economists' research about optimizing outcomes, and they closely resemble the dimensions of relational coordination:

1. Develop a shared purpose.
2. Create an open and safe environment (that is, psychologically safe), and encourage diverse views.
3. Include all those who share the common purpose.
4. Learn how to negotiate agreement, and teach these skills to all stakeholders.
5. Insist on fairness and equity in applying all norms and rules.[4]

The STRICU team leadership—the medical director and the nurse manager—made a commitment to model these behaviors in all their interactions. They codeveloped a statement—that is, a credo—of their shared purpose to improve the outcomes of the patients for whom they cared, and they shared this credo with all their colleagues. The medical director and nurse manager committed to publicly demonstrate their cooperation. When they developed care protocols that guided many of the processes in the STRICU, for example, how to treat elevated blood sugar values or how to liberate patients from mechanical ventilation, they did so together, and then they invited all members of the STRICU community to offer their candid input about those protocols before they were implemented. Recognizing that ICUs sometimes have an implicit hierarchy in which caregivers who are not physicians can sometimes feel intimidated by the physicians' presence, the doctors in the STRICU would reach out individually to seek all STRICU stakeholders' (for example, nurses' and respiratory therapists') views.

Negotiation training was developed and made available to all members of the STRICU team. They were all encouraged to be hard on problems and soft on people and, whenever possible, to use hard metrics and data to guide decisions. Finally, they committed to apply rules equitably to all STRICU stakeholders. For example, when deadlines for comments on new protocols were announced, late input was dismissed from physicians and other caregivers alike. Conversely, input from all was actively invited during the announced comment periods on the protocols.

The results of this four-year effort to improve patient outcomes in the STRICU were impressive. Practices in sedating patients and using powerful paralytic drugs for various STRICU procedures improved. Control of important blood chemistry values like potassium and blood sugar levels improved. And the use of antibiotics, which when overused can have an adverse impact by creating resistance of the infecting microorganisms to these agents, was enhanced. And, as a bonus, all of these clinical improvements were accompanied by a 30 percent decrease in STRICU costs of care and a 19 percent decrease in the overall hospital cost of care for these patients. Clearly, collaborative teamwork matters. Figure 5.2 features a checklist and an assessment tool that can help strengthen collaboration. Check one area that would most strengthen performance for your team.

High-Performing Team

- Teammates care about each other, and each teammate has a voice.
- Teammates feel safe to take risks with team members.
- Teammates feel confident that no one on the team will be embarrassed or punished for admitting mistakes, asking questions, or offering new ideas.

Low-Performing Team

- Teammates don't feel like they belong to the team.
- Teammates fear what will happen if they fail, even when they take intelligent risks.
- Teammates do not feel they are treated with respect and dignity.

Ask Yourself

- Are teammates hesitant to ask questions?
- Is there a lack of accountability for results?
- Is there a fear of asking or giving constructive feedback?

Figure 5.2 A Checklist and Assessment Tool That Can Help Strengthen Collaboration

2. LEVERAGE STRENGTHS

Teams learn faster when they are strengths-based because a focus on weaknesses—not strengths—diminishes performance. Gallup compared 50,000 teams in 192 organizations that ranged in performance from high to low. Almost none of the variance in performance was about pay and career opportunities. Instead, the statement that explained most of the variance in performance was, "At work, I have the opportunity to do what I do best every day." Teammates who reported "strongly agree" on this item, were 44 percent more likely to earn a high customer satisfaction score, 50 percent more likely to be retained, and 38 percent more likely to be productive.[5]

Performance evaluation systems can undermine strengths-spotting when leaders deliver some version of a "crap sandwich": say something nice, point out "areas for growth," and then say something nice. Deloitte offers a subtle, though powerful, "crap sandwich" alternative. Don't ask leaders what they think about a teammate's skills. Ask what they would do to help their teammate.[6]

While we stink at rating others, we are highly consistent in creating actions to support a teammate's growth and learning. Of course, evaluations on compensation still need to be made. Importantly, we should separate in time the extrinsic part of evaluation (pay) from the intrinsic part of development (learning and growth). When we mix pay and development, all we hear is pay as a proxy for whether we are valued.

Traditional performance assessment involves infrequent judgment, which means evaluation is often limited to a once-a-year event. As an alternative, imagine a system and a culture that relied on the science of high performance by focusing on teamwork, resilience, and regular coaching. Deep learning is about *recognizing* strengths and then *reinforcing* and *refining* strengths. A leader could say to an impressive teammate, "When I observe how you help others, this is what you made me think about (recognize). When members of the team were struggling to get back up after getting knocked down, you helped the team focus on what they needed to learn in order to get better."

Good coaches ask questions rather than offer answers. For example, before you take on the problem of people feeling discouraged, ask what's working now. When you have had a problem similar to this, what worked? What do you already know you need to do? The emphasis is on *what* and *how questions* rather than *why* because asking *why* implies judgment. *What* and *how* are the questions of a skilled coach.[7] All this is to say, let's just see if we can do a better job leveraging strengths and managing weaknesses.

How Well Does Your Team Leverage Strengths?

But let's face it. As we saw, humans are deficit-based animals. We see the potholes in the road instead of the beautiful horizon. The issue is not, "What is broken and how do I fix it?"—a distinctly deficit-based approach—but rather, "Who are we when we are at our best?" and "What skills do we have that, when developed yet further, can improve our work?" Organizational thinkers call this an *appreciative approach*. Words create worlds, and the way we frame the issue informs the answers we generate. And appreciative framing informs better answers than deficit-based thinking.

Consider another context: marriage counseling. One approach to marriage counseling involves partners describing how each person drives the other one nuts. The remedy is for each partner to correct their annoying behavior—usually with disappointing results. In contrast, research reveals that marriages destined for success involve two people overlooking each other's flaws. When a spouse messes up, their partner grants them the benefit of the doubt. When we overreact to negative events, we lose perspective and make matters worse.

Fear is the engine of negativity and becomes a prediction of what will happen, even when that outcome is unlikely. About 85 percent of what we worry about never happens, and the remaining 15 percent often wasn't as bad as we feared. When we acquire a more precise account of what is actually happening, we can read our fears accurately and gain a bit of wisdom and perspective. So, when your fear story kicks in, consider asking three questions to reduce the power of negativity:

- What is the worst that could happen?
- What is the likelihood that the worst will happen?
- If the worst happened, could we handle it?

If we increase the amount of time that each person uses their strengths, then performance increases. And we will also increase personal satisfaction. Figure 5.3 features a checklist and an assessment tool that can help strengthen the ability of teams to leverage their strengths. Check one area that would most strengthen performance for your team.

High-Performing Team

- Team reliably completes quality work on time.

- Teammates leverage each other's strengths while acknowledging each other's weaknesses.

- Teammates assume responsibility for a member's weakness, and the person who offloaded responsibility will contribute to the team in another way.

Low-Performing Team

- Team culture is deficit based.

- Team's primary focus is improving weaknesses.

- Teammate responsibilities are fixed with limited consideration to how strengths can be leveraged.

Ask Yourself

- Do teammates think they can make a difference?

- Do teammates believe they are encouraged to leverage their strengths?

- Do teammates actively adapt to serving business partners or customers by leveraging strengths and managing weaknesses?

- What do we do well, and how can we do more of it?

Figure 5.3 A Checklist and Assessment Tool That Can Help the Ability of Teams to Leverage Their Strengths

3. CREATE CLARITY

The third step asks the question, "What does good look like?" The answer helps teams develop shared clarity and structure in the work. A shared vision clarifies what is expected. Otherwise, good people get discouraged working at cross-purposes.

Chartering at the beginning of a team's work is an effective way to achieve clarity and alignment. In chartering, every member of the team is invited by the leader to weigh in on the question, "If our work together is successful, what do we do?" Answering this question at the front end of the team's work enables people to identify, discuss, and resolve differences. Do this work at the front end, to avoid misalignment at the back end. Part of chartering is clarifying the roles and responsibilities of each team member. Two questions and two statements can help here:

- Ask teammates and partners, what do you expect of me?
- Ask teammates and partners, what don't you expect of me?
- Tell teammates and partners what you expect of them.
- Tell teammates and partners what you don't expect of them.

These simple questions can go a long way to aligning expectations and efforts. In the following section is a checklist to assess whether your team has clarity.

Is Clarity a Strength of Your Team?

In addition to being clear on goals, roles, and responsibilities, how people treat each other predicts performance more than who is on the team. Specific ground rules of team behaviors are important to high-performing teams. These behaviors include the following:

- Listening by summarizing what others said—also referred to as *active listening*
- Admitting what we don't know
- Making sure everyone speaks
- Avoiding interrupting teammates
- Encouraging people to express frustrations

- Encouraging teammates without judgment
- Calling out conflicts and resolving conflicts openly[8]

An especially important behavior in a high-performing team that is essential to creating clarity is ensuring that everyone has a voice. Leaders must invite—indeed insist on—full participation. In turn, every teammate is obligated to make the team stronger. Before the meeting ends, ask each person, "What are your thoughts?" "What do you see that we are missing?" "What do you know that I should know?"

Figure 5.4 features a checklist and an assessment tool that can help strengthen clarity for teams. Check one area that would most strengthen performance for your team.

High-Performing Team

- Team understands what's expected and follows processes to fulfill these expectations.
- Team knows how their performance affects organizational performance.
- Team uses specific, measurable, actionable, results-based, time-bound (SMART) goals.

Low-Performing Team

- Team has poor visibility into priorities or progress.
- Team responsibility is diffused—no clear owners for tasks or problems.
- Team is unclear what successful performance means.

Ask Yourself

- Do teammates feel they are empowered?
- Do teammates understand their goals and how to get there?
- Do teammates knock down silos and prioritize collaboration across disciplines?

Figure 5.4 A Checklist and Assessment Tool That Can Help Strengthen Clarity for Teams

4. DEFINE PURPOSE

The fourth step in creating high-performing teams is defining purpose. When we can align our team around how we treat each other and having a shared purpose, we are on a mission. While purpose has a powerful impact on performance, the idea is abstract. We can be more concrete about purpose by considering how we treat others and whom we serve.

Let's start with how we treat others. People are not changed by programs. We know people are changed by relationships. Virtue is the most pro-social relationship practice of all. So, our aspiration, not always our reality, is to treat each other by practicing virtue.

The second question asks, "Whom do we serve?" We define our purpose based on value sought by the people we serve, *not* based on what we think others need. The point of purpose isn't to pat ourselves on the back but to actually help others. How do we know what would help someone? We don't guess. We ask them. If we get this right, then we are on a purpose-driven mission. When our purpose is clear, inevitable problems become speed bumps rather than impenetrable walls. In the following section, consider the checklist of attributes of purpose-driven teams.

To What Degree Does Your Team Have a Shared Purpose?

Figure 5.5 features a checklist and an assessment tool that can help your team members determine the strength of their shared purpose. Check one area that would most strengthen performance for your team.

High-Performing Team

- Team feels part of something bigger than themselves.
- Teammates live by conviction to practice virtue regardless of circumstances.
- A sense of purpose is personal and can vary— financial security, supporting family, helping the team succeed, or practicing virtue. What's common is a commitment to teammates, customers, and/or the community, as well as a commitment to high performance.

Low-Performing Team

- There is a lack of gratitude and recognition for contributions or achievements.
- Work assignments are based solely on ability, expertise, and workload. There is little consideration for individual development, strengths, interests, and meaning.
- There is a lack of shared commitment to whom the team serves and who they strive to be.

Ask Yourself

- Do teammates feel that their efforts matter?
- Do teammates feel proud to be part of the culture?
- Do teammates demonstrate grit and a growth mindset?

Figure 5.5 A Checklist and Assessment Tool That Can Help Strengthen a Team's Sense of Shared Purpose

5. DRIVE RESULTS

The fifth step in creating a high-performing team is to drive results. Effort is laudable, but results are what matters. It's one thing if a team misses its plan by a little. It is quite another when a team misses its plan by a lot. The consequences of a big miss can limit an organization's ability to serve others and limit teammates' ability to grow, or worse, it can cost hardworking people their jobs.

We all want to work on a team that makes a positive impact. Impact can be defined by both tangible and intangible results. Tangible results include objective metrics, such as financial performance. Intangible results include ideals that are subjective but not as easy to measure, such as whether a team feels their work stands for something that matters.

What Is the Impact of Results on Your Team's Performance?

Figure 5.6 features a checklist and an assessment tool that can help your team determine the impact of results on their performance. Check one area that would most strengthen performance for your team.

Because results are so important, a growth mindset is a healthy way to think about effort and results. Carol Dweck, in her work on the growth mindset, shared these three strategies:

1. **Your brain is like a muscle—exercise it.** When we do something that is hard and important, something we haven't done before, our brain fires up new neurons. When we keep doing the same thing no matter how hard we work, the result is no new neurons and no new smarts. Our brain doesn't care if we succeeded or failed. It just knows when we are trying to learn something new, and it responds by connecting new neurons to develop new abilities.
2. **Adopt a growth mindset.** Understand the difference between a growth mindset that sees talent as something that is developed versus a fixed mindset that is limiting because it sees talent as something we either have or we don't.

3. **See "not yet" as opportunity.** If we fell short of our targeted results, we need to learn and consider what capabilities we need to develop and with whom we should form a partnership in order to succeed. In other words, we are *not yet* where we want to be. "What now?" Not, "Why me?"[9]

Let's go the other way. You delivered results, though team satisfaction is in the dumpster. While the tangible financial results are impressive, intangible results feel empty. This isn't just fluffy philosophy. Getting results that don't feel meaningful certainly isn't sustainable. Peter Drucker viewed profits like breathing: necessary for life, but not a reason to live.

Consider if intangibles can be strengthened, such as trust and care among the team. Perhaps there is value in doubling down on teammates' strengths or improving clarity. Ultimately, the issue is getting clear about a team's purpose:

1. How do we strive to treat each other with dignity and respect?
2. Practice virtue, even if imperfectly.
3. Whom do we serve?
4. Define the people we serve, their pain points, and their alternatives.
5. Why is our value superior?

Perhaps teams can learn from the Navy SEALs' training about purpose. Cadets are told to put away gear in the following order: team gear first, buddy gear second, self-gear third. After cadets receive this instruction, they are tied together to swim the cold water of Coronado Bay in San Diego until they are exhausted. They return to shore so physically spent that they are unable to think straight. Inevitably, the cadets take care of self-gear first, then buddy gear, then team gear. Loads of pushups in the sand help remind cadets of the original priority. Good luck asking a colleague to drop and give you 50 pushups. But it is within our reach to consider our teammates' and buddies' concerns before our own.[10]

High-Performing Team

- Team's subjective judgment is that results make a difference and are important.

- Team's objective performance data demonstrates results contributing to organizational success.

- Team increases its performance by applying deliberate practice.

Low-Performing Team

- The team frames work as "treading water." They work hard but don't see the impact.

- The team regularly misses performance targets.

- There are too many goals, which limits the team's ability to make meaningful progress.

Ask Yourself

- Do teammates feel their work matters for a higher-order goal?

- Do teammates see their work as creating change for the better?

- How do the current team's processes affect well-being and burnout?

Figure 5.6 A Checklist and Assessment Tool That Can Help a Team Determine the Impact of Results

PLAYBOOKS TO STRENGTHEN TEAM PERFORMANCE

With the goal to increase team flourishing in mind, we offer a three-tiered performance sandwich. Relationships are the foundational bun, which can be strengthened by a *team user manual*. *Psychological safety* is the meat, which is a sophisticated task that includes assessment, understanding what promotes and inhibits team performance, and then practice. An *after action review* (AAR) tops off the sandwich, which is a concrete way to practice team learning. So, relationships first, psychological safety second, and after action review third.

Team User Manual

Since trust is efficient, how can trust be earned quicker and deeper? Regrettably, the worst way is the most common way: people just get to work. We assume that everyone wants to work the way we do though this is rarely the case. Let's call this *teamwork by chance*. Big surprise, teammates who don't know how to get the best out of each other underperform. Let's call the alternative approach *teamwork by design*. We assume that people differ significantly in how they best function on a team and a *team user manual* leverages differences:

> Step 1. Create a team user manual: Teammates write brief answers to a series of questions.
>
> Step 2. Members share their teammates' answers with the larger team.
>
> Step 3. The team creates a *team user manual* composed of one-page summaries of each teammate's answers to *who they are, the best way to interact with them*, and *their motivations and strengths*.

Now, team members have the insights they need for individual teammates to perform at their best.

Here are questions that can be used to create a team user manual:

Who You Are
1. What should people know about you to get your best effort?
2. What drives you nuts?
3. How can people earn a gold star with you?

Best Way to Interact with You
1. What are the best ways and worst ways to communicate with you?
2. What are the best ways to give you hard news or critical feedback?
3. What are three things that help you best respond to pressure and uncertainty?

Your Motivations and Strengths
1. At your funeral, which virtues do you want people to say were your strengths?
2. Name three to five of your greatest competencies.
3. What are your best hopes and greatest concerns?
4. Describe when you leveraged your character and competency strengths to serve others.[11]

You can think of a team user manual as an anti-drama tool. It's about intentionally getting to know your teammates at a much deeper level rather than slamming a group together and telling them to get to work. It creates more predictability and accelerates trust. Team performance is enhanced when turmoil is reduced.

Psychological Safety

When Harvard Business School Professor Amy Edmondson originally studied high-performing teams, she wasn't looking for "psychological safety." She was looking for determinants of high performance. What she found, though, was that psychological safety was a necessary condition for high performance.[12]

When people fear being humiliated, blamed, or ignored for bringing their ideas forward, they will shut down and disengage. Their teams or organizations will then underperform. Think about the absence of psychological safety as a giant brake on performance. Until you release the brake of fear, hitting the performance accelerator won't help. It is that important.

Psychological safety isn't a "soft phrase" because the point isn't comfort. It's candor. The goal isn't psychological safety. The goal is motivation and accountability for results. The method doesn't need to be tender and hypersensitive. Teams can learn to be tough, not rough.

What psychological safety does involve is getting the order right: relationships first and performance second. If trust and care are limited or missing in action, the candor needed to increase team performance will be missing. Constructive advice is best offered from a position of care and concern for our colleagues to do their best work.

Think about it. You can offer advice to criticize—a "gotcha" moment—or you can offer advice to express authentic concern and compassion for your colleagues and their performance. Some of the best teammate relationships are so candid that people regularly bust on each other. Candor reigns when people have full confidence that their teammates have their back.

To achieve psychological safety, start with a team self-assessment. How psychologically safe is our work together? The assessment in Table 5.1 helps teams consider which of the four quadrants shown in Figure 5.7 best describes their team.

Table 5.1 **Assessment of a Team's Psychological Safety**

	Strongly Agree	Agree	Sometimes	Disagree	Strongly Disagree
Individual Safety					
In this team it is easy to discuss difficult issues and problems.					
It is difficult to ask other members of this team for help.					
I won't receive criticism or retaliation if I make a mistake.					
I don't feel safe offering new ideas that are not fully formed plans.					
Team Respect					
My teammates welcome my ideas and give them time and attention.					
In this team, people are sometimes rejected for being different.					

	Strongly Agree	Agree	Sometimes	Disagree	Strongly Disagree
Members of this team can easily describe the value of each other's contributions.					
Team Learning					
We take time to find new ways to improve work processes.					
When someone makes a mistake in this team, it is often held against him or her.					
Members of this team raise concerns they have about plans and decisions.					
We try to discover our underlying assumptions and seek counterarguments about issues under discussion.					

Source: Adapted from Amy Edmondson, "Psychological Safety and Learning Behavior in Work Teams," *Administrative Science Quarterly*, vol. 44, no. 2, June 1999, pp. 350–383.

The *comfort zone* reflects a team with high psychological safety and low motivation and accountability for results. People enjoy lattes in the morning and each other's company, but they are not getting much done.

The *apathy zone* is defined by low psychological safety and motivation and accountability for results. No lattes in the morning, and we don't like each other either. Unemployment for all will probably come next.

The *anxiety zone* is the most common team experience defined by low psychological safety and high motivation and accountability

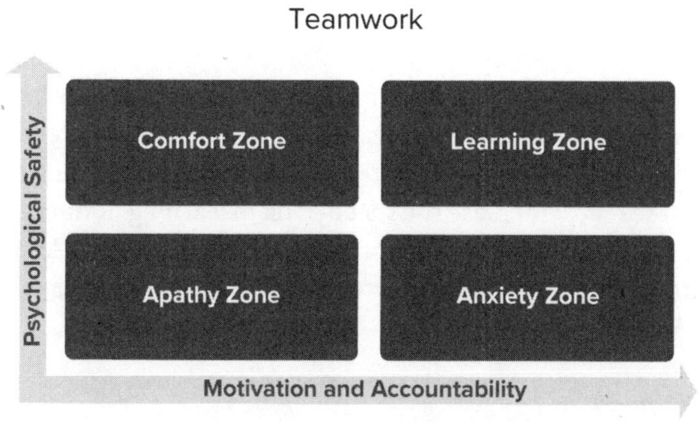

Teamwork

Figure 5.7 The Four Quadrants of Psychological Safety

for results. People want to deliver results, though they fear being humiliated, blamed, or ignored. This isn't just about hurt feelings. This is about performance. When anxiety goes up, performance goes down.

Ideally, teams are in the *learning zone*, defined by high psychological safety and high motivation and accountability for results. These are the highest-performing teams.

Lock in on three behaviors that *destroy* psychological safety—humiliate, blame, and ignore. And three behaviors that *create* psychological safety—vulnerability, questioning, and learning. Start with vulnerability. We don't trust arrogant leaders. We trust leaders who acknowledge their fallibility. When leaders "tell one on themselves," for example, describe a time when they failed, we can all relate to that. All of us have screwed up. When the air of "do no wrong" is dismantled, then humility becomes contagious and binds people together.

Next, strong teams ask questions such as the following: "Do we provide the level of service we are capable of providing?" "Are we certain that we understand what our partners and customers need?" "What skills do we lack?" When questions like those are being asked, team learning can be kicked up a notch by using an after action review (AAR). This tool will be most impactful when relationships have been established with a team user manual and when some degree of psychological safety has been achieved.

After Action Review

Anyone interested in high-performing teams can quickly get behind the reality that the team that learns the fastest wins. The challenge is how to do this. Think of an *after action review* (AAR) as a concrete way for teams to increase the speed of team learning. Rather than presume that team learning will somehow just happen, an AAR assumes that team learning has to be intentional. Here are the basic steps for an AAR:

Purpose
- Repaint an accurate picture of what happened. This isn't as easy as it might appear because people view the same experience differently based on their perspective.

Foundational AAR Questions Include These
- What was expected to happen?
- What actually occurred?
- What went well and why?
- What can be improved and how?

How Should the AAR Be Facilitated?
- Everyone on the team participates.
- In fact, one key objective is that everyone on the team speaks. Trust has been established when everyone feels obligated to strengthen the team.
- An AAR aligns with psychological safety because the goal is candor, not comfort.
- The team that struggles the most learns the most. An effective AAR pushes people beyond their comfort zone while being respectful.
- Someone other than the senior leader facilitates the discussion. The AAR is an effective leadership development experience. Senior leaders can guide less experienced leaders to plan and facilitate an AAR.
- Brief and frequent is better than long and infrequent.

- The length of the AAR can be 15 minutes. The goal is to make the AAR a habit, and that won't happen if it's a burden.

PUTTING THE THREE-TIERED TEAM PERFORMANCE SANDWICH TOGETHER

The team user manual is trust by design rather than trust by chance. Psychological safety comes next, though this is exceedingly rare for reasons that take us back to preferring comfort over discomfort. It is far easier to hold back ideas, avoid asking questions, and view a disagreement with the boss as a career-limiting move. Even the term *safety* can be misunderstood. No one is completely safe. Perhaps the word *security* defined as the absence of deliberate harm is a more realistic standard, and even this definition doesn't come with a 100 percent warranty.

Creating a psychologically safe culture is a sophisticated task. The first step is getting clear that the goal is performance, not psychological safety. The second step is getting clear that the goal is candor, not comfort. The third step is understanding that vulnerability, questioning, and learning need to be practiced.

One way to practice psychological safety is to reflect on an important project that has not made progress.[13] Choose an important project that cuts across silos, so that no one person or function can solve the challenge. In a hospital setting, this might include access to care, which is a perennial challenge for all healthcare institutions. The physicians, nurses, and scheduling staff will likely be the first to see that patients can't make timely appointments. In a psychologically safe culture, vulnerability, questioning, and learning kick into gear. Those who are seeing the problem will speak up to executive leadership. The executive team will ask questions to assess the scale and scope of the access issue. The executive team will assign a group of leaders to define the skills, teamwork, and processes needed to increase access to care.

When the project has seen some progress, learning is accelerated by conducting an after action review that involves a team reflecting on four questions:

1. What did we want to happen?
2. What actually did happen?
3. What did we do well?
4. Where can we do better?

It is hard to get an AAR to work as designed if trusting and caring relationships are missing in action. This is where a team user manual can make a valuable contribution. In addition, our brain learns better when we are psychologically safe. We can't take trust or psychological safety for granted when people who don't normally work together are tasked to solve a challenge, such as access to care in a hospital, that cuts across an organization. This is the kind of issue that will be viewed differently by clinical staff, administrative support, and executive leaders. Gaining insights from diverse perspectives to knock down organizational silos requires that vulnerability, questioning, and learning are not left to chance. They depend on intentional practice.

KEY TAKEAWAYS

Thomas Friedman concluded that we now live in a world of defined contribution rather than defined benefits.[14] Just as 401(k) plans require that we learn to invest for retirement, so too do teams need to invest in their learning.

Rapid periods of change result in not knowing the questions, never mind the answers. That is why we need teams that sense emerging disruptions. We need teams that will rapidly self-govern fueled by trusting and caring relationships. Increasingly, we are unable to steer away from the storm. We need stronger teams capable of steering through the storm.

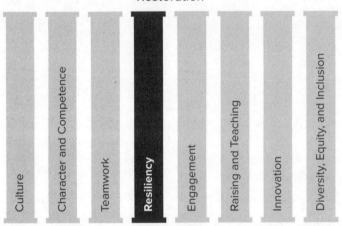

ARETÉ

Excellence

Habits
Coaching
Restoration

Culture

Character and Competence

Teamwork

Resiliency

Engagement

Raising and Teaching

Innovation

Diversity, Equity, and Inclusion

Character

Trust   Compassion   Courage

Justice   Wisdom   Temperance   Hope

RESILIENCE

We don't rise to the level of our expectations;
we fall to the level of our training.[1]
—ARCHILOCHUS

Taking Archilochus's, the Greek poet's, wisdom to heart, the military adopted this credo to train personnel for resilience to perform well under adverse conditions. Under pressure, people default to their training, so trainers repeat the same exercises again and again, until the desired behavior is a habit or second nature.

Whether people volunteered to be put in harm's way or harm found them, we all need to recover, persist, and even thrive in the face of adversity. For these reasons, resilience is among the greatest moral quests of our time or any time for that matter.

Humans vary widely in how well they respond to stress, pressure, and uncertainty. So, where is the training to which more people could default, since resilience is often the difference between those who succeed and those who struggle?

During the COVID-19 pandemic, the resilience training described in this chapter was offered to more than 2,000 people, ranging from senior leaders to entry-level professionals. It was also offered to people working in sectors other than business—for example, caregivers (physicians-in-training and established physicians); professional and college coaches and athletic performance professionals; and students (medical, MBAs, undergraduates). The goal of this training was to normalize discomfort by preparing for when, not if, things go off the rails.

The strategy was to get the brain to work for, rather than against, us by considering three factors or the 3Rs—*regulation, relationships,* and *reason*:

1. **Regulation:** Am I safe?
   - Regulation starts with homeostasis, which means the body needs stability before it can change.
   - Homeostasis involves adjusting one's physical state, which can be affected by factors like sleep, diet, and exercise.
   - Homeostasis also involves one's psychological response, the drivers of which include factors like anxiety, uncertainty, and fear.
2. **Relationships:** Do I belong?
   - Relationships are enhanced by trust and compassion.
   - Do I feel valued as a person in my team or organization?
   - Do I add value to others?
3. **Reason:** Do I matter? Do I make a difference?
   - When we are well regulated and relationships are sturdy, it is then that we are best positioned to reason well. I am able to effectively manage my emotions.
   - Do I feel that my strengths are valued and that I value the strengths in others?
   - Do I feel that I make a difference in the lives of others and help other people make a difference in their own lives?

The recurring theme throughout this chapter is that pro-social behavior—that is, behavior that benefits others—contributes mightily to resilience and that virtue is the most pro-social behavior of all. When we intentionally prevent fatigue, strengthen our relationships, and lead purposeful lives, we become more useful when we are most needed.

REGULATION: FEELING PHYSICALLY AND PSYCHOLOGICALLY SAFE

Homeostasis is a key principle of life for all living organisms. First coined as a term by Walter Cannon in 1932 in his book *The Wisdom of the Body,* homeostasis describes the body's imperative—tightly regulated—to maintain a steady state in elements like body temperature, serum electrolytes (or salts in the bloodstream), and oxygen and carbon dioxide levels in the bloodstream.[2] The term *homeostasis* derives from the Greek words for "same" and "steady," which capture the essence of homeostasis.

The body likes a Goldilocks solution to its temperature. Not too hot and not too cold, but just right—homeostasis. This is why we sweat to cool when we get hot and we shiver to get warm when we get cold. The body's temperature will be determined by the balance between the forces generating heat (like metabolic processes and muscular movement) and those that cause heat to be lost (like exposure to cold).

Yet, just as homeostasis is necessary for life, so is change inevitable in life. This is the challenge: how to maintain homeostasis (or return to it) within a process of ongoing change. When we are out of control or dysregulated, we cannot effectively change. When forced to change, people do. Yet, to initiate change takes tremendous mental, emotional, and physical energy. Said differently, when we are emotionally stable, we can better muster the intellectual capacity, the resolve and resilience, and the physical ability to change. Hence, homeostasis and change can—indeed must—coexist.

Everything you learn today determines how your brain will predict tomorrow. Based on past experiences, our brain guesses when to spend and when to save energy. We can get clearer about what we control. We can become more disciplined in deciding what we want to pay attention to. We can self-regulate by developing new habits with sufficient practice. Habits are formed when our brain makes novel connections and prunes itself to make different predictions of the future. Even when our brain inaccurately evaluates our circumstances, it can learn from mistakes and change how we predict the future.[3]

Think of the brain as the chief financial officer (CFO) for our body budget. In business, a CFO uses the concept of generating and deploying cash for the organization to survive. The brain coordinates overall changes in creating and deploying energy to help the body survive. When we manage energy well, we prevent fatigue and handle stress better. Just as a CFO deploys cash to generate even more cash, our brain deploys resources like water, salt, and glucose to generate even more energy. When we sleep well, eat healthily, and maintain hydration, it is like generating cash that can be deployed later to better function and learn. Like any budget, our body budget has limits. When we spend energy we don't have, a body deficit limits our ability to function and learn.

We are built to handle brief acute episodes of high-intensity stress. What wears us down is chronic stress resulting from multiple stressors that rarely turn off, such as job pressure, sleep deprivation, and constant electronic device stimulation. Chronic stress can take a toll on our health by weakening our immune system and our mental fitness. How do we cope? Put your CFO body budget—your brain—to work by prioritizing sleep, diet, and exercise.

So, is calm under pressure something you either have or you don't? While DNA does matter, consider again the word *epigenetics*. This remarkable concept challenges the old debate about whether we are determined by nature or nurture. Conventional wisdom long held that genes affected human development. Genes were viewed as the independent variable that caused personality. Now we know that our experiences influence genes. So, the answer to the question "Does nature or nurture influence our development?" is yes. Both do.[4]

Taking neurology, genes, and human development back to adversity, we must acknowledge that building resilience and bouncing back is easier for some than for others. Whether our current state is survivor, bend but don't break, or thrive, here is how we are fundamentally the same. We all benefit from a sense of belonging to people who know us, who love us, and who can calm us. When we feel safe with the people in our families, friends, and teammates, we are amazingly resilient.[5]

RELATIONSHIPS: FEELING LIKE WE BELONG

Connections with others are enhanced when we practice the virtues. For example, relationships thrive when we show compassion.[6] Interestingly, studies show that compassion shrinks the amygdala, which affects our fight-or-flight mechanism residing in the brain. This is a remarkable finding. When we strengthen the muscles of trust and compassion, we become better humans and, in the process, more resilient.[7]

Our relationships do not need to be Hollywood perfect. In fact, trust deepens as our relationships swing back and forth between rupture and repair. A Harvard longitudinal study showed that even couples who were cranky toward each other lived well, as long as both knew that in a pinch, their partner had their back. The study made clear that trusting and caring relationships reduce the odds that we will get sick and increase the odds of recovery from a serious illness such as cancer or heart disease.[8]

The Harvard study followed 724 men for 75 years beginning in 1938. (Of note, only men were admitted to Harvard College in 1938, so initially no women were included. The study has since expanded to include women and now more than 2,000 children of these men.) Medical records were reviewed, blood samples were taken, brains were scanned, families were interviewed, and employee records were collected. So, what happened? Some climbed the social ladder from the bottom to the top, and others went from the top to the bottom. Some had successful careers and marriages, and others became alcoholics and were haunted by mental demons.

Perhaps you are a 20- to 40-year-old woman wondering how a study of old white guys is relevant. Consider that the key finding was simple and universal—trusting and caring relationships are really good for every human's happiness and health. That's it. The study found those who lived life well didn't have more stuff. They invested in relationships. The quality of close relationships matters more than the quantity of family and friends.[9] You might also wonder, are you kidding me? It took 75 years to figure out that relationships matter? Well, if this idea is so widely understood, why don't we invest more in our relationships? Perhaps, the answer is that relationships are messy and complicated, and they require significant effort. Perhaps the answer is relationships often take a back seat to fame and fortune.

By now, we hope it is clear that resilience is not about our circumstances. Our response can help us and those around us flourish even independently of our circumstances.[10] Despite our human shortcomings, we have the ability to guide our behavior by virtue and not be limited by the forces acting on us. The virtues toughen us.

Being tough, not rough—that is our goal. We need toughness to remain resilient and supportive of others in the face of adversity. Paradoxically, we become tougher by practicing the so-called soft stuff like compassion . So, what gets in the way? Things like fear. Even those who excel are not exempt from the barrier of fear, though they manage to weaken its grip.

Fear

"I'm leaving the world of technology and entering the world of Epictetus," is what James Stockdale said to himself about 30 seconds before he was captured after his jet was shot down over Vietnam.[11] Stockdale survived seven years in Hanoi Hilton, a prisoner-of-war camp where he was tortured, starved, and isolated. He credits the Stoic Epictetus in particular and Stoicism in general for saving his life. His experience became known as the Stockdale Paradox:

Retain faith that you will prevail, regardless of difficulties. At the same time, confront the brutal facts of your current reality, whatever they might be. As retired Navy SEAL Brent Gleeson, put it, "Embrace the suck."[12]

While inspirational, Stockdale's courage seems out of reach for most of us. We can more easily relate to Michel de Montaigne who over 500 years ago wrote: "My life has been filled with terrible misfortune; most of which never happened."[13] Studies have proven Montaigne's insights to be correct. Humans fear loss, most of which doesn't actually occur and, if it does, is milder than imagined. The punch line: 97 percent of what people worried about turned out to be no more than exaggerated fear.[14] Our brains don't distinguish between experiences that are intensely imagined and experiences that are real. So, perspective is lost, while fear and anger spread rapidly. Past dangers and their associated fears stick with us. To extinguish fear, our exposure in a safe environment needs to last long enough for the brain to form a new memory. Once safety is established, we are ready to perform. While it's not easy to dial back our primitive brain, we aren't served well to medicalize normal experiences of discomfort with terms like "depression" or "anxiety." When we do, the point that discomfort is a normal part of life gets missed. And when framed in the right way, discomfort can improve us rather than diminish performance.[15] Let's be clear: fear is normal. The question is how much priority do we want to give fear? To strengthen our courage requires that we come to grips with our response to risk, uncertainty, and fear. We conquer or at least manage fear by facing it. This is what resilient people do. Winston Churchill reminded us, "When you are walking through hell, keep walking."[16]

We can more easily take on risk in the calm of the day than in the heat of the moment. To this end, teammates can share their hopes and fears before taking on a difficult mission. Each teammate then commits to helping others realize their best hopes and mitigate their greatest concerns. Our brain wants control and stability. So, when we name and discuss our fears with people who want to "en"-courage and support us, we better our chances to conquer our fears. We can't manage what we can't name. So, naming emotions is critical to managing them.

REASON: FEELING LIKE WE MATTER AND MAKE A DIFFERENCE

Does stress make us sick? A study tracked 30,000 Americans over eight years, asking how much stress they experienced each year and whether they believed that stress was harmful to their health. Public death records determined who died during the course of the study. People who experienced loads of stress in the previous year had a 43 percent increased risk of death. But, and it's a big BUT, this was only true for people who believed that stress was harmful to their health.

In other words, those who experienced loads of stress and didn't view stress as harmful were no more likely to die than those who reported little stress. So, if we think stress will hurt us, it will. Time to reframe!

Another study asked 1,000 Americans two questions:

- How much stress did you experience last year?
- How much time did you spend helping friends, neighbors, and people in your community?

Again, public records were used for five years to find out who died. People who experienced significant stress related to events such as family crisis or financial difficulties had a 30 percent increased risk of dying. But again, there was a counterintuitive insight. People who spent time caring for others showed no increase in risk of dying. What is fascinating about these findings is that people who viewed stress as helpful and who took care of others, became courageous and resilient.[17]

Here is what is both amazing and hopeful. Changing how we view stress, combined with being well supported and supporting others, can deactivate our amygdala, thus improving our response to stress.

WHY ME? OR, WHAT'S NEXT?

Edie Eger cautions us to be wary of asking "Why me?" She states that "Why me?" is the question of a victim. Instead, she suggests that we ask, "What's next?," the question of the liberated. "What's next?" can be the key to release us from our mental prison. It is a question about the future . . . where hope lives. Fear also lives in the future. Learn to hope instead of fear. It may be surprising to learn that most people become resilient or grow after a traumatic event. About one-third or less get stuck, about one-third stretch like elastic and return to normal after the band snaps back, and about one-third are stronger than before the trauma. They are not necessarily cured, but the trauma and subsequent healing yielded a wiser, braver, and more caring person.

Most of what we have known about trauma is defined as *post-traumatic stress disorder* (PTSD). PTSD is the inability to move on after an intense traumatic experience, causing the person to continue reliving the experience.[18] PTSD is more likely in a culture that is dangerous or violent, or one in which the person feels ignored.

Decades of research show that most people exposed to violent or even life-threatening events do not develop PTSD. Most people exposed to potentially traumatic events are able to adapt relatively quickly without suffering long-term consequences. For example, a cohort study of over 100,000 soldiers tracked PTSD symptoms before and after military deployment. Nearly 83 percent of participating soldiers experienced few or no PTSD symptoms.

The antidote to developing PTSD is having a supportive social network. James Stockdale said, "True resilience and courage were measured by acts of generosity, compassion, and altruism."[19] A study of 2,490 Vietnam veterans with low social support found they were 2½ times more likely to suffer from PTSD than those with high social support. Similarly, the lack of social support is twice as reliable in predicting PTSD as the severity of the trauma itself.[20] By telling your story to compassionate family members and friends, you are more likely to grow beyond your adversity.

Even for those who experience PTSD, it is important to know it is not a lifelong condition; rather, it is a diagnosis for a specific period of a person's life. Sadly, fear of PTSD has become greater than the disorder itself, according to Daniela Montalto, Department of Child and Adolescent Psychiatry at NYU Langone Health. We have medicalized our language by saying "I was traumatized," or "I'm depressed" rather than saying "I had a bad day." Dr. Montalto said, "Ninety percent of people who develop post-traumatic symptoms have complete remission within eight months. And remember, we're talking about 90 percent of the 10 percent who have significant symptoms."[21]

We have made significant progress in not stigmatizing PTSD and encouraging people to receive the support they need. It goes without saying that everything should be done to support people who have had traumatic experiences, whether on the battlefield, in mourning the death of a loved one, or in braving a life-threatening illness. However, our insights are limited when the only perspective we think is possible is PTSD. There is room for tragic optimism that acknowledges the pain we experienced without crushing our spirit.

Psychologist George Bonanno studied people who had experienced the same traumatic event—for instance, soldiers in a platoon during times of war or doctors and first responders during a crisis like the terrorist attacks of September 11. He often found that between one-third to two-thirds of any population seemed to have had no lasting ill effects. This doesn't mean they didn't grieve. It does mean their ability to function wasn't compromised.

So, what do you do for those who struggle? While it is not exactly clear how people bounce back, there does appear to be a path that puts people on a resilience trajectory made possible by a flexible mindset composed of three mutually reinforcing qualities:

1. A growth mindset makes clear that resilience is a learned skill. We can learn to both accept the brutal facts of our circumstances, while being realistically optimistic about creating a meaningful future.
2. We are confident in our ability to cope. Confidence is a by-product of applying our greatest strengths to our circumstances.
3. We think about our circumstances as a challenge rather than a threat. All three combined are more powerful than practicing one without the other.[22]

Oddly, even though most people experience resilience and growth after a trauma, the less commonly experienced PTSD is more widely known. For example, a survey revealed that 97 percent of West Point cadets were familiar with PTSD, while only 10 percent had heard of *post-traumatic growth* (PTG). PTSD can become self-fulfilling when it appears that this is what happens to people after a trauma. In the mid-1990s, research by Richard Tedeschi and Lawrence Calhoun showed that people can experience growth after trauma.[23] Growth does not mean that pain is absent, but rather that trauma's negative impacts are diminished.

PTG isn't about glorifying suffering. Statements that trauma builds character feel like total hogwash when we are in the midst of a horrible event. We certainly need more than happy thoughts and pixie dust to get back up after being slammed to the ground. *Trauma* is the Greek word for "wound." Rumi, the thirteenth-century poet, offers hope: "The wound is a place where the light enters." Those like Edie who liberate themselves from their jailers create a place where light enters, enabling the following PTG qualities to emerge:

Empathy: Once we have been knocked to our knees, we can become more understanding and caring toward others who have suffered a tough blow.

Relationships: Big surprise, people like us better when we are empathic. As we become more empathic, our relationships become deeper and more meaningful. When we flex our empathy muscles, we strengthen our relationships.

Purpose: Trauma can lead us to reorder our priorities. We seek a life that involves something bigger than ourselves. Frederic Nietzsche, the German philosopher, said, "He who has a 'why' to live can bear almost any 'how.'"[24]

Vulnerability: A traumatic event makes it clear that whom we love and what we love can be swept away in a heartbeat. As we become more aware of our vulnerability, we also become more aware of another person's vulnerability. We become more caring in ways that otherwise may not have happened.

Sense of urgency: Trauma shows us that our life is short, encouraging us to not waste the time that we have. We learn to engage deliberately with the most meaningful parts of our lives while we can.

PTG is cultivated when people feel accepted, feel loved, and have a sense of belonging and connection.[25]

In other words, individuals can start to look forward when they are part of a safe place, a place where people find words to capture their feelings and where their trauma won't be held against them.[26] Now, the possibility of achieving PTG shouldn't endorse blaming people who experience post-traumatic stress. Events that befall us are not necessarily our fault, though ultimately, notes Viktor Frankl, "when we are no longer able to change a situation, we are challenged to change ourselves."[27]

CRISIS: SMALL T AND BIG T TRAUMA

Knowing that *trauma* means "wound," we know if we live long enough, we will experience "small *t*" and "big *T*" traumatic events. When it comes to collective trauma, 2020 was a whopper. The world hit the trifecta of a pandemic, a global recession, and social unrest caused by racial injustice. Travel plans were kicked to the curb, businesses were shut down, and kids were removed from school. Physicians and nurses worked around the clock, some businesses and jobs did not come back, and, sadly, many people died in isolation from loved ones. Global trauma has continued with the pandemic through 2022, when the trauma of COVID-19 and social injustice was compounded by the Russian invasion of Ukraine and the humanitarian crisis that ensued. There is no shortage of trauma, and no one escapes it. And now we face the potential trauma of climate change.

The trauma of COVID-19 created a shared experience of uncertainty. Among the many inequities laid bare by the pandemic were the differences in the ways people navigated the pandemic. Greg Boyle suggested some folks traveled the coronavirus waters on an ocean liner, some in a rubber boat, and some clinging to a piece of driftwood.[28] Those on the ocean liner had to limit their interactions, though their jobs and pay remained intact while they worked relatively safely from home. At the same time, houses were upgraded thanks to carpenters, toilets flushed thanks to plumbers, and store shelves were stocked thanks to truckers and retail staff. Those in rubber boats had their lives turned upside down, doing jobs that put their health at risk. Those clinging to driftwood battled to hang on to their jobs and lives. And many lost their lives.

Whether 2020 was a big *T* or a small *t* trauma for you, shared adversity raises a question that defines the human condition: what are our responsibilities to each other? Two behaviors emerge during disasters: fear that breeds conflict and solidarity that generates collaboration and commitment. We can expect the best more than the worst in most people. Our mental health improves when situations require sacrifice, which strengthens our need to connect and work together. At our best, emergencies increase our need for social solidarity to survive. As a result, selfish instincts and individual differences melt away when the only way we can survive is by relying on each other. COVID also laid bare our dark side with outcries over systematic racism and political instability flamed by misinformation and mistrust of our institutions and leaders. However, the bleak side of human nature is never the whole story. Most people understand that a crisis calls for caring and collaborating with strangers.[29]

So, why are most people transformed to embody compassion, courage, and hope during a tragedy? During normal times, we are just living our lives. We don't spend loads of time thinking about our obligations to others. In fact, busyness can be the next best thing to having a purpose. In contrast, a crisis forces us to become more reflective, wiser, and focused on others. When we look out for each other, we learn some resilience for ourselves, so the world won't topple us easily.

Here is what doesn't build resilience: my big T or small t trauma is worse than your big T or small t trauma. Heartache isn't a competition. Misery and fragility are well fertilized by being aggrieved and entitled. Here is what does build resilience—a moral compass fortified by people who bring out our best self. People who strengthen our courage even when we feel like we will buckle. After watching neighbors take care of each other after the 1906 San Francisco earthquake, Dorothy Day wondered why people can't treat each other this way all the time?[30]

We will end a chapter on resilience by looking at a small t trauma experience of job loss. While not often life-threatening, losing a job is a significant wound nonetheless. In 1981, the term *hardiness* emerged from a 12-year longitudinal study of Illinois Bell Telephone employees after a layoff. Legislation swept away the company's monopoly and tossed everyone into a hypercompetitive pool without swimming lessons. The economic disruption that ensued devastated some Bell Telephone employees but invigorated others. Why did the same event affect people so differently? The answer was "hardiness" defined as commitment to the task at hand rather than dwelling on what was lost; belief that there are conditions that can be controlled; and the ability to see the circumstances as a challenge rather than as a threat. Since this study was completed, hundreds of studies have confirmed that hardiness converts disruption and potential disasters into growth opportunities.

Hardy people believe they are involved in meaningful work and that they have agency to affect change, and they view success and failure as the path to learn and grow. Hardy people learn to accept the world as it actually works, not as they want it to be. In contrast, the fragile yearn for a world that never existed and struggle to accept the reality of their circumstances. Hardy people push forward with the view that going backward is not an option. However, people must be hardy with humility. Forcing the reluctant to jump into a moving river when they are not ready will go about as well as you might expect. At the same time, the hardy need to make clear that you can't stay on the riverbank where you are now.[31]

Think of Edie's question, "What's next?" as the way to understand the details of hardiness. Commitment implicates a sense of purpose and meaning in life. Hardy people view change as an opportunity to live life well. They see their work as important and worthy of their best efforts and creativity. They are gritty; they have a deep sense of purpose, which drives persistence. They view withdrawal from stress as weak and stepping into stress as strong.

There are lessons for leadership here too.[32] A resilience study of 25,000 adults working in 25 countries revealed that neither gender nor nationality determined how well a country had handled the COVID-19 pandemic. Instead, the more clearly the leaders defined the threat, the more resilient their people became.

The implication for leaders is that there is no need to sugarcoat brutal facts. When threats are clearly defined, resilience kicks in.[33]

During COVID-19, many people experienced disruption in their routines, loss of financial security, and disconnection from teammates, friends, and families. Events are objective though our interpretations are not. Our interpretations are a guess or a story as to what happened and what it means. The story we tell ourselves influences whether we react with anger and fear or understanding and forgiveness. Do we yell at our teammates, or do we listen and coach? In every situation, we can find a better story to tell ourselves. Applied to COVID-19, we can create a constructive story by asking questions such as these:

1. During COVID, what was the greatest loss you experienced?
2. During COVID, what was the greatest gain you experienced?
3. Upon reflection, what did you learn about yourself?
4. What would it look like if you applied your greatest areas of growth from COVID to your future?[34]

At this stage in the book, it should come as no surprise that employees in organizations that help their people face significant challenges feel more satisfaction and commitment to their work and experience less burnout and absenteeism. The importance of prosocial behavior defined by virtue replaces angst with a sense of belonging. In 2022, an unpublished study that involved Oxford and Harvard Universities showed that a treatment group that practiced the virtues significantly reduced anxiety and depression while angst and depression in the control group continued.

The door that opens to optimism is agency or free will, at least the belief in free will. The best way to open this door is caring for others— being empathic. We better handle discomfort, lower angst, and improve performance when we focus on others. In music, this is called the *empathy shift*. At first, a violinist gets better at their craft when tutored by a skilled teacher. The teacher amps up discomfort by having the violinist practice with an orchestra. They see if they can squeeze even more out of the violinist when they experience discomfort in front of a live audience as part of an orchestra. At each step, the violinist plays better, but their performance is suboptimal until they make the empathy shift, which means that they start to listen to the sound of fellow artists, not just themselves. When they make this empathy shift, their performance improves.[35]

In sum, the hardy teach us that if we practice fear, we multiply fear. If we practice resilience, we grow resilience. If we practice virtue, we get better at who we are, and we get better at what we do.

KEY TAKEAWAYS

To recap, resilience is a key attribute that comes from being pro-social—that is, caring for others. The 3Rs—*reason* (Do I matter? Do I make a difference?), *relationships* (Do I belong?), and *regulation* (Am I safe?)—provide the basis for being resilient, as does the awareness that we can grow from trauma and that post-traumatic growth is possible.

But how do we develop resilience? Here is a baker's dozen toolkit of positive habits to strengthen resilience.

Fear is a reaction. Courage is a decision.[36]
—WINSTON CHURCHILL

1. APPLY VIRTUE STRENGTHS TO CHALLENGING SITUATIONS

We live life operating on a continuum from service before self to grumpy to downright nasty. A goal is to become the best version of our self. How would you use virtues in a challenging situation that you are facing now?

2. REALISTIC OPTIMISM

While we can't control events, we can control our response. We don't live in Disneyland. Reality means that we get clear about the factors that we can't control. Optimism means that we kick into gear everything possible to contribute to a favorable outcome for others and for ourselves. Accordingly, put tasks into one of three groups:

A. Those you can control
B. Those you can influence
C. Those you can neither control nor influence

Prioritize those in group A and B, and ditch those in group C.

3. WHAT WOULD YOU DO IF YOU WEREN'T AFRAID?

Our brain's threat detector creates a negativity bias in us. Yet, 85 percent of the things we worry about never actually happen, and most that do happen are not as bad as we thought they would be. When events are scary, ask three questions to help keep fear in perspective:

- What's the worst that could happen?
- What's the probability that the worst will happen?
- If the worst happened, could I handle it?

4. SUPPORTING SELF AND OTHERS

For whatever you are doing in the moment, is it helping you or others? If so, keep it up. If not, cut it out.

> *Sometimes it is very easy to hold a grudge;*
> *however, it harms no one but you.*[37]
> —NELSON MANDELA

5. BENEFIT-FINDING EXERCISE

One way to move past resentments is to identify the hidden benefits of negative experiences to make the costs seem smaller and less controlling of our lives. Think about being harmed by another person from your recent past. It could be something minor or something serious. Then, take a few moments to identify some positive consequences of the event that you were not expecting. Perhaps you became aware of personal strengths that you did not realize you had. Perhaps a relationship became better or stronger as a result, or perhaps you grew or became a stronger or wiser person. Here are some common benefits for you to consider:

- I discovered strength I didn't know I had.
- I became wiser (that is, slower to trust in relationships, less naïve).
- I gained confidence in myself.
- I became more kind, less selfish.
- I learned the importance of forgiving.
- I learned more about how to be a good teammate.
- I became less worried about pleasing others.
- I learned about qualities to look for in friends.
- I learned how to deal constructively with my anger, and I learned how to keep a cool head.
- I learned how to be grateful for what I have.
- I learned to stand up for myself.
- I learned the importance of learning to stand up for others.

Pressure is a privilege.[38]
—BILLIE JEAN KING

6. PERFORMING UNDER PRESSURE

Practice three steps to perform better under pressure:

- **Step back.** Buy some time. Step back to figure out what is happening. Take a deep breath to tamp down your primitive brain and to activate your thinking brain.
- **Step up.** Sort out how you want to show up under pressure. Which virtue is being called for: compassion, courage, hope?
- **Step in.** Time to act. Strive to be the person you want to be.[39] Remember that it isn't a virtue until you act.

I am a fool, but I know I'm a fool and
that makes me smarter than you.[40]
—SOCRATES

7. CONSTRUCTIVE VERSUS DESTRUCTIVE

When someone shares good news with us, our response can strengthen them and our relationship, or it can diminish and weaken our relationship. We can be active and constructive (genuinely offer enthusiastic support); passive and constructive (lame or lazy support); passive and destructive (ignore the good news); or active and destructive (focus on the negative). Here is what these four different responses look like after someone tells us they got a promotion:

- **Active-constructive:** "What a wonderful opportunity. What most excites you about your new position? Whom do you look forward to working with? What a great way to build on your strengths."
- **Passive-constructive:** "That's great."
- **Passive-destructive:** "What are we going to have for lunch?"
- **Active-destructive:** "That sounds like loads of work and hassle. You would be crazy to take that job."

One aspect of neighborly love is that we must not merely will
our neighbor's good, but actually work to bring it about.[41]
—THOMAS AQUINAS

8. PEOPLE WHO BRING OUT YOUR BEST SELF

Write down the people who bring out your best self. Figure out how to spend more time with them. People who contribute to our character and strengths contribute to our resilience.

We had the experience but missed the meaning. And approach to
the meaning restores the experience in a different form.[42]
—T. S. ELIOT

9. REFLECTION QUESTIONS FOR BIG KIDS

Once a week, ask four questions of yourself. Or, as a family, ask these four questions together:

- Did I reflect on the virtues?
- In what acts of compassion was I involved? (Relieving the suffering of another person.)
- In what acts of social justice was I involved? (Righting a public wrong where I live or work in the community.)
- Did I learn from my mistakes? (Not, "Did I make mistakes?" Rather,"Did I learn from my mistakes?")

10. REFLECTION QUESTIONS FOR KIDS

First, the parent makes it clear that unconditional love means the kid didn't do anything to earn parental love and couldn't do anything to lose it. Once that is established, make it clear that the purpose of school is not to be the valedictorian, first chair violinist, or starting quarterback. The purpose of school is to ask three questions every day:

- Were you brave?
- Were you kind?
- Did you learn from your mistakes? (Again, not, "Did you make mistakes?" Rather, "Did you learn from your mistakes?")

11. REFLECTION QUESTIONS IN THE SPIRIT OF BENJAMIN FRANKLIN

- Ben started the day by asking, "What good can I do today?"
- Ben ended his day by asking, "What good did I do today?"[43]

I want to say thank you to all the people
who walked into my life and made it outstanding,
and all the people who walked out of my life
and made it fantastic.

—UNKNOWN

12. HUNT FOR THE GOOD STUFF

At the end of each day, reflect on what went well. Write down three or four things that went well as a result of practicing virtue.[44]

13. *HO'OPONOPONO*

Ho'oponopono reflects an ancient Hawaiian forgiveness practice that roughly translates to "cause things to move back in balance" or to "make things right." It is practiced by expressing four sentiments to someone facing a life-threatening illness: "I'm sorry." "Please forgive me." "Thank you." "I love you."[45]

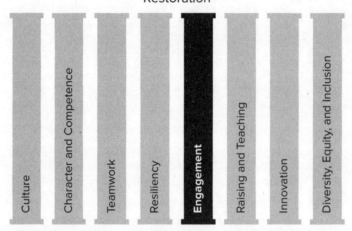

ARETÉ
Excellence

Habits
Coaching
Restoration

Culture

Character and Competence

Teamwork

Resiliency

Engagement

Raising and Teaching

Innovation

Diversity, Equity, and Inclusion

Character

Trust   Compassion   Courage

Justice   Wisdom   Temperance   Hope

ENGAGEMENT

To win in the marketplace,
you must first win in the workplace.[1]
—DOUG CONANT, FORMER CEO OF
CAMPBELL'S SOUP

n March 2020, at the very beginning of the global pandemic, models developed by staff at the Cleveland Clinic estimated that 8,000 patients would be hospitalized with COVID-19, necessitating 1,700 ventilators. This number did not include serious non-COVID-19 illnesses such as heart attacks and strokes. Disaster planning based on this worst-case scenario identified that these issues needed to be resolved by May 2020.

To be able to accommodate the surge of COVID-19 patients, elective surgeries were canceled and outpatient visits fell as patients wrongly thought that hospitals were unsafe. Though many hospitals instituted layoffs and issued furloughs in an attempt to survive, Cleveland Clinic CEO Dr. Tom Mihaljevic took a different tack. Despite the financial pressures facing the Cleveland Clinic, like every hospital in the United States, he announced at the outset of the pandemic that clinic caregivers would go through this as a team—there would be no layoffs and no furloughs.

The result? Employee engagement scores from items such as "I would recommend the Cleveland Clinic as a good place to work" and "Executive leadership provides open and honest communication" soared from already high baseline values established in 2017. Although a global pandemic robs us of our control over much in our lives, it does not control how we treat each other.

The Clinic promised their staff that they would keep their jobs, jobs that were about to become very physically and emotionally challenging, with the possibility of exposure to a deadly virus with no pay raise. And yet, engagement went up. Why?

BELONG, MATTER, AND
MAKE A DIFFERENCE

The leaders who have developed their noncognitive abilities are successful in making people feel like they belong, matter, and make a difference. As a by-product, engagement goes up. This point is not widely understood. And, based on Gallup's reporting that 70 percent of employees are not fully engaged, these insights are not widely practiced. Whether times are calm or chaotic, and despite countless leaders of good faith investing millions to boost sagging morale, the engagement needle is consistently stuck at 70 percent disengaged. If company picnics, casual dress, Ping-Pong, more volunteering, and clear career paths did the job, engagement would be easy and soaring. While these might all be good things to do, they are all unlikely to budge engagement.

How about pay? Researchers like Edward Deci synthesized results from 128 controlled experiments that showed that pay incentives had a consistent negative effect on intrinsic motivation. These effects were especially strong when the tasks were interesting or enjoyable rather than boring or meaningless. Deci's conclusion was that extrinsic rewards run the risk of restraining, rather than enhancing, intrinsic motivation.[2] Another meta-analysis of 92 quantitative studies that included over 15,000 individuals showed that the correlation between pay and job satisfaction was very weak. Furthermore, job satisfaction is not related to nationality or whether a person holds an entry-level, middle management, or senior-level position.[3]

Just so there is no misunderstanding about compensation, let's be clear that job satisfaction doesn't pay the mortgage. People must be paid a living wage or better yet, offered bonus pay when the organization does well financially. Just understand that the relationship between pay and performance is like a sugar high that fades quickly. Over the long term, money can be more a source of dissatisfaction than satisfaction. If engagement could be bought, plenty of financially secure organizations would have solved this problem long ago. The biggest cause of disengagement is underinvestment in leadership—something to which we will return.

The evidence is in. Most approaches currently used to increase engagement simply don't work. The main point of this chapter is that engagement is largely an intrinsic issue that cannot be solved with extrinsic tools, such as pay. Engagement is affected by three drivers (the 3Rs we discussed in Chapter 6, as they are also the cornerstones of resilience):

1. Do I feel like I belong?
   - I feel included and supported.
2. Do I feel like I matter?
   - I understand why my role matters to my organization and my strengths are leveraged.
3. Do I feel like I make a difference?
   - I feel valued and I add value.

We need to feel appreciated to contribute. Appreciation without contribution is narcissism. Contribution without appreciation is discouraging. To matter is to contribute to the organization in a way that leverages my strengths. To make a difference is about doing meaningful work and contributing to helping other people create meaningful work.

The "eureka moment" is to understand that engagement or morale is actually a moral issue. This point becomes clear once we understand that *moral* is the root word of *morale*. How people treat each other is core to morality. Compassion is an especially important engagement ingredient. For example, Gallup research has repeatedly demonstrated a clear link between having a best friend at work and engagement.[4] If engagement is really low, there is good reason to suspect the absence of compassion.[5]

A strong moral culture deepens the bonds between us, so people feel connected. In contrast, an amoral or toxic culture is characterized by teammates feeling disconnected, resulting in poor performance or worse—teammates actively working against the goals of the enterprise.

At Parker Hannifin, virtue has been practiced both because it is worthy in and of itself and because it affects engagement. Over a 12-month period, when leaders and teams consciously practiced virtue, engagement scores consistently increased between 10 and 20 percent. Should this come as a surprise? Well, let's invert the case for virtue. If virtue doesn't affect engagement, then what does? We know that carrots and sticks—reward for doing good work and punishment for not—don't increase engagement. Would we bet that distrust, callousness, cowardice, and despair would favorably affect engagement over trust, compassion, courage, and hope?

The hopeful outcome is that we don't have to practice virtue perfectly. But we do need to try. The moral life defined by virtue isn't about a purity code. In fact, practicing virtue involves setbacks, tensions, and misunderstandings. However, when we get it right—or even try—we continually exercise our altruistic muscles and, accordingly, deepen trust that results in the higher levels of engagement that all leaders seek.

WHAT IS ENGAGEMENT?

If you ask your teammates what engagement is, answers will likely range from blank stares to work ethic to motivation and more. While everyone is for engagement, we often don't know what it is. Organizations can't affect something that is ill defined. Truth be told, there isn't a single definition of engagement. However, defining engagement as giving "discretionary effort" gets us off to a good start. People who exhibit discretionary effort act like owners rather than employees. They are committed to the organization's success.

People who demonstrate discretionary effort work with others to create solutions to make things better. They do the right thing and fix problems, even when no one is looking. Discretionary effort happens best when people trust and care about their teammates, when leaders leverage teammates' strengths, and when people find purpose in their work.

Why Is Engagement Important?

One way to answer this question is 70 percent × 4:

1. 70 percent or more of a typical workforce is disengaged.[6]
2. 70 percent of the variance in return on investment is attributed to the leader and the team, not the strategy.[7]
3. 70 percent of teammates report to a frontline leader.
4. 70 percent of the variance in engagement scores is attributed to the direct leader.[8]

Point 1

Let's start with 70 percent disengagement levels. Gallup's research shows that the distribution of engagement is about 30/50/20. This means that about 30 percent of a typical organization is fully engaged—loads of discretionary effort. About 50 percent will do what you ask, but not much more—limited, if any, discretionary effort. Sadly, about 20 percent are disengaged, with some percent of those actively working against the goals of the enterprise. Worse still, the 30/50/20 engagement distribution has been largely static for years. The key insight of this distribution isn't to disparage the disengaged. At some point in your career, have you been disengaged? Are there times when you mailed in your effort? The best engagement cure for all of us is to feel like we belong, matter, and make a difference.

Point 2

About 70 percent of the variance in return on investment is attributed to the leader and the team, not the strategy, according to MIT. An organization's strategy will and should change. A great leader and/or team will fix a bad strategy. A middling leader and/or team combination will mess up even a brilliant strategy. The implication is clear. Ultimately, return on investment is a bet on the leader and the team more than on the strategy.

Point 3

About 70 percent of teammates report to a frontline leader, not to senior leaders. These leaders go to work every day wanting to do a good job. They are frustrated by working with disengaged teammates. Disengaged teammates spin (waste effort and talent on tasks that don't matter); settle (lack commitment though not dissatisfied enough to leave); and split (they quit).[9] Disengaged teammates view their jobs as an exchange of time for a paycheck. They arrive and leave on time, take their breaks, and offer minimal effort. The actively disengaged teammates are the most destructive. They undermine their teammates' performance by sharing their unhappiness in words, attitudes, and actions.

Point 4

About 70 percent of the variance in engagement scores is attributed to the direct leader. The business literature is chock-full of advice on how leaders can motivate teammates. Yet, the reality is that organizations don't have to motivate their teammates. They have to stop demotivating them! Leaders inadvertently make it difficult for teammates to do their jobs. Endless paperwork, micromanagement, fuzzy strategy, and most important, lack of trust and care—all contribute to frustrated teammates. People don't leave organizations. They leave their leaders.

To be clear, a 70 percent disengagement level is not an indictment of leaders. It is an indictment of putting leaders into their positions without educating them on what engagement is, why it is important, and how it can be strengthened. One study showed that 58 percent of leaders received no training at all, never mind insights about engagement.[10] As a result, few leaders are aware of the 40/20/1 disengagement distribution. This 40/20/1 calculus means that leaders achieve the highest level of disengagement (40 percent) by simply doing nothing! Apathy is a killer for engagement. When leaders focus on teammates' weaknesses, then 20 percent are disengaged, so criticism beats apathy. However, when leaders focus on teammates' strengths, only

1 percent are disengaged. Now that's good math.[11] This observation suggests that we should look for strengths and teach leaders to do so.

An effective engagement strategy is focused on leadership development, the cost of which is well worth the investment. Study after study has found a strong correlation between engagement and organizational performance, such as increased profitability, customer satisfaction, and growth, and decreases in safety incidents, turnover, and absenteeism. These results are consistent across different organizations from diverse industries and regions of the world. In other words, these are human issues, not industry or nationality issues. These findings make it clear that taking care of teammates—being pro-social—is the best way to take care of organizational performance.

The punch line is this: the most powerful drivers of engagement have to do with creating a sense that we belong, a feeling that we matter, and a belief that we are making a difference. With these three ends in mind, we offer an engagement playbook.

Engagement Playbook

While surveys have their role, the goal is not to chase engagement scores. Asking someone to sit down for a cup of coffee to share their experiences and their aspirations is far more powerful for understanding an organization than reporting survey results. When we start asking people how they are doing, what is getting in their way, or how we can help them, we begin enhancing engagement. When we actively take an interest in someone, engagement scores are a happy by-product.

DO I BELONG?

A sense of belonging is a basic human need that acts as an effective buffer against economic and health uncertainty. In contrast, when people feel excluded, their ability to focus and engage declines during uncertain times.

Employees with a strong sense of belonging are over six times more likely to be engaged than those who don't feel like they belong.[12]

A sense of belonging builds grit and boosts motivation to persist in the face of challenging work.[13] A study of people exposed to rejection showed a drop in their ability to reason by 30 percent and a decline in their IQ by 25 percent.[14]

Our sense of belonging underscores our desire to be "with"—with family, friends, colleagues, and teammates. We want to belong to a community and be part of a culture that nurtures the sense of belonging among all members. We know that certain behaviors enhance our sense of belonging, community, and engagement. These behaviors are related to achieving trust, compassion, stability, and hope.

Now here's the evidence. Between 2005 and 2008, about 10,000 followers from 16 different countries were asked to name what they wanted from their leader. The answers: trust, compassion, stability, and hope. Three of the four qualities sought by followers in their leaders are virtues. The fact that followers seek virtue and stability, rather than strategy and pay, can leave some leaders scratching their heads. As a leader, you are paid to deliver results. You might say, "Look, we don't have time to get to know people. We have work to do. If they want a friend, they should get a dog." Besides, leaders feel it is risky to form emotional ties with teammates who have to be held accountable. Yet, it is very unlikely that people will be engaged when no one cares about them. So, the reluctant leader who manages the downside risk of a relationship going south misses the upside of engagement going north.

Here are hard facts on trust, compassion, stability, and hope. When followers trust their leaders, 50 percent are engaged compared to 13 percent when they view their leaders as untrustworthy. When people feel either their leader or someone at work cares about them, they are more likely to be engaged with customers and more profitable to their employers. When followers believe they work for an organization with a secure financial future, they are nine times more likely to be engaged. Infusing hope was especially powerful: 69 percent of followers were engaged when their leader made them "feel enthusiastic about the future," compared to only 1 percent of those who disagreed with that statement.[15]

So, what is hope? Hope isn't wishful thinking. It is about realistic optimism fueled by courage to accept the brutal facts that confront the team. Hope is a function of a struggle to focus on resolutions within the team's control. Without hope, uncertainty and paralysis can take the upper hand. With hope, teams come to grips with their collective fear to get out of a jam. Einstein said, "It's not that I'm so smart. It's just that I stay with problems longer."[16] That is hope in the face of challenge embodied.

How do we have this happen more often? Daniel Kahneman, the Nobel Prize–winning behavioral economist, believes that the key to behavior change is understanding driving forces and restraining forces. *Driving forces* push us in a particular direction, and *restraining forces* prevent change. Kahneman says, "It turns out that the way to make things easier is almost always by controlling the individual's environment, broadly speaking. Is there an incentive that works against change? Then let's change the incentives. If there is social pressure, then let's reframe the pressure."[17] Though counterintuitive, Kahneman reminds us that the key to achieving behavior change is to weaken what restrains us

Despite this insight, we tend to do the opposite. We often start with the question, "How do I get this person to do something?" The driving force toolkit includes incentives and threats—sweeter carrots and sharper sticks. In contrast, a focus on eliminating restraining forces starts by asking, "Why is the person not already doing something?" Instead, we can start from the perspective of the individual and ask what restrains her. By weakening or perhaps removing restraining forces, the new behavior emerges with less tension and change is more sustainable. But when we rely on driving forces, the behavior is likely to snap back to what it was.

We start by asking questions about driving forces that push us in a particular direction, which might include these:

1. Is the pressure to achieve metrics limiting a sense of meaning?
2. How do teammates respond to pressure and time limitations?
3. Is there a practice of keeping emotional distance from teammates whom you need to hold accountable?

We ask what restrains people from feeling they belong, which might reveal forces such as these:

1. We may not be sure how to start conversations that increase a sense of belonging.
2. We may not be sure how to integrate conversations into standing meetings.
3. We may not be sure if these conversations would be viewed as cheesy and disingenuous.

We then explore ways to weaken or remove restraining forces that might yield ideas such as these:

1. Listen more, talk less. Ask more, tell less.
2. Select a learning partner to help each other listen and ask more.
3. Practice conversations that matter to contribute to a sense of belonging.

Listening is more than being quiet while others speak. Listening is about presence as much as hearing; it's about connection more than observing. Real listening is powered by curiosity, vulnerability, and a willingness to be surprised. Deep listening leads to deep conversations. These are the kind of conversations that build trust, which is the oxygen of a healthy organizational culture. Admittedly, not everyone is necessarily curious, though curiosity can be cultivated.

For example, in medicine, caregivers learn to listen actively by paraphrasing when taking a medical history: "This is what I heard you say. Did I get that right?" The caregiver listens carefully to affirm to the patient that they and their symptoms have been understood. As much as active listening is a mainstream reflex for seasoned clinicians taking medical histories, caregivers and leaders have a long way to go to make active listening a routine part of their everyday interactions with colleagues. There is the opportunity to enhance a sense of belonging in medicine and in all organizations. We have more control over this reality than we might think. We also have more responsibility than we might realize.

DO I MATTER?

Peter Drucker said, "The task of leadership is to create an alignment of strengths in ways that make a system's weaknesses irrelevant."[18] To this end, *appreciative inquiry* is an evidence-based way to leverage strengths to effect positive organizational change.

Have you ever heard of a business, university, or hospital trying to compete based on weakness? Let's take our worst products and services and see if anyone will buy this junk! We compete based on our strengths, not on our weaknesses.

Does this mean that we ignore weaknesses? Of course not. That's called "narcissism," which annoys people and undermines teamwork. In fact, leveraging strengths and managing weaknesses requires that we are forthright about both our strengths and our weaknesses. So, of course, we need to deal with weaknesses. The debatable part is, how?

If we can increase the amount of time that each person uses their strengths, then performance increases. If we can offset one teammate's weakness with another's strength, then performance increases. If the leader integrates a strengths-based approach into the business, then performance increases. We all have to do things we don't like or things that don't play to our strengths. Let's just see if we can do a better job of using our strengths more often.[19]

Switch from the individual to the team. A good teammate attempts to address the better part of all teammates, hopefully through subtle diplomacy, rather than heavy-handed judgment. Good teammate relationships are built on mutual forgiveness, since we inevitably annoy even people we like. All teammates are capable of saying and doing the wrong thing at the wrong time, and yet they forgive each other. Good teammates help us see ourselves through another person's perspective and are gracious when, not if, we act like a dunce. Since teams are composed of imperfect people, without graciousness, teamwork declines. Good teammates encourage the best in each other less by judging our limitations and more by leveraging our strengths.

But strengths-spotting isn't as easy as it seems. As deficit-based thinkers, we are more skilled at defining weaknesses than strengths. For example, organizations use green, yellow, and red colors to measure progress on their key performance indicators (KPIs). Green means goal achieved or exceeded. Yellow means caution—more work to do. Red means expectations not met. Typically, teams start with red numbers, since these areas demand attention. We ask, who is accountable and when will results be achieved? A strengths-based approach differs in two ways. First, we visibly write the virtues above the list of KPIs, including those coded as green, yellow, and red metrics. Second, we ask which virtues were present that made the green results possible. After all, can you imagine green results being achieved in the presence of distrust, cowardice, and despair? The goal is to start by defining what the team did right to achieve green results, including practicing virtue, so they can make progress on red results.

A strengths-based approach isn't about self-esteem booster shots. Its purpose is to move an organization closer to "creating an alignment of strengths that makes a system's weaknesses irrelevant." The hard part is shifting from a focus on deficits to strengths. Deficit-based thinking is particularly difficult to change in work that centers on diagnosing and fixing problems, such as the work done by physicians, lawyers, car mechanics, and plumbers. Anyone whose livelihood is about diagnosing and fixing a problem is at risk for being a deficit-based thinker.

A strengths-based approach to engagement starts by making your strong stronger. Study your version of the 30 percent highly engaged, and find out what they are doing right. This doesn't mean that you ignore your version of the most highly disengaged. Just don't lead with your chin. Start with the people who are engaged, and apply those lessons to the disengaged. Besides, organizational success is tied directly to the retention and support of your best performers.

What doesn't work is studying divorce to understand happy marriages. Studying low morale doesn't teach us about cultures where people flourish. Studying disease doesn't teach us about fitness. Referencing healthcare again, doctors especially need to work on adopting an appreciative approach to engaging teams. Why? The reason is that the entire process of figuring out what is wrong with the patient in front of you is based on a time-honored, highly effective, but deficit-based process called *differential diagnosis*. Patients tell us their story and their symptoms, and doctors generate a list of possible causes—the "differential diagnosis"—which informs what other questions to ask or tests to recommend in order to figure out *the* cause of the patients' problem.

This is all in service of figuring out the best treatment to make the patient well because identifying the best treatment requires accurately understanding the underlying cause. As much as this process works for clinical practice, deficit-based thinking can poison the way that physicians lead. If they apply the same deficit-based thinking to their organizational lives, like figuring out how to improve quality or eliminate wrong-side surgery, the solutions are less imaginative and more limited than if they frame the question appreciatively—for example, "When we are at our best, what are we doing? And how do we do more of that?" Physicians must be mindful of which mindset they are in—clinical (where deficit-based thinking works) or organizational (where appreciative thinking is recommended)—and be able to pivot nimbly between the two in order to deploy the best listening approach.

DO I MAKE A DIFFERENCE?

For 30 years, Susan was a waitress at a university restaurant for campus leaders, faculty, and special events. She served drinks and meals, laid linen and cleaned tables, and slogged heavy piles of dishes to the dishwasher. Yet, Susan viewed her job as hospitality. The word *hospitality* originates from the Latin *hospes*, meaning "guest" or "stranger." In Spanish, the word for "guest" is *huesped*. *Hospes* is the root of words such as *hospice*, *hostel*, *hotel*, and *hospital*. Susan embodied hospitality. She befriended faculty, their spouses, and their kids. She taught international students about American culture and helped them improve their English. She comforted homesick students, so they would stay focused on their studies. In brief, she made people feel like they belonged.

Annually, the university selected an Employee of the Year to honor at its holiday party. Usually, senior leaders and faculty were selected, but this year Susan's name was called for recognition. About 800 people spontaneously rose to give her a standing ovation. She accepted her award with a clear statement about hospitality: "I may not be on the faculty, but that doesn't mean I don't know how to teach."

There is a name and process for how Susan defined her work: *job crafting.* This term was an outcome of a study on hospital janitors. Interviews with janitors showed that some defined their job as a paycheck, others as a way to get ahead, and others viewed their job as caregivers. All janitors had the same job description. What differed was how they did their job. The "caregiver" janitors paid attention to patients who were upset because no one had visited, and they took time to talk and listen to them. They walked elderly patients to their cars so they wouldn't get lost. They paid attention to those who were in a coma by moving pictures around in the room with hope that changing the environment might spark recovery. When one janitor was asked if this was part of his job, the answer was, "No, but this is a part of me."

Finally, one more real-world example. At the Cleveland Clinic, a consistently top-rated healthcare organization, all employees of all types—doctors, nurses, health science workers, bus drivers, environmental service workers, secretaries, and others—are called "caregivers" because each has an opportunity to touch the patient in profound ways. Imagine your experience when you are confused by trying to navigate your way to your appointment in a big medical center and any one of the more than 72,000 caregivers at the clinic sees your confused look and stops to ask you how they can help. Imagine your experience then when they offer to guide you to your destination! When everyone is a caregiver and sees their role through a caregiver lens, the patient experience skyrockets. That is what the "hospitality" in "hospital" should do! Who wouldn't want that patient experience?

PALEOLITHIC EMOTIONS, MEDIEVAL INSTITUTIONS, AND GODLIKE TECHNOLOGY

According to social biologist Edward O. Wilson, the real problem of humanity is the following: "We have Paleolithic emotions, medieval institutions, and godlike technology."[20] COVID-19 laid bare the normal human folly of "Paleolithic emotions," such as fear, greed, and hubris. Some refused to wear masks or take the vaccines despite the evidence that it protects others. Others put their lives at risk to take care of the rest of us, including the infected who didn't wear masks.

In 2020, our "medieval institutions" were not always up to the task of fighting a pandemic that killed millions of people globally. Some institutional leaders argued for personal rights over washing hands, social distancing, and wearing masks. Other institutional leaders actively shared clinical evidence to reduce the percentage of patients who died from COVID-19. Their efforts saved lives, including the lives of those who claimed that COVID-19 was a hoax.

Our "godlike technology" produced and tested multiple vaccines with efficacy rates of about 95 percent. Miraculously, effective vaccines were created in record time—tested and ready to be distributed in less than one year. This was an unprecedented achievement in the history of developing vaccines.

We are more skilled at producing "godlike technology" than managing our "paleolithic emotions." We are still humans seeking to cure our human failings. We can limit, but not eliminate, human folly by choosing to live our twenty-first-century life in accordance with the virtues that emerged more than 2,000 years ago.

KEY TAKEAWAYS

The insight is both simple and hidden in plain sight to many. When we practice virtue, people feel like they belong, matter, and make a difference. And that's when engagement thrives.

TOOLS FOR BELONGING: CONVERSATIONS THAT MATTER

If we are of interest to each other, then we need tools to have conversations that matter. We best put these tools into practice with humility, which is the companion to curiosity. Humility is being grounded. Humility isn't about getting small. Humility is about encouraging others to get big. Remember: our purpose is for people to feel like they belong. To this end, here is set of prompts and activities to begin "conversations that matter." These prompts are evidence based. They have strengthened a sense of belonging among teammates in multiple countries:

1. **4Hs:** Ask teammates to take turns sharing their history, heroes, heartbreaks, and hopes. In about 10 minutes, even people who know each other well gain new insights about their colleagues.
2. **Hopes and concerns:** Ask teammates to express their greatest hopes and concerns, based on the premise that we can manage what we define.

Teammates then accept the responsibility to help each other realize their best hopes and mitigate their greatest concerns.

3. **Inside scoop:** On a single slide, all team members provide pictures of people who mean the most to them and what they most enjoy doing. Every team member then takes five minutes to talk about his or her slide. This enables each person to express to the team, "This is what matters to me."

4. **Bucket list:** Identify 5 to 10 experiences you want to do before you die. Teammates share bucket lists to learn what matters to each person, as well as to identify shared interests.

5. **Defining experiences and people:** Identify 5 to 10 experiences and people that shaped the person you have become. Focus on how you grew both in grace and grit based on both positive and negative experiences and people. Look for what matters to each person, as well as experiences that people share.

6. **Personal timeline:** Take your age and divide it by 3. In each part of your life, who were the people and experiences that shaped who you have become? Include both positive and negative experiences and, importantly, when you were at your best. What is your life story so far? Going forward, what do you want your life story to be?

7. **Who am I?** Each teammate answers the question, "Who am I?" Clearly, this is a challenging question that may freak out some teammates. Remember that the critical point of conversations that matter is vulnerability, not comfort. The deeper the vulnerability, the deeper the bond among teammates. Each person is given time to prepare how he or she wants to answer this question. A timekeeper lets the person know when 5 minutes are left, then 3 minutes, then 2 minutes with a firm cut off at 10 minutes.

Which of these tools works best? The tool that deepens trust and compassion among teammates. We weaken forces that restrain a sense of belonging when we make deposits into each other's emotional bank account. We decrease a sense of belonging by making excessive withdrawals.

JOB CRAFTING FOR MATTERING AND MAKING A DIFFERENCE

We will close the engagement chapter with a powerful engagement method entitled *job crafting*. This evidence-based tool increases engagement, performance, satisfaction, and resilience. Job crafting can also address burnout, which is where we will start in describing how it can be used.

It is hard to feel engaged when we are emotionally exhausted and feel depleted. Professions defined by high demand and low control such as police, teachers, and social workers are especially prone to burnout. Healthcare workers also experience particularly high levels of burnout. For example, a study found that 38 percent of physicians exhibited burnout, compared to 28 percent of the population.[21]

So, sometimes burnout isn't between a person's ears. The problem is a job designed by a crushing workload and inadequate resources. Here's an example from healthcare. Few caregivers put the words "ease of use" and "medical records" in the same sentence. To address increased workloads and stress imposed by the electronic medical record (EMR), the Cleveland Clinic launched a task force to simplify data input, and the clinic hired *scribes* to free up time for caregivers to be with patients.[22] Scribes listen to the doctor engage with the patient, and they record the history and physical examination into the EMR. They then record any orders for laboratory tests or prescriptions. They thus unburden the caregiver, allowing her to focus on the patient. The task force also automated the process of calling pharmacies for refills and engaging with insurance companies to preauthorize tests that were ordered. Scribes have become a much-desired resource at the Cleveland Clinic, and the scribe program is actively growing.[23]

Burnout isn't always about overwork. It can also be caused by "under-meaning." People are less cynical and more resistant to the stresses of organizational crisis when they understand the significance of their efforts. For physicians and nurses, this might include remembering why they got into healthcare in the first place. So, let's switch from burnout to job crafting focused on strengthening engagement and performance.

There are different job-crafting methods, some more sophisticated than others, though the basics are easy to understand. Our approach to job crafting will be organized with the goal in mind to strengthen people's feelings that they belong, matter, and make a difference:

1. **I belong.** Whom do you work with? (relationship crafting)
   - **Appreciation: I feel valued as a person.** Who brings out the best in you? How could you spend more time with them? Encourage people to build relationships by asking for help. Asking for help can be viewed as a sign of weakness, so the cultural shift is viewing support as an act of strength—a gift, not a weakness.

- **Contribution: Do I add value?** Perhaps operations people actively form relationships with a sales team so that quality, cost, and delivery results are aligned with customer expectations.

2. **I matter.** What do you do? (task crafting)
   - **Appreciation: My strengths are acknowledged.** Start a "stop list" to create capacity to grow. By defining what we will stop doing, we can reduce crushing workloads that prevent us from learning a new skill, such as *motivational interviewing*. Motivational interviewing places the caregiver in the role of a coach whose responsibility is to probe whether the patient is motivated to change. Motivational interviewing shifts responsibility of behavior change to the patient because the patient's behavior change isn't something the caregiver controls. The caregiver only controls helping the patients uncover what does motivate them in addition to offering sound clinical advice. Getting clear about what you can and cannot control reduces burnout.
   - **Contribution: Recognize other people's strengths.** Ask people, "What do you do well, and how can you do more of it?" Increase the amount of time that a person spends using their strengths. Apply the 80/20 rule (20 percent of our activities contribute to 80 percent of our value). Increase the 20 percent activities, and reduce the 80 percent activities. In other words, focus efforts on those activities that have the greatest impact on those you serve.

3. **I make a difference.** Why does your job exist? (cognitive crafting)

When it comes to purpose or making a difference, start with the challenges that are right under your nose: (1) "What problems are around me?" (2) "What competencies, strengths of character, and passions prepare me to address some of these problems?" (3) "How can I apply my greatest strengths to help find solutions to these challenges?"[24] Each of these strategies can help mitigate burnout, but none has the power of compassion. Applied to medicine, compassion isn't just good for patients. It is also good for caregivers. The best buffer against burnout is for clinicians to cultivate the skill of compassion.[25]

Job crafting might be good for individuals, but what about organizations? Research shows that job crafting contributes to greater satisfaction and commitment. Performance and mobility in new roles are enhanced. If people are going to job craft anyway, it makes sense to endorse an approach that serves the organization, the team, and the individual. For example, imagine a performance evaluation discussion about what you do, whom you work with, and why your job exists, all guided by organizational priorities.

When the Cleveland Clinic instituted the policy to call everyone a "caregiver," every caregiver spent a half day engaged in an activity (with randomly chosen other caregivers) that plotted the patient experience—from the time they parked their car, to their visit, and to finally finding their way out. Every caregiver in this activity imagined themselves as the patient, providing each caregiver an opportunity to job craft.

Teams can start job-crafting meetings by discussing what people want more of and what they want less of. One person's troubles are another person's gift.[26] One teammate may enjoy creating a sense of team among sales and operations folks, who normally don't work well together, and they would gladly give up compiling reports on delivery times to a highly structured teammate who enjoys this work. Another teammate enjoys statistical analysis on quality issues. That teammate would appreciate being freed from preparing speeches on quality trends by giving that work to the teammate who enjoys giving presentations.

A sense of meaning is missing too often for too many. Job crafting puts teammates in the driver's seat to create meaning in their work. When job crafting is aligned with organizational strategic priorities, both the individual and the organization benefit.

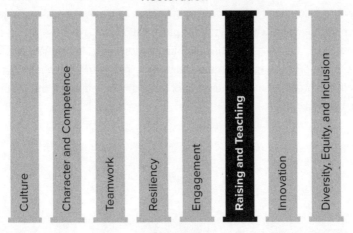

ARETÉ

Excellence

Habits
Coaching
Restoration

Culture

Character and Competence

Teamwork

Resiliency

Engagement

Raising and Teaching

Innovation

Diversity, Equity, and Inclusion

Character

Trust   Compassion   Courage

Justice   Wisdom   Temperance   Hope

RAISING AND TEACHING BETTER HUMANS, BY JULIE REA

*We must remember that intelligence is
not enough. Intelligence plus character—that
is the goal of true education.*[1]
—**MARTIN LUTHER KING, JR.**

For over two decades, we have delivered seminars on the virtues to leaders. Frequently, after discussing and implementing practices to facilitate better performance in the workplace through the application of the virtues, leaders have asked whether these practices translate to home and family. They perceive the need to help their children develop as positive contributors to the family, their schools, and their communities, and they are curious how to use what they have learned at work in the family setting. Furthermore, the underpinnings of a successful society and successful organizations are the people in them, all of whom grew up under the influence of teachers, parents, and friends.

Julie Rea is an experienced teacher and thinker about virtue-based performance. The use of the first-person voice in this chapter reflects her expert observations and experiences.

Thus, beyond leaders' inquiries about the impact of virtues on their homelife, the business case for practicing the virtues at home and in school is that the practice makes young people better, and better young people perpetuate high performance in their work and for society. Furthering the business case for helping people practice virtue with their families, remember that what occurs at home invariably makes its way back to work.

Another rationale for including a discussion of practicing virtue in families and in school in a book about high performance in organizations and society is that leaders know that the purpose of practicing virtue is to make an investment in their professional and personal growth, which includes supporting how they want to parent. Again, the method matters—pull, not push. Share the research and tools, and grant people freedom to apply what they learn at work and home. What follows are some suggestions for helping caregivers create a culture that supports children in developing into their best selves.

"Research suggests that almost all parents say they are deeply invested in raising caring, ethical children, and most parents see these moral qualities as more important than achievement."[2] Data from the teacher survey conducted by the Making Caring Common Project of the Harvard Graduate School of Education suggests that most teachers also view preparing youth to be caring as more important than their achievement."[3] Children, however, hear differently. What they hear the adults in their life saying is that achievement and happiness are more important than being a caring community member.

What is going wrong? How did our children hear, "You must be at the top of the class and be the best [musician/athlete/artist]," when we thought we were saying, "You must be kind and caring"?

Adam Grant and Alison Sweet Grant wrote in *The Atlantic*, "Kids learn what's important to adults not by listening to what we say, but by noticing what gets our attention. And in many developed societies, parents now pay more attention to individual achievement and happiness than anything else. However much we praise kindness and caring, we're not actually showing our kids that we value character."[4]

Ironically, the more attention we pay to individual achievement and happiness, the more anxious our children become. Psychologist and author Madeline Levine notes, "As it stands, we are not preparing our children (or ourselves) very well for confronting an unpredictable, rapidly changing future. Just the opposite: in our efforts to protect our children from experiencing distress, we are unintentionally setting up the circumstances that nurture distress today and will surely exacerbate it tomorrow."[5]

These tendencies toward anxiety persist into adulthood. As a tutor for adults pursuing a General Education Development Test (GED), I hear students apologize again and again for making mistakes or rationalize why they made an error in pronunciation or computation. Sometimes they cry; sometimes they quit in frustration. Their previous schooling experiences have taught them that the goal is not the journey to understanding. The goal is the correct answer, the first time, without hesitation. Such an outlook impedes progress greatly, as tutors must take time repeatedly to reassure the students that they are learning, that mistakes are part of the process, and the length of time it takes to understand a topic is not a mark of intelligence. When schools and parents value achievement over character, the anxiety produced in school becomes a fearsome barrier.

We want our children to be kind and caring people who make their communities better places to live and grow. We want our children to be prepared to live confidently and grow in an uncertain future. We want them to be resilient, able to withstand, and even grow, in the face of failure, setbacks, and disappointments. Our goals as parents resemble the goals for organizational leaders, who wish to build climates in which their work colleagues have resilience and do the right thing when nobody is watching. How do we accomplish this?

CHANGING THE MESSAGE

If we want to change what our children hear, we need to change our message and how we present it. In *Self-Theories*, Carol Dweck presents her research on the development of mindsets, an individual's assessment of the malleability of intelligence. According to Dweck, based on our experiences, we develop an idea that either we can change our intelligence or we can't. We believe that our efforts make a difference in what we can learn or achieve, or we believe that we are stuck with what we were given at conception. Dweck calls the belief that we can control our intelligence a *growth mindset*. In contrast, the belief that, regardless of effort, our intelligence is limited is a *fixed mindset*.[6]

At first glance, it is surprising to learn that some students with the highest grades have a fixed mindset. You might assume that these high achievers would have ample support for believing that hard work would generate results. Yet, in K–12 education, high achievers are frequently the ones for whom school has come easily. They have the self-control, fine motor skills, and inclinations to literacy and numeracy to make the routine tasks of school effortless. They not only tolerate but frequently welcome the repetition of content presentation followed by worksheet completion. They have been praised for getting right answers and getting them quickly. They know the game and excel at it.

Ask these same high achievers to tackle open-ended projects or complex questions common in the workplace and they may freeze. Because they have been rewarded for knowing the right answer, it stands to reason that not knowing the right answer immediately calls into question their intelligence. Maybe they are not as smart as everyone, including themselves, thought. Maybe they should retreat to the work they already know how to do. Continuing to put in effort, trying a new solution, or looking for help means that they have failed.

On the other hand, students with growth mindsets attack open-ended, complex, challenging tasks with relish. Not knowing the answers right away is an opportunity to apply new thinking or new strategies, to learn something new. They see these tasks as challenges. Rather than the defeatist self-talk of the fixed mindset students, the growth mindset students use encouraging self-talk, reminding themselves of what they know or motivating themselves to persist.

Dweck reports on research documenting ways to help students change the self-defeating narratives that hinder success on challenging tasks. In one study, students with a fixed mindset were given *attribution retraining*. That is, they were taught to assign an explanation for failure to not offering enough effort, rather than assigning it to not having enough intelligence. By reframing the reason for failure, these students improved in task-persistence (asking for help appropriately) and confidence.

Even more importantly, Dweck and fellow researchers demonstrated that when children are given the opportunity to correct errors with the instruction "to think of another way to do it," they developed a mastery-oriented response to failure. They were more able to develop solutions to the problem; they expressed more positive attitudes about their experiences; and they believed more in the inherent goodness of people.

This repeated exposure to opportunities to learn from so-called failure is supported by experience from the Harvard Center for the Developing Child. In a report entitled *8 Things to Remember About Child Development,* the center noted, "It is the reliable presence of at least one supportive relationship and multiple opportunities for developing effective coping skills that are the essential building blocks for strengthening the capacity to do well in the face of significant adversity."[7]

So, What Do We Do to Help Children Develop a Growth Mindset?

Remember to ask your child if there is another way to do whatever they are trying to do.

As hard as it is to do, let your child fail. Then encourage them to figure out what to do next. If needed, offer suggestions to get them started. If an apology, atonement, or repair is in order, let them know you expect that will happen and will follow up until it is done.

Make sure to let your children know that we all fail, it is OK to fail, and that what is important is what we do next.

Model and encourage a *not-yet attitude*: I haven't been successful yet, but with persistence, I can be.

Discuss examples of your own failures and what steps you took to atone for and repair your mistakes.

Point out examples of failures that turned out to be happy surprises—better than the original expectation had you (or someone else) not failed.

Consider using the items on the 4Gs scorecard (Chapter 4) as a series of question prompts to help you and your child focus on what is most important. For example: Did I practice compassion today? Did I get back up and try harder after a failure? Did I help others succeed? Did I deal with frustration positively?

RECOGNIZE THE PATTERNS

Teaching Algebra 1 to high school students who believe that math is unrelated to their life and adds nothing to their functioning as humans in the real world can be challenging. While coteaching math to a group of reluctant math learners, I heard many complaints of the "Why do we have to learn this?" and "When will I ever use this?" variety, even though my colleague and I spent hours creating engaging lessons targeted directly at these very questions.

One day, a student named Robert began his usual round of moaning about the math task of the day, and I started to say something motivational, such as, "Please stop talking and get to work," when my incredibly talented coteacher said, "Oh, Robert, that's the sound of you learning." She had heard and recognized the pattern of Robert's brain revving up by voicing his resistance, getting it out in the open so that he could clear the way for the learning to happen.

In *Seven and a Half Lessons About the Brain*, Lisa Feldman Barrett describes the brain as a "predicting organ."[8] My colleague had tapped into what Robert's brain sounded like as it made a prediction of what he would experience in the next 40 minutes. Robert's brain remembered that at 9 a.m. every weekday, he was in algebra class; his teachers expected that he would exert effort to comprehend and remember some information; and that in the past, that effort had not led to satisfactory results. Robert's brain was rapidly seeking ways to avoid this unproductive energy expense. His brain had learned that whining and complaining sometimes earned him time away from the task, often enough that it was worth expending some energy to see if he could avoid the task this time.

Once my colleague identified Robert's pattern, we could see and hear other students' learning routines. Some seemed helpful—getting materials neatly stacked on a desk or finding a compatible partner to work with. Others seemed less so—bathroom trips, asking someone else for pencil and paper, putting heads down on desks. Yet when we could identify these patterns, frame the behaviors, annoying or not, in this way—that's the sound or sight of this student learning—we became more tolerant of these behaviors and less likely to see them as disruptive. We could privately ask students if they found the behaviors were truly helpful in kick-starting the learning process. With a change in our perspective about these behaviors, we could sometimes help students create better, more efficient patterns leading to more productive work routines.

So, What Do We Do to Help Children Develop Effective Patterns?

Remember what it is like to be a beginner, perhaps by attempting a brand-new skill yourself. What does it feel like when you don't know exactly what to do when or how?

If you have a reluctant learner at home, spend a few days observing how they approach homework time. Notice the behaviors that occur at the beginning of the session, midsession, and the conclusion. Are there avoidance behaviors at the start? What are they? Does concentration wane halfway through? Does your learner shift to daydreaming, or restless movements, or leaving the area altogether? Is there a rush when the end is in sight? Do papers get filed or shoved higgledy-piggledy into the backpack or left on the desk? Which patterns are useful? Which are not?

Once you have identified some patterns, have a talk with your learner about what you have observed. Discuss which patterns seem helpful and which do not. For example, it may surprise you to learn that, although it doesn't appeal to you, walking in circles while thinking actually helps your child improve concentration. Choose one pattern that your child identifies as not helpful and help your child design a more productive alternative.

For example, if getting up repeatedly to find needed materials derails your child, what can be done to eliminate those disruptions? Maybe putting a range of supplies in a bin that is kept near the homework desk would be an answer. Or if homework is frequently completed but left at home, set a new pattern. Your child repeats the mantra "Homework is finished only when it is in the homework file," and a trusted partner checks every day for three weeks to make sure the new pattern is set. Be open to suggestions even if they don't seem plausible to you.

Let your child direct the process. Your most helpful stance is to ask if the experiment has been successful with the understanding that both of you need to agree on its success. Once that new pattern is solidly in place, select another problem pattern and try to address it.

This approach works well not only for homework but for chores, instrument practice, work schedules, and in any number of other contexts.

RECOGNIZE THE ALTERNATIVES

As an instructional coach, I was often in classrooms to observe the learning process and to support teachers as they went about creating their learning communities. Sometimes, if a teacher was called away, I served as an impromptu substitute, continuing a lesson for a few minutes while the teacher was out of the room. One day I was in a roomful of kindergarteners when the teacher needed to step out of the room. The lesson was about shapes, and we were discussing circles. Since the children seemed antsy, I thought they needed to move a little. I invited them all to stand up and make a big circle with their arms.

As I demonstrated with my own arms, I had visions of all these beautiful children beaming up at me with their arms in circles, feeling very circular and knowing exactly what a circle was. What happened next was mind-boggling. These kindergarteners were feeling so circular they began to swing their arms, bodies, and legs around and around, bumping into each other, knocking over chairs, and somehow stepping on each other's fingers and toes. In two seconds, the room was chaos. What went wrong? Exactly that. I had failed to predict what could go wrong. I had failed to get into the mind of a kindergartener.

In *How Children Succeed*, Paul Tough introduces us to Elizabeth Spiegel, a middle school chess teacher in Brooklyn. Spiegel's chess teams were incredibly successful because, as Tough notes, she taught her students to "resist the temptation to pursue an immediately attractive move"—think kindergarteners with their arms in circles. Instead, she taught her students to look for alternative solutions and new and creative ideas. Her students learned not to hide from what could go wrong but to go looking for it. After each chess game, won or lost, Spiegel and her students replayed the game, move by move, analyzing key turning points in the game, thinking about what would have been a better move and what would have happened if that better choice had been made. Spiegel helped her students get comfortable with what is inherently uncomfortable: staring down your mistakes.[9]

So, What Do We Do to Help Children Recognize Alternatives?

Model thinking through a better move. When a project doesn't work out, you miss a deadline, or you forget a friend's birthday, think out loud about where you went wrong. Ask yourself what would be a better move: How could I do this better? Let your children see the process in action.

When things go well, ask why they went well. What decisions were made, or what strategies were used to ensure that the project, activity, or game was a success. Talk about how those decisions and strategies can be replicated and carried over into other areas of life.

SWIM BUDDIES

A conversation I had with a colleague many years ago has stuck with me, long after I have forgotten other details about our work situation. Her teenage daughter was doing typical teenage daughter things for the time, like hanging out at the mall, going to parties, and visiting friends' homes with varying degrees of parental supervision. My colleague and her daughter had developed a unique system for handling these social opportunities. They had discussed each of her friends and classified them into two groups: those who had good sense and those who didn't. No one was banned or shunned, but wherever the friends went, there had to be more in the good-sense group than in the bad-sense group. If the groups were out of balance and the have-nots were in the majority, the daughter needed to recruit enough good-sense friends to tip the balance.

Looking back, I can see that my colleague was creating a *swim buddy system* for her daughter. Her message was this: surround yourself with people whom you can count on to help you do the right thing. In the adolescent years with a brain wired for reward more than pain, having swim buddies who support your desire to exercise caution and good sense is extremely practical. It eliminates the need for the parent always to be in control and calling the shots, and it helps the adolescent develop guardrails and learn independence.

A corollary to the swim buddy system is the *trusted-advisor system*. Every child should be able to name several adults outside the family unit they count as trusted advisors. Teachers, faith group leaders, coaches, and parents of friends are all possible candidates. We knew that our young son had learned this concept when, as a Cub Scout, he entered the Pinewood Derby. At the time, we had no power tools at home, so he carefully used a handsaw, sandpaper, and a hammer to build his car, under my supervision, but without much technical input, since I didn't have any to share. His efforts resulted in race times that placed him in the top three of his pack and earned a spot in the District Pinewood Derby.

On the day of the district meet, in the first heat, his car sped down the track, hit the bumper at the end, bounced back, and lost a wheel. We were dismayed. Our son, however, was not. He calmly picked up the car and the stray wheel, looked around the room and headed our way. We had no idea what to do next. Fortunately, our son did not come to us for help. He was actually headed for his trusted advisor, the assistant Cub Scout leader, who had thought about what could go wrong at the Pinewood Derby, and who had brought a toolkit with him. Together, they assessed the situation, our son made a repair, and he was ready for the next heat. I do not remember the outcome of the event, which surely means his car did not end up in first place. I do remember that we were extremely grateful to the leader who thought about what could go wrong and to our son who wisely used his trusted advisors.

So, What Do We Do?

Discuss with your child how impulsiveness, a temperance issue, can lead to poor decision-making, and poor decision-making can lead to hurtful, sometimes even dangerous, outcomes. Talk about children you know who are inclined to be impulsive and make poor choices. Then talk about how helpful it is to have more friends around to support you in making good choices. Come to an agreement about how your child should cope in situations where the poor decision makers outweigh the good decision makers.

Ask what your child might do in an emergency situation. What if parents or caregivers aren't available for some reason? Which adults might your child reach out to for help? Make sure your child has a list of trusted adult advisors who can be counted on for help and advice. No trusted-advisor list? Think about ways to connect your child to competent, caring adults. Big Brothers and Big Sisters, Scouting or Guides, faith groups, recreational sports, school clubs, or activities are some structured relationships that might be helpful. Informal relationships with neighbors and friends' parents are also good candidates for trusted advisors.

Make sure your child knows that it is a mark of intelligence and maturity, not weakness, to ask for help when needed.

RESTORATIVE PRACTICES

When I was teaching in a middle school, the principal stopped me in the hall one day to let me know that one of my students had been suspended.

"We found cigarettes in his locker. He says his dad borrowed his coat and left them in his pocket, but I'm not buying it," the principal said. "He's out for three days."

I asked, "Was he smoking at school?"

"No, but I won't have any student bringing illegal substances into my school."

I responded, "Isn't it his school too? How is he supposed to learn if he's not in school? And how do you know they aren't his dad's? And if they are Sam's, shouldn't we help him? I mean, he shouldn't be smoking! No one should! And if he's at home, isn't he just going to have more opportunity to smoke? Isn't that the real problem?"

The principal looked at me with annoyance. "I could have given him five days, you know."

On his return to school after his suspension, Sam was behind in all his classes, overwhelmed by trying to catch up and angry with all of the adults at the school. The principal's strong stance, however, was secure.

Had I known about restorative practices at the time, I might have had a more productive conversation with the principal. It would have centered around who was being harmed because Sam had cigarettes in his pocket and because he was most probably smoking somewhere, though not at school. We would have discussed how we could help Sam and all the other students who might try smoking. Maybe we could have had a productive meeting with Sam's parents, who might very well have been the source of the cigarettes. Sam would definitely be part of these conversations because he was at the heart of the issue. Unfortunately for all of us, restorative practices were not part of our culture, and we were left with the consequences of a broken system.

The concept of restorative practices has deep roots in many cultural traditions. Today, we are looking back to these deep roots to help us create a "civil society that pursues the need for individual human dignity through the development of more just communal engagement and social structures," according to John Baile of the International Institute for Restorative Practices. Baile's work at the institute and his review of restorative practices scholarship reveals "three areas of universal human need. These are the needs to belong, to have voice, and to have agency."[10] Sounds a lot like "I belong. I matter, and I make a difference."

In response to the mass incarceration of convicted individuals as a result of "tough on crime" legislation in the United States, many organizations in the country and the world have implemented restorative justice practices in the criminal justice system.[11] Such practices provide offenders and their victims the opportunity to meet, hear each other's perspectives, and possibly develop a plan in which the offenders make some sort of restitution for the harm they have caused.

In a similar vein, schools have turned away from those zero-tolerance policies that resulted in record rates of suspensions and expulsions but not in more acceptable behaviors, better test scores, or improved sense of community. Instead, schools are implementing an "approach to behavior management and youth development that focuses both on intensive proactive relationship development and responding to misbehavior as harm done to relationships"[12]—in other words, restorative justice practices.

At the heart of the restorative practices process is the recognition of the responsibility of the individual to the community, and vice versa. There are both proactive practices of community and relationship building and restorative practices of repair and atonement. In schools, routines such as community circles help build a sense of trust and care in the classroom community. When trust has been broken and harm has occurred, those involved meet and discuss the wrong and how it can be repaired. The following restorative questions are used:

- What happened?
- What were you thinking about at the time?
- What have you thought about since?
- Who has been affected and in what way?
- What's been the hardest thing for you?
- What needs to happen to make things right?[13]

Those who were affected by the poor choices may be asked these questions:

- When you realized what happened, what did you think?
- How did these insights affect you and others?
- What was the hardest issue to resolve?
- How can you make things right?[14]

These conversations can range from informal to formal and from quick to lengthy, depending on the number of people involved, the context, and the degree of harm committed. But inherent to all these conversations is this consideration: "Human beings are happier, more cooperative, more productive and more likely to make positive changes in their behavior when those in positions of authority do things with them rather than to them or for them."[15]

So, What Do We Do to Promote Restorative Practices?

- Be proactive. Implement a circle time to discuss issues that are important to your family.
- Create norms about how and when circle time happens and how to be sure every voice is heard.
- Be responsive. When harm has occurred, use the restorative questions to guide your discussion and your actions.
- Remember that "each of us is more than the worst thing we have ever done."[16]
- Be curious.

Find out more about restorative practices at www.iirp.edu.

This focus on restoring trust replicates the importance of developing virtue-based cultures in organizations that is so critical to encouraging high performance. In raising children, as in leading organizations, when you get better at who you are, you get better at what you do. And the added value of raising good, resilient children is that it sets up the societies they will populate when grown to be the kind of worlds we all covet—worlds grounded in trust, compassion, wisdom, hope, temperance, and justice.

KEY TAKEAWAYS

Helping children become individuals of character is a heavy lift. It requires that the adults in a child's life have a clear idea of exactly what "character" means. The virtues described in this book provide a solid foundation for understanding character. The tools provided in each chapter can be adapted for use with children.

A close look reveals that the tools in this chapter are geared to helping children recognize that they belong, they matter, and they make a difference. By including children in discussions of virtues and by modeling your own acceptance of mistakes and challenges, children learn that they belong, even when they have stumbled. By teaching children to look for what can go wrong, they learn that what they do matters. By encouraging restorative practices, children learn that they can help others belong and that they can make a difference. When children get better at who they are, they get better at what they do.

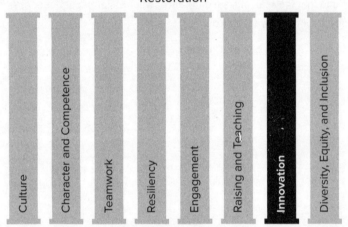

ARETÉ

Excellence

Habits
Coaching
Restoration

Culture

Character and Competence

Teamwork

Resiliency

Engagement

Raising and Teaching

Innovation

Diversity, Equity, and Inclusion

Character

Trust   Compassion   Courage

Justice   Wisdom   Temperance   Hope

DRIVING INNOVATION

If you want something new, you have to
stop doing something old.[1]
—PETER DRUCKER

The key to innovation is the idea. This statement is the greatest myth of innovation according to Bill Aulet, the managing director of entrepreneurship at the Massachusetts Institute of Technology. MIT launches 900 companies a year, so when it comes to innovation, they know what they are talking about. MIT conducted a study to determine which factors contributed more to a new venture's return on investment (ROI): the idea or the leader and team. They found that about 66 percent of the variance in ROI was attributed to leaders and teams and about 33 percent was explained by the strategy or idea. Ideas matter, but leaders and teams matter more. Innovation is not a linear pursuit of a predetermined idea but rather, an iterative process that requires the practice of virtue. In fact, a linear approach defines why so many innovations fail. Ideas will and should change as the venture bumps into real customers.

In this chapter, we don't claim that what we have to say about innovation is unique. Amazon lists over 70,000 books on innovation, which would take 2,397 years to complete if you read 20 pages a day. However, you can read this chapter in a day! We do think that what we have to offer about innovation and virtue is distinct. Today, we need not only product innovation but also relationship innovation, and there is no better way to strengthen relationships than to practice virtue.

A virtue-based culture isn't just important from a moral point of view. It is important from a success point of view. A strong mission and culture are much stronger glue to develop and retain innovators than money. To be fair, we need to pay people to innovate, but we need to practice virtue to cultivate innovative performance. To these ends, the first part of the chapter will focus on the critical shortage of innovators. The second part of the chapter will focus on an equally rare organizational asset—an innovative culture.

ADAPT OR DIE

Now, some might say, wait a minute, if you want to succeed in life, you need to subscribe to Darwin's "survival of the fittest" rather than virtue. Success has to be grabbed, taken. You need to take what you want or someone else will get it. The kicker is that Darwin did not coin the phrase "survival of the fittest." Herbert Spencer did. Darwin's insight, which he wrote in *On the Origin of the Species*, is this: "Those communities which included the greatest number of the most sympathetic members would flourish best and rear the greatest number of offspring."[2] What Darwin called "sympathy," we call "compassion."

So, planet Earth's evolutionary prodigy actually concluded that compassion, rather than selfishness, is our strongest instinct, and that compassion would spread through natural selection. Increasingly, social scientists are building a case that "survival of the kindest" more accurately captures Darwin's insights.[3]

Fear not, there is no rush to place selfishness and ruthlessness on the endangered species list. The human capacity to be self-serving and self-absorbed is alive and well. Daily, we observe callousness openly competing with compassion where we work and live. What Darwin and social biologists such as E. O. Wilson are saying is that when teams and cultures are composed of self-interested people, they will fail more than they succeed. In contrast, teams composed of people who care about each other will win more than they lose. From an evolutionary perspective, altruistic morality has been passed down to us from our ancestors for practical reasons. We survive and thrive best by living in large social groups where people treat each other well, at least most of the time.

"Survival of the kindest" aligns with *homeostasis* (Chapter 6)— our brain and body's need for stability. When we are regulated or stable, and when relations are strong, we can better reason our way to adapt. When we feel unsafe or dysregulated, and we feel excluded, our ability to reason is compromised. Virtue creates safe environments where people will not be humiliated. Rather, they are encouraged to speak up, raise questions or concerns, or risk making mistakes, all of which are vital to adapting to changing circumstances.

Here's a story about how collaboration promotes our ability to adapt to external change. During COVID-19, knowing that ventilators could not be manufactured fast enough to meet the projected need, Cleveland Clinic pulmonologists and respiratory therapists teamed with engineers at Parker Hannifin. Together, they cracked the daunting challenge of multiplex ventilation—how to take care of two patients with a single ventilator. Rapid prototyping and fluid interdisciplinary collaboration across organizations produced this outcome in fewer than 30 days. Publications shared this knowledge with the medical community throughout the nation and the world.

BETTER HUMANS, BETTER INNOVATORS

Innovation involves more than knowledge. Innovation is also who we are. It is our character. The case for character to guide innovation is not based on sentimentalism or hopeless idealism. Character is a hardheaded way to promote innovation and lower its inherent risk. Ultimately, innovation is a bet on the leader and the team more than the idea. The importance of pro-social qualities such as teamwork, collaboration, intelligent risk-taking, and learning from failure takes us back to virtue—the best pro-social invention available to humans.

Innovation starts with *trust*. Organizations with high-trust cultures outcompete low-trust organizations as measured by increased innovation, as well as higher productivity and improved engagement.[4] We learn and grow from uncertainty better when we trust our team and when the quality of the idea matters more than who suggested it.

Innovation deepens with *compassion*. Innovation depends on connecting to whom we serve. Whether we serve customers, patients, or students, as compassion increases, we learn how to provide value better than competitors.

Innovation depends on *courage* to do as Peter Drucker suggested: "Put your products out of business before your competitors do."[5] It takes courage to step into the unknown. Innovation depends on vulnerability, grit, and resilience.

Innovation requires *justice*. A sustainable organization continually strives to look out for the interests of customers, teammates, business partners, and investors. Without a purpose greater than profits, an organization might survive in the short term, but over a long term, this kind of enterprise isn't sustainable.

Innovation is lifted by *wisdom*. Wisdom creates a *what-if* culture rather than a *no* culture. Innovation is an experiment without assurance that it is going to work. So, innovation is doomed in cultures that lack tolerance for mistakes.

Innovation takes *temperance*. Temperance involves balancing daily operations that pay today's bills and future innovations to pay tomorrow's bills. Structures and processes that support operations are not the same as those that cultivate innovation.

Innovation always requires *hope*. Few people want to take or can afford to take crazy risks. We can better manage fear of failure by defining and managing the level of loss we are willing to accept.

IDEA RISK, INNOVATOR RISK

Experienced investors expect innovators to be enthusiastic about their ideas. But new ideas come with risk that investors sort out during the due diligence process that includes these:

1. **Commercial risk:** Failing to attract enough customers
2. **Operational risk:** Failing to meet quality, cost, or delivery expectations

3. **Financial risk:** Failing to achieve adequate return on investment

Yet, the trickiest risk of all are *dark-triangle leaders*, defined as people competent in managing commercial, operational, and financial risk though at a price—dark-triangle baggage. If you are looking to create a toxic culture that causes agony for others, you can do no better than select *Machiavellian, narcissist,* and *psychopathic leaders*:

1. **Machiavellian:** The ends justify the means.
   - Machiavellians can turn on the charm to work with others and then switch to using others to achieve their goals. They are characterized by doing things that others see as immoral, coercive, dishonest, and impulsive.
2. **Narcissus:** Self-absorbed.
   - Narcissus admired his own reflection at which he stared until he died. Narcissists have an inflated view of their self-worth, and they are often insecure and entitled.
3. **Psychopaths:** What Germans call "suffering souls."
   - In German, *suffering souls* is used to capture the downside of being a psychopath. However, it is hard to work up much empathy for people who are dishonest, egocentric, and cruel. What's worrisome is that "not all psychopaths are in prison—some are in the board room."[6]

Virtue and the dark-triangle leader are more of a continuum than a stark either/or choice, with each of us falling somewhere along the spectrum. When leaders hold the dark side somewhat in check, they can rise to the top of corporate, military, and political leadership by being politically savvy, by excelling at networking, and by managing well. If dark-triangle leaders are not to menace others, they need to be toned down with positive qualities such as openness to new experiences and curiosity. When the dark side isn't checked, these qualities work brilliantly in toxic cultures where parasites thrive, thereby contributing to bullying, theft, absenteeism, turnover, and sabotage.[7]

E. O. Wilson put competition this way: "Competing is intense among humans, and within a group, selfish individuals always win. But in contests between groups, groups of altruists always beat groups of selfish individuals."[8] Wilson's use of the word "always" is probably too strong, but the key caution is this: the success of dark-triangle leadership comes at the expense of the organization's success, and most importantly, its culture.

HIRE FOR CHARACTER, TRAIN FOR INNOVATION

The competencies of innovation include making the product, selling the product, and counting the money, among other areas of expertise such as legal, engineering, and software as a service. These competencies are amplified when character is present and diminished when character is absent. For this reason, investors are wise to hire for character (who) and train for competence (what) when building an innovative team. Without character, a fledging organization is at risk. With character, a new venture hasn't eliminated risk though it has taken steps toward mitigating the greatest risk of all—an ethical scandal that takes down the company.

You might excuse away entitlement and arrogance for the benefit of exceptional competence. The problem is that self-absorption isn't just annoying. It destroys teamwork and innovation.

It's not that investors don't value character. We underestimate what we can't define, and investors can lack the language of virtue to define what excellence looks like. Investors may not know that character defined by virtue is a better predictor of performance than competence. Without the lens of virtue, it is tempting to hire dark-triangle rock star surgeons, sales rainmakers, or uberinnovators whose heads are large and whose hearts are small.

INNOVATE WITH INTEGRITY

Clearly, you can learn to innovate without being virtuous. For some businesses, the desired end is a high margin. Innovation then becomes the means to profitability. This approach can work. Alternatively, the desired end can be integrity that creates sustainable profitability. Too idealistic? Consider how trustworthy leaders who care about others are more willing and able to suspend their judgments to better understand a customer's or teammate's perspective. Courageous and hopeful leaders encourage others and are less afraid to make mistakes. Just leaders effectively balance safety and efficiency. They cut costs and improve quality, and they train people with new skills when innovation makes old skills obsolete.

Absent virtue, leaders punish people for making mistakes, taking risks, or challenging past practices, all of which will decrease, not increase, the likelihood of innovation.

Lastly, even well-intentioned leaders who want to rely on integrity to innovate come up short without knowing what integrity means or how it can be practiced. These are the leaders who are served well by understanding that integrity is defined by virtue, which can be practiced with evidence-based tools. So, if the goal is sustainable innovation, then the approach is for leaders and teams to get better at who they are by practicing virtue.

Just as character is formed as a result of habituation, so too is innovation. A six-year study conducted at Harvard uncovered habits of innovation defined by five *discovery characteristics*.[9] The important insight was that innovative entrepreneurs spent 50 percent more time on the art of discovery than did senior leaders who lacked a record of innovation. The hopeful news about these habits is they can be learned and practiced. What is more hopeful is that even successful innovators do not do all five well. Success means that we do at least one or two well. It means that those who fail to innovate lack all of these habits. Here is an adaptation of the five discovery characteristics uncovered by the Harvard study:

1. Associating
   - The backbone of creativity and innovation is made possible by those who see nonobvious connections between two seemingly unrelated ideas. For example, roof gardens first built between 4,000 and 600 years BCE in ancient Mesopotamia are an unobvious connection. In the 1890s, roof gardens became popular in New York City, which

is where Madison Square Garden gets its name. Today, companies around the world make possible the unobvious connection between a roof, a garden, and saving energy. Rooftops are built sturdy enough to take the extra weight of soil so that residents can grow tomatoes and lower their heating bill.[10]

2. Observing

- Start with customers' needs, wants, and values to ensure that your solution resolves their problems better than competing alternatives. The population of Curitiba, Brazil, is about 2 million people. Like all major cities, traffic jams made getting to work inexpensively and quickly a daily struggle. Curitiba urban planners significantly reduced this struggle by building an aboveground subway system. Passengers are protected from bad weather by large, attractive glass cylinders. People pay before they get in the line to board the bus rather than wait in line while people fumble for correct change. In less than a minute, over 300 people enter and exit bus doors that are level to a platform, similar to an underground station. Buses travel in dedicated lanes so they can move more quickly than cars stuck in traffic. The system was built for a fraction of the cost of an underground system. And, unlike fixed rail, the system is fluid, so, bus lines can adapt whenever people shift where they live and work.[11]

3. Questioning

- Innovation starts by asking the right questions. *Voice of the customer* (VOC) is a powerful way to cocreate innovation with a customer. The best questions are founded on earning a person's trust and caring about their "pain points." Voice of the customer doesn't have to be at the level of transforming urban life the way the Curitiba bus system did. It could be recognizing that car ownership manuals are big and unwieldy. Mercedes converted voice of the customer insights into designing a phone app that replaced the printed manual and monitors critical car and driver data.[12]

4. Experimenting
   - The future of work will require leaders run ongoing experiments to balance belonging with flexibility. Here's why. About 50 percent of people work in organizations such as manufacturing or healthcare that cannot be done from home. About 10 percent of people work in jobs such as IT support or editing that can be done remotely indefinitely. About 40 percent of people can work under a hybrid model—some remote and some in person.[13] COVID tore away any illusion that job flexibility is distributed evenly.
   - The performance impact of remote versus in person depends on the task at hand. Trusting and caring relationships are the engine of collaboration, teamwork, and coordination to complete complicated projects. Relationships built on virtue are critical to resolving conflicts and creating novel solutions that are not easily achieved remotely. On the other hand, uninterpreted tasks such as writing reports or coding can be completed more productively remotely.
   - The impact of remote versus in person on life-work balance varies widely depending on someone's circumstances. A person raising a family has different needs than someone taking care of aging parents or someone managing a difficult health issue. The challenge is a temperance issue that calls for a Goldilocks solution. Individuals need to balance flexibility with staying connected with leaders and teammates so their value is known when promotion decisions are made.
   - Flexibility sounds great, though choices create justice issues of fairness and equity. Whenever we bump up against justice, wisdom will be needed. For all these reasons, wise leaders make clear that the future of work is an ongoing experiment that requires continual adaption to avoid walking back a policy that people thought was fixed.[14]

5. Socializing
  • *Social capital*, defined by the number of authentic
    relationships one has, is the best predictor of who will
    innovate. Building social capital includes meeting people
    with different ideas, backgrounds, and points of view to
    expand our insights. Strengthening social capital requires
    the skill of trustworthiness and compassion.[15]

Clayton Christensen helps us see the importance of social capital by comparing how identical twins might approach innovation differently. Say you ran an experiment involving two identical twins that have similar brains and talent. One twin puts her head down and works tirelessly, though alone. She imagines what people would want and how to fill an unmet need. The other twin talks to 10 diverse people, including artists, teachers, physicians, scientists, the poor and the wealthy, the conservative and the liberal. This twin visits a half dozen companies to observe their approach to innovation. She also asks 30 potential customers lots of questions about their pain points and competing alternatives, and she experiments with a half dozen prototypes and services to create a compelling value proposition. Kick genetics to the curb; social capital beats diligent isolation hands down.[16]

It's virtue that builds social capital. It's virtue that gives innovators convictions to navigate whatever circumstance come their way. It's virtue that makes the life of the innovator simpler guided by conviction and not circumstance. But practicing virtue to guide innovation is anything but easy.

BETTER CULTURES, BETTER INNOVATORS

When good innovators meet a bad culture, it's the culture that leaves with its reputation intact. When good innovators meet a good culture, now they have a fighting chance. The elements of a good culture include a compelling purpose, as well as structures and processes that enable innovation.

Purpose: Why Does a Business Exist?

Adam Smith thought of business this way: "It is from not the benevolence of the butcher, the brewer, or the baker that we expect our dinner, but from their regard to their own interest." In 1776, Smith's *Wealth of Nations* stated that the reason the butcher curates, cuts, and sells good meat is to make money to feed himself and his family.[17] The same is true for the brewer and baker. Some might view this motivation as greed. Smith viewed it as an "invisible hand" that yielded unintended social benefits when the pursuit of self-interest cultivated collaboration and mutual benefit. "Enlightened self-interest" means that we best serve our own interests by serving others.

In 1962, Milton Friedman, a Nobel laureate in economics, created the Friedman Doctrine. Friedman was heavily influenced by Smith's ideas when he wrote, "There is one and only one social responsibility of business—to use its resources and engage in activities designed to increase its profits so long as it stays within the rules of the game, which is to say, engages in open and free competition without deception or fraud."[18]

For the last half century, most business leaders and business educators have relied on the Friedman Doctrine to define the purpose of a business. Today, it comes as no surprise that antibusiness voices are challenging the Friedman Doctrine. But here is what is surprising. It's not the opponents but rather the proponents of capitalism who are calling for reform. Increasingly, business leaders and business educators are advocating that companies redefine their purposes from an exclusive focus on profit to one that includes people and the planet.

For example, the Business Roundtable, composed of the CEOs of America's largest companies, has stated that long-term shareholder value isn't a company's only purpose. Corporations also need to invest in and train employees, create value for customers, develop ethical supplier relationships, and take care of the environment. Prior to the Business Roundtable statement, Laurence Fink, the CEO of BlackRock, made clear that if a company lacked a sense of purpose and failed to engage with the community, "it will ultimately lose the license to operate from key stakeholders."[19] Fink's concerns are that "widespread aversion" to capitalism requires that companies do more than focus on profit. As the world's largest investor managing $6 trillion in 401(k) plans, exchange-traded funds, and mutual funds, Black-Rock has the financial muscle to hold companies accountable for delivering social value, not just economic value.

To be clear, creating social value doesn't mean that profitability takes a back seat. Businesses still need to create wealth for shareholders to generate and deploy capital that makes it possible to hire and invest in people and to deliver value to customers and business partners. Nonprofits have to make more money than they spend too. They might not be for profit, but nonprofits can't be for loss either.

The broader justice point is this. When society's sense of justice shifts, behavior and laws follow, not the other way around. If enough people believe that it is "just" that businesses adopt a broader purpose than profit, then this might shift a narrow focus on quarterly earnings to a broader focus on stakeholders.

We started with Adam Smith's *The Wealth of Nations*, which focused on enlightened self-interest.[20] We will end with his treatise on *The Theory of Moral Sentiments*.[21] Smith was not just the founder of economics. He was also a moral philosopher who thought deeply about self-interest and sympathy. Like Darwin, Smith used the word *sympathy* to mean "empathy." Smith concluded that it is prudent that we look out for our own interests. At the same time, we are wise to have empathy for others and for others to have empathy for us. He was clear that we demand that business leaders adhere to the law; otherwise, society would break apart. Justice and the rule of law limits the harm we cause others.

Smith also thought that our conscience reminds us that other people matter. He stated that we welcome business leaders who are benevolent but that we can't demand they be so. In other words, we can cultivate compassion, but we cannot command it. Clearly, Smith's two-century-old insights about self-interest and empathy are still with us today.

This is why we can count on an endless debate about how to best create value for both shareholders and stakeholders.

Converting Purpose into Action

We don't need much convincing that when it comes to innovation, purpose comes in handy. A compelling purpose can help teams react to innovation's inevitable barriers more as speed bumps than as impenetrable walls. While purpose has a powerful impact on innovation, the idea is abstract. How do we create a purpose that leads to action at the organizational, team, and individual levels to adapt to change? The Cleveland Clinic London provides an interesting case study to answer this question.

Organizational Purpose

Your mission should you choose to accept it is this: build a hospital from scratch in another country during a global pandemic. The Cleveland Clinic chose to open an innovative hospital in London, England. Why London? The goal was to combine the insights of 100 years of care achieved by the Clinic in Cleveland with the learning and innovation of nearly 500 years of Royal Society of Medicine leadership. What was Cleveland Clinic London's purpose? "Compassionate caregivers transforming health and care for the world." This would be achieved by integrating the best of US and UK medical practice and research.

The English are proud of their National Health Service (NHS), and the royal family has a long history of recognizing UK healthcare professionals. In 2021, the queen awarded UK healthcare professionals with the George VI Cross for "acts of the greatest heroism or of the most courage in circumstances of extreme danger."[22] The Cleveland Clinic sought an ongoing relationship with the NHS to share insights on how to best "transform health and care for the world." Here is where making a purpose gets messy. During the pandemic, London experienced three economic lockdowns when about 160,000 people died and nearly 19 million COVID-19 cases were confirmed. Lockdowns meant construction milestones were missed. Supply chain disruptions meant that materials and labor expenses soared.

The Cleveland Clinic London is across the street from Buckingham Palace in one of the world's most expensive cities. London's cost of living means clinical talent is expensive. So, a global pandemic and raising costs were the conditions under which the Cleveland Clinic London had to build a culture as well as a hospital.

The pandemic meant most of the 1,000 staff members who were hired had to be interviewed remotely. Of course, staff physicians were selected for excellent clinical expertise, but recruiting for character was the performance differentiator to navigate disruptions caused by a pandemic. Scenarios were used to evaluate how well candidates possessed Cleveland Clinic values such as compassion, empathy, teamwork, inclusion, innovation, quality, and safety. Candidates also were selected for a growth mindset.

The battle for discretionary effort was constant. To win in the marketplace, the Clinic had to win in the workplace. In healthcare workplaces, people seek meaning and purpose as well as the opportunity to learn and grow. Staff had to learn not to wallow in fear but not to deny it either. An important way to push through fear is to know whom you serve and how your purpose and values help in making decisions.

Even with all of those challenges, in the fall of 2021, outpatient services were opened. In spring of 2022, inpatient services opened.

From the time hiring started until inpatient services were launched, what was the impact on engagement? It would be reasonable to assume that Brexit, a global pandemic, and building a culture remotely would tank engagement. Instead, over two cycles of engagement studies, the Cleveland Clinic London had among the highest scores in the Clinic system that employs approximately 72,000 people.[23]

The Cleveland Clinic London story offers important insights about the impact of purpose on engagement, which in turn is related to how we treat others and whom we serve. Recall that how teammates treat each other is a better predictor of performance than who is on the team. The best way for teammates to treat each other well is for them to practice virtue.

Answering the question "Whom do we serve?" sounds simple. However, ask your team this question, and odds are high that you will be impressed with the range of answers. Furthermore, if we ask only our team why we exist, we are quite likely to be off the mark. This is why we define our purpose based on value sought by the people we serve, *not* based on what we think they need. The point of purpose isn't to pat ourselves on the back but to actually help others. How do we know what would help someone? We ask them.

STRUCTURE FOLLOWS STRATEGY

Terrorists hijacked a cruise ship to capture passengers for ransom. Recapturing a ship in the middle of an ocean sounds like a wickedly hard problem to solve. If you are the Navy SEALs, you airdrop boats and a platoon out of the back of a C-17 and chase bad guys. The airdrop happens after a 20-hour flight. The commute to work has already been long, and SEALs then need to get into boats to be pounded by waves to catch a ship of passengers yet to be rescued. A SEAL officer wondered why the plan was to airdrop behind the ship, then race to catch up, rather than airdrop in front of the ship and let it come to you. This option hadn't been considered because catching up to ships (rather than dropping in front of ships) "is how we always do it." Even SEALs bang their heads against bureaucracies. This is why Admiral Hyman Rickover cautioned, "Good ideas are not adopted automatically. They must be driven into practice with courageous patience."[24]

Too often, the bottleneck is at the top of the bottle. Old hierarchies and silos are just too slow to keep up with the pace of change. For this reason, decisions need to be pushed deeper down into organizations. But for this to work, the structure of the organization and its strategy must be aligned. There is a challenge when the structure is "command and control" while the strategy is to empower the front line.

In 1962, Alfred Chandler coined the term "structure follows strategy," which means that all aspects of an organization's structure should keep the organization's strategy in mind. Where things get tricky is when the structure that supports operational strategies differs from the structure that supports innovation. The chart in Figure 9.1 compares an operational structure on the left with a growth structure on the right.

Operational Structure Values	Growth Structure Values
• On-time delivery	• Customer experience
• Variance reduction	• Seek deviations and novel solutions
• Cost reductions	
• A feel for crop production	• Innovation protected in a "greenhouse" environment
• Inside-out thinking	• Outside-in thinking
• Control and compliance	• Commitment and creativity
• Metrics-driven performance	• Meaning-driven performance

Figure 9.1 Comparison of an Operational Structure
with a Growth Structure

Of course, organizations benefit from both innovation and operational excellence. Yet, organizations tend to excel more at either innovation or operations rather than both. Innovative organizations often suffer from poor operations. Organizations that excel at operations often struggle with innovation. Organizations that do neither well are placed on Darwin's endangered species list. Organizations are served best by understanding that innovation and operation strategies require different structures.

Operational structures are more like crop productions—sturdy and stable. The goal is to reduce variance. Decades of agricultural science guide steady crop production by relying on healthy soil, managing water wisely, reducing pollution, and promoting biodiversity. We certainly need reliable crop productions to pay today's bills.

Innovation structures are more like greenhouses. The warmth, moisture, and light of a greenhouse promotes plant growth by protecting plants from extreme conditions. A greenhouse offers a safe place to experiment and to seek deviations or novel solutions. A greenhouse relies on tools such as voice of the customer that uncovers "pain points." We need greenhouses to cultivate innovations to pay tomorrow's bills that just might secure an organization's future.

The punch line is this. When an innovation meets a static, calcified operational bureaucracy, the outcome is certain. Operational bureaucracies attack innovations like monoclonal antibodies attack the coronavirus. Innovators need greenhouses where they have a chance to grow something new. Once the innovation is sturdy enough, then it can be transferred into large-crop production.

A concrete example of what it would mean to create structures that encourage innovation is at Intuit, located just down the street from Google in Mountain View, California. Quicken and Turbo Tax are among their most well-known products. Intuit has a single mission: "improve customer financial lives so profoundly they could never go back to another way." This mission requires that innovation is everybody's job at Intuit. The company's leaders rely on cross-functional teams to uncover deep empathy with the customers. The teams work hard to fall in love with a customer's problem rather than the solution. They eventually land on a solution through rapid prototyping and experimenting.

At Intuit, innovation happens both through bottom-up and top-down approaches. Bottom-up happens by granting people time to innovate on a project of interest with people they want to work with. When teams have demonstrated that they are onto a critical customer pain point, then senior leaders weigh in. Before senior leaders make additional investments, they consider who is on the team more than the nature of the idea.

The second way that innovation happens is top-down. Senior leaders propose "big challenges" for their 8,000 teammates, whom they call "entrepreneurs." Again, the process for establishing "deep customer empathy" is followed to ensure that the correct pain point is identified. Once ideas show merit, senior leaders merge teams and provide funding to accelerate commercialization.

The process isn't flawless. In both bottom-up and top-down approaches, senior leaders have received feedback that they need to learn to coach more and judge less. So senior leaders go through training to learn how to coach better.

Intuit's way to harness 8,000 entrepreneurs is impressive. Yet, for most organizations, this strategy might be more aspirational than realistic. Perhaps the more realistic goal is to create a culture where those not involved in innovation directly look for ways to help rather than hinder innovators.[25]

AFFORDABLE LOSS:
WHAT RESTRAINS INNOVATION?

If asked to vote for the greatest restraints to innovation, fear of failure would be a good candidate. Remember that we fear loss twice as much as we hope for gain. This part of our evolutionary biology isn't something we can change. For this reason, an experienced innovator makes decisions more on acceptable downside risk than on upside gain. Hidden in full view is the necessity to cultivate courage. A way to help innovators replace fear with courage is called the "real, win, worth it tool." It is an approach guided by three sequential questions:

1. Is it real?
2. Can we win?
3. Is it worth it?

Those questions help teams deal with the uncertainty and fear associated with innovation by providing a structured way to take on an unstructured task. Teams learn to fail fast and cheap by knowing when to stop and when to proceed.

Is It Real?

The purpose of innovation is to acquire paying customers. To this end, we need to answer two fundamental questions:

1. Who is our customer?
2. Will this customer pay us for what we have to offer?

We start by putting the customer at the center of the innovation. In too many organizations, the boss is at the center of the innovation—not the customer. Sometimes, the boss is an engineer who has a strong influence on product development. When you put technology first, you risk creating products and services too far ahead of customer priorities, too cumbersome for people to use, or too expensive to produce. When you rely too much on sales, products can get pushed based on price, promotion, volume, or increasing market share without understanding the customer's real pain point.

For the sake of an example, let's say you know there is a shortage of truck drivers. So, the question is this: Who is the customer? Is it truck drivers, human resources, safety directors, or CEOs of trucking companies? The best tool to answer this question is *voice of the customer* (VOC). The purpose of an effective VOC exploration is to listen, not sell. The goal is to define your customer and their *pain point*. A pain point isn't just mildly annoying. It is what keeps your customer up at night. No one is going to pay to solve a problem that is only mildly annoying or something they can resolve on their own. A skilled VOC interview asks questions such as, "Tell me more about that. How big is this problem for you? How do you address this issue now?" This sounds simple, but it is incredibly difficult to ask questions and not jump out of your shoes wanting to solve the problems that come up.

Let's say a series of VOCs with truck drivers, human resource directors, safety directors, and CEOs shows that a shortage of drivers is the number one barrier to a trucking company's growth. CEOs describe their pain as "trucks against the fence." If you can get a $150,000 piece of equipment (that is, the truck) off the fence by attracting and retaining drivers, the CEO will pay you. Human resource and safety directors will also support anyone who can solve this issue, though this problem is so painful that it has the full attention of the corner office. But truck drivers are not the customers since they won't pay your invoice. The CEO will. However, getting trucks off the fence requires that you understand how to attract and retain trucks drivers. Your VOCs of truck drivers shows that they struggle to comply with the Federal Motor Carrier Safety Administration (FMCSA) regulations.

Companies such as Walmart and Amazon that hire thousands of drivers have automated compliance records to manage FMCSA requirements. But VOCs show that companies with a fleet of 50 to 200 trucks who rely on manual records struggle to keep drivers. Also, manual records put the company at risk during an FMCSA audit, which can result in the company being fined. So, the value proposition is to convert paper records to electronic records to better comply with FMCSA regulations. Drivers are given an easy-to-use mobile app that informs them when and how to remain compliant with FMCSA regulations. So, the answer to the VOC analysis is that one important way to get trucks off the fence is to offer an automated, easy-to-use process by which truck drivers and the company can comply with federal regulations.

How many VOCs with drivers, human resource directors, safety directors, and CEOs do you need to conduct? As many as it takes to define the customers and a pain point that someone will pay you to resolve. Don't stop until you have addressed the key factors in the question, "Is it real?":

- Who are the customers?
  - In this example, the customers are the CEOs of trucking companies with fleets of 50 to 200 trucks.
- Will these customers pay you for what you have to offer?
  - You get paid when you get trucks off the fence by retaining licensed drivers.

When, and only when, you have sorted out a compelling value proposition for a well-defined customer can you then ask the next question, "Can we win?"

Can We Win?

By now, it is clear that leaders and teams are more important than ideas such as automating driver compliance records to retain licensed drivers. So, do you have a leadership team that can win? A point that is often lost when it comes to innovation is this: people innovate because they want to, not because they have to. If you are an innovator, you cannot delegate the idea. You need to own the idea. You cannot expect your organization to help you unless you help them. Be very clear how the project is important to the business, and be diligent in managing loss.[26]

In addition to being motivated, the right leaders and teams possess high character and competence. Either intuitively or by design, the best teams practice the 4Gs and innovative habits. They also build a team of anthropologists, technical experts, and experts with business savvy:

1. Anthropologists
   - These are astute observers of human behaviors and cultures. Skilled at VOC, the anthropologists uncover that CEOs of trucking companies hate trucks against the fence.
2. Technical experts
   - They have expertise in testing the proof of concept to validate that the product satisfies the customers' pain points. Skills in engineering, software, and industry knowledge are often needed to test product feasibility. Skilled at developing user-friendly apps, they make it easy for truck drivers to comply with FMCSA regulations.
3. Experts with business savvy
   - They can evaluate the business model to ensure that the organization has the resources and processes to deliver the value proposition at a profit. Expertise in finance, marketing, and operations is needed to evaluate the business model. A subscription model that keeps drivers FMCSA compliant 24/7 enables the company to make money while they sleep by not having to manage a system once it is launched.

If the team lacks the necessary motivation, character, and competence, then stop investing until you have the right team. When you have the right team, then ask the next question: "Is it worth it?"

Is it Worth It?

The question about whether the loss associated with the innovation is affordable considers questions such as these:

- Is the cost of the investment worth the potential financial return?
- Is the opportunity cost worth it? In other words, when you say yes to this opportunity, what opportunity are you saying no to since resources are finite?

- Is the reputational risk affordable? Consider whether the organization could handle the reputational hit if the venture flopped.

Ideally, the market is large enough to warrant the investment. Better yet, customers are prepared to cocreate the product or service, which means you are making money while you refine the product.

Clearly, commercial success rates are vital, but the intangible value of creating innovators is often overlooked. Often innovation succeeds only 10 to 30 percent of the time. However, innovator and interdisciplinary learning can be a success 100 percent of the time.

People and teams grow only if given the opportunity to "fail faster to succeed sooner."[27] Organizations only grow when their people grow.

KEY TAKEAWAYS

According to Harvard Business School Professor Clayton Christensen, about 30,000 consumer products are introduced annually and 95 percent fail.[28] These are the kind of odds that caused Gimli from *Lord of the Rings* to say, "Certainty of death. Small chance of success. What are we waiting for?" Perhaps a 95 percent failure rate is too pessimistic. Certainty of death unlikely. Still, small chance of success is the reality of innovation.

The courage to innovate can be developed when you know what you are up against. For this reason organizations can en-"courage" innovation by creating a purpose that is actionable, by creating structures that provide protection to test ideas, and by relying on processes to fail fast and cheap. The best innovators are clear about their character and competency, strengths and flaws, and hopes and concerns, and they actively seek feedback to get better. This is the foundation to solving problems with solutions that didn't exist before. Concern and even compassion for others is at the heart of innovation. Better humans, better performance.

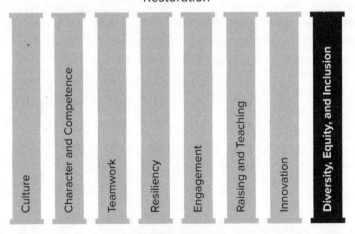

ARETÉ
Excellence

Habits
Coaching
Restoration

Culture

Character and Competence

Teamwork

Resiliency

Engagement

Raising and Teaching

Innovation

Diversity, Equity, and Inclusion

Character

Trust   Compassion   Courage

Justice   Wisdom   Temperance   Hope

Creating Diversity, Equity, and Inclusion

We are more alike, my friends, than we are unalike.[1]
—Maya Angelou, "Human Family"

n 1978, Vusumzi Mcongo's arms and legs were shackled by chains when he scuffled into a maximum security cell on Robben Island in South Africa. On the same day, Christo Brand started as a prison warden, or warder as South Africans call it. Christo was warned that the men he guarded, like Vusumzi, were no better than animals. For his part, Vusumzi kept his distance from all the warders on Robben Island since his job was to share information with prisoners from one section of the prison to another. If caught, the warders would revoke his educational privileges. Since education offered hope for a better future, this was the punishment that prisoners feared most.

Nelson Mandela spent 18 of his 27 years in prison on Robben Island. He was committed to educating the uneducated by turning Robben Island into a university. When Christo was put in charge of Mandela's educational program, the dangerous prisoners he was told about were not to be found. Instead, he found that prisoners were polite and friendly. Eventually, warders permitted literature, philosophy, political theory, and history seminars on the condition that they could listen in.

When apartheid ended, Vusumzi and Christo both applied for and gained positions to become tour guides at the Robben Island Museum. Two people who did not have any relationship with each other for nearly 20 years were now peers and tour guides. You would expect them to be bitter toward each other. Remarkably, working together strengthened their affection for each other. While their friendship transcended race and power, they readily acknowledged that some prisoners and guards remained angry and full of hate. A South African democracy formed in 1994 couldn't completely erase three centuries of racial friction from apartheid.

If these men can reconcile and become friends, then the rest of us can surely stop from slipping into hopelessness in a world that is inevitably flawed and troubled. In 1759, Voltaire wrote *Candide*, in which he suggested that the cure for hopelessness was to "cultivate one's own garden."[2] Voltaire suggested that we let go of trying to cultivate all of humanity and focus on where we can make a difference.

On a remote island off the coast of Cape Town, South Africa, Vusumzi and Christo did just that by sharing their own story about reconciliation with Robben Island visitors.[3] This story is not a one-off example of reconciliation. Evidence shows that when people from different backgrounds work side by side, people's stereotypes start to melt away.

Vusumzi and Christo's friendship illustrates a profound and simple point captured in a body of research entitled *contact hypothesis*. In 1954, Gordon Allport, a Harvard professor of psychology, first suggested that interpersonal contact between groups could reduce prejudice.[4] He proposed that four conditions were especially important: equal status, common goals, cooperation, and institutional support. Allport's caution was that when one group was treated as subordinate to another, prejudice could actually get worse. Vusumzi and Christo's story supports Allport's insight: "Only the type of contact that leads people to do things together is likely to result in changed attitudes."

Let's start by taking stock of the level of diversity in US organizations that have been both part of the problem of discrimination and part of its solution. In the United States, about half of the labor force is composed of women; Hispanics and African Americans represent 18.5 and 13.4 percent of the labor force, respectively. Yet, corporate boards and executive teams are largely composed of white men.[5] Business has the capacity and opportunity to transform the broader society. When groups that were previously excluded gain access to good jobs, they can better support their families and communities. In addition, stereotypes are reduced when different groups work together.

To attract, develop, and retain a diverse workforce, American companies spend $8 billion a year on diversity, equity, and inclusion efforts. A central point in this chapter is that sadly, this investment has delivered disappointing results.[6] For example, research suggests that mandated anti-bias training does not increase diversity or decrease stereotypes. Rather, research reveals that providing mentoring opportunities and offering voluntary rather than mandatory education are interventions that do increase diversity and decrease stereotypes. This chapter takes a deeper dive into the strategies that don't work and those that do.

Earlier, we suggested that engagement in organizations soars when people feel like they belong, matter, and make a difference. For this to happen, more of us will need to actively help others feel like they belong, matter, and make a difference.

More of us will need to see our human differences as a challenge rather than a threat and an opportunity to be embraced rather than to be feared. More of us will need to enhance rather than deny human potential so that a wider range of talent can be expressed.

When we embrace only our own perspective, we deny others the opportunity to contribute. Differences do not diminish us. Differences enlarge us. Gandhi put the task of humankind this way: "Our ability to reach unity in diversity will be the beauty and the test of our civilization."[7] Martin Luther King, Jr., gave humanity realistic optimism: "We shall overcome because the arc of the moral universe is long, but it bends toward justice."[8]

DIVERSITY, EQUITY, AND INCLUSION:
WHAT DOESN'T WORK?

Frank Dobbin, sociology professor at Harvard, and Alexandra Kalev, sociology professor at Tel Aviv University, analyzed diversity data from hundreds of employers across dozens of years. Their findings reveal some counterintuitive insights. For example, diversity training does not increase opportunities for women and underrepresented groups, either in the short term or even over a decade. In addition, training does not significantly affect bias. Research shows that anti-bias training can reduce bias slightly, though the effects don't stick.

A short-term program is not likely to make much of a dent in biases ingrained over a lifetime starting with the ways we were raised and the cultures in which we have lived.

The limitation of short-term training on behavior change is not unique to diversity, equity, and inclusion (DE&I) efforts. Training of all sorts often falls short of its goal to effect lasting behavior change. For example, safety training rarely sustainably reduces safety incidents. Worse still, training can have unintended adverse consequences. When it comes to mandated diversity training, the results may actually increase complacency and decrease commitment to diversity goals. It allows us to tick the box that training was completed rather than do the hard work necessary to authentically create a diverse culture. We are compliant but not changed.

Diversity training can also cause resentment when any group feels blamed or shamed. Over 70 years of social science research shows that "blame and shame" do not lead to behavior change. Just as shame about one's weight doesn't cause healthy lifestyle changes, shame about one's advantages does not cause inclusive habits. A brain full of shame doesn't learn, grow, or change.

Lastly, bringing a global perspective to diversity adds another layer of complexity. In the United States, if you discussed diversity without mentioning race, people would appropriately look at you cross-eyed. In homogenous nations such as the Nordic countries, Japan, and South Korea, diversity might rather be better understood by discussing immigration, income, or social class differences. Gender is relevant in every country, though the history and social aspects of gender vary widely among regions as diverse as Saudi Arabia and Sweden.

Many people of goodwill are trying to create a more inclusive and equitable society today. For this reason, there is no shortage of profit, nonprofit, and government institutions scrambling to put DE&I initiatives in place. No matter how well intended, however, research suggests that diversity training falls short of its stated goals to increase inclusion and diversity.

DIVERSITY, EQUITY, AND INCLUSION: WHAT DOES WORK?

If typical diversity training doesn't work, what does?

Start with Inclusion

Research suggests that we should reverse the order of diversity, equity, and inclusion to inclusion, equity, and diversity. An exclusionary culture will often lose the very diverse people that an organization worked so hard to recruit. If the promise of diverse perspectives is to be realized, then inclusion needs to be the bedrock.[9]

Find Ways to Limit Bias

Some orchestras use curtains to hide the gender of an auditioning musician. Before they used curtains, conductors were quite confident in both their ability to judge talent and in their indifference to gender because all they wanted were capable musicians. In the 1970s, before curtains were used, about 5 percent of musicians in orchestras were women. After curtains were used, the number of women went up to about 40 percent.[10]

The takeaway? We don't think we are biased; we just think other people are. Since unconscious bias is a reality, training seems like a reasonable response. The trouble is, without curtains to prevent us from being biased, we can't train bias out of ourselves. Becoming aware of bias doesn't turn off our brain's threat detector that lumps people into "us and them" categories. The bad news is that to keep us alive, our evolutionary reflexes quickly and often inaccurately judge whether someone is friend or foe. The good news is that we can increase whom we put into the "us" category by intentionally learning the story of people who are different from us.

Offer Voluntary Education

Mandatory diversity training sends the wrong message that we are doing this only because we have to comply with the law. As a consequence, studies have found that five years after requiring training, companies had no improvement in the proportion of white women, Black men, or Hispanics in management. Worse still, the percentage of Black women had declined by 9 percent.

Even voluntary education isn't necessarily a rousing success, though at least with voluntary education, we make progress rather than go backward. For example, one study found that voluntary education increased the percentage of managers of Asian American men and women and Hispanic men and Black men from 9 to 13 percent after five years.[11]

Establish Meaningful Partnerships

Programs don't change people. People change people—one person at a time. While mentoring programs are common, it is less common that they are used as vehicles to support inclusion and diversity. When an organization establishes a formal mentoring program without specific strategies to include women and people of color, participation is often limited to white men. In addition, while some organizations rely on informal mentoring, formal mentoring with clear goals and structures is more effective.

Mentoring and coaching also create opportunities for cross-race and gender relationships so everyone can learn from each other. However, people don't mentor well just because they want to. Careful selection and development to learn how to coach and mentor well is critical to success. In the strongest relationships, mentors transfer their hard-earned reputation to the person they are supporting.

And it works. Dobbin and Kalev's research reported that a mentoring experience increased leaders among Black, Hispanic, and Asian American women, and Hispanic and Asian American men from 9 to 24 percent. One study showed that the people of color who advanced the furthest in their careers were the beneficiaries of mentors and sponsors who advocated for them.[12]

Leaders become invested in supporting the women and underrepresented people whom they coach. After all, we think that anyone we sponsor is deserving of opportunity!

Integrate DE&I into Daily Operations

Rather than create a stand-alone program on DE&I, consider ways to integrate evidence-based inclusion strategies into daily operations. DE&I needs to define how people work together rather than count how many people attended a program.

Anchor DE&I in the organization's strategy and ask, how could a sense of belonging, mattering, and making a difference be cultivated to deliver strategic results? Inclusion becomes a habit when its practice supports existing priorities.

Create Psychological Safety

This is both the means and the ends in establishing an inclusive culture. The absence of psychological safety contributes to exclusion and sunders teamwork. The presence of psychological safety cultivates inclusion. Inclusive behaviors start with the leader who then encourages three behaviors among the team, as we have already seen: *vulnerability*, *asking questions*, and *learning*. In contrast, three behaviors that increase exclusion, deception, and pretense are *humiliation*, *blaming*, and *ignoring*.

Including people won't happen without education and effort.[13]

Diversify Recruiting

Expand where you look for talent. For example, in the United States, recruit at historically Black colleges and universities, not just majority white colleges. It also means involving leaders to define and generate solutions to attract and retain diverse talent.[14]

There is wide agreement among neuroscience, psychology, and social science researchers that our perspective and capabilities are enlarged rather than threatened by people who are different from us. So, the task is to practice evidence-based inclusion strategies that help majority and diverse teammates feel like they belong, they matter, and they make a difference.

The virtues underlie each of these strategies. Inclusion and diversifying talent require compassion and justice. Mentoring and coaching are founded on compassion and hope. Psychological safety and integrating inclusion into daily operations involves courage, temperance, and trust. And all of this work will lead us to wisdom. When we get better at who we are by practicing the seven classical virtues, we get better at practicing inclusion and diversity.

SOCIAL JUSTICE STARTS WITH KINSHIP

A good place to start is understanding how inclusion and exclusion affect engagement.

Rather than start with how we are different, start with how we are the same by asking teammates three questions:

1. Recall a time when you felt like you belonged, mattered, and made a difference.
2. Recall a time when you felt humiliated, blamed, or ignored.
3. How did each experience affect your engagement and performance?

Of course, some groups feel more included or excluded than others. That said, the universal experience is that when we feel included, we engage. When we feel humiliated, blamed, or ignored, we disengage.

When we extend being inclusive to all of humanity, far more is demanded of us. Confucius offered a standard to do just this. The word *ren* in Chinese means "co-humanity" or "humaneness." *Ren* is an inward expression of the Confucian ideals of benevolence, compassion, and empathy. These ideals represent the key behaviors that cultivate a flourishing human community. The first step on this inward journey is to practice benevolence toward our kin and friends, not just ourselves. It's a good first step, to be sure, though if we stop here, we end up with nepotism. We can extend our benevolence further to include our community. This is an upgrade from nepotism, though if we stop here, we become provincial. We can extend our benevolence to include our country. Caring for our fellow citizens is terrific, though if we stop here, that leads to nationalism.

The best among us pursue an inward journey that extends benevolence to all of humanity. This is especially impressive since our journey will include working with people who practice nepotism, provincialism, or nationalism. The Confucian standard to practice *ren* is incredibly demanding: the goal is to practice benevolence toward others independently of how they treat us.

The concept of *ren* aligns with Howard Thurman's teachings. In 1936, Thurman, the grandson of slaves and a mentor to Martin Luther King, Jr., met Mahatma Gandhi, who was leading a nonviolent struggle to remove the yoke of British rule from the neck of the Indian people. Thurman and Gandhi explored strategies to end the oppression faced by Indian people and by African Americans. Gandhi concluded at the end of his meetings with Thurman, "It may be through the Negroes that the unadulterated message of nonviolence will be delivered to the world."

Thurman was a teacher who was both strong and kind. He was a pastor who was an outspoken critic of Christianity for not supporting marginalized people whom he described as having their "backs against the wall." Prior to World War II, he founded a church where people of different races and religions worshiped together. He believed that spirituality was best explored experientially and in a diverse community rather than through dogma. He taught that only an inward journey removes the power that fear, hypocrisy, hatred, and even violence have over us. He was unimpressed by our ability to get on well with others on our own terms and reject others when our terms are not acceptable. The more impressive person overcomes relationships marred by hatred, anger, and hypocrisy. Our great internal battle is to see fear, hatred, and hypocrisy for what they are and then destroy their hold over us.[15]

STORIES

In 1954, Gordon Allport offered a way to strengthen relationships among diverse people in his book *The Nature of Prejudice*. Allport's research suggested that bigotry often boiled down to a lack of acquaintance. Its antidote was just as simple: bring people together and awaken their shared humanity. This was the view Mandela also held. He was convinced that only through personal contact among people can stereotypes, prejudices, and discrimination be reduced. This is the very heart of the story about Vusumzi and Christo's reconciliation.

Prior to Allport, some scholars had argued that contact among different groups increased prejudice and conflict. However, a meta-analysis of over 500 studies examining what was called the "contact hypothesis" demonstrated that increased contact actually led to greater understanding between groups in all but the most hostile conditions.[16] While hatred of outsiders is ancient, it isn't inevitable.

After all, empathy is more appealing than conflict, which most people want to avoid. Contact and interaction make it harder to avoid being empathic.

We are capable of caring for the stranger in our midst and looking beyond our differences to see our common humanity. When people work, live, and play alongside each other, divisions melt. We become wiser when we view compassion as being muscular, not wimpy. This is how Abraham Joshua Heschel expressed the wisdom of this insight: "When I was young, I admired clever people. Now that I am old, I admire kind people."[17]

Allport cautioned that contact would not always work. When diverse people are brought together, nuances need to be considered. For example, treating everyone as an equal works for the majority since they walk away with a warmer view of the minority. On the other hand, minorities often report that they already understand the majority's perspective because their survival has depended on this understanding. For example, women are more likely to be aware of the male experience, but males haven't always needed to understand the female experience to survive. For this reason, instead of offering equal status, the minority could be offered the opportunity to report hardships facing their group to the majority who takes notes. Minorities have reported feeling better about the majority after sharing their challenges first.[18]

Demographics like race and gender certainly matter, though if we stop at demographics, we don't fully understand a person's past and current story nor their desired future state. We are also shaped by socioeconomic status, physical differences, immigrant status, or for that matter being a parent, being a caregiver of aging parents, recovering from a serious medical condition, pursuing an advanced degree, and on and on and on. No matter how thinly we slice a category, we cannot account for everyone's differences. So, how do we understand someone's story? We ask. This could be as simple as asking, "What will it take to support your best hopes and to reduce your greatest concerns?" This approach is truly inclusive. When we make clear that DE&I is for everyone, we relieve the us-versus-them view that can result from some DE&I initiatives.[19]

CULTURE

Cultures are the property of groups, not individuals. Groups have the power to make people benevolent, indifferent, or ruthless. So, our tendency to be virtuous is not just about individual commitment to virtue. It is also shaped by our groups. In sociology, an *ingroup* is defined by a social group with which a person identifies psychologically. An *outgroup* is a social group with which a person does not identify.

Humans divide into groups and create rules and institutions that disproportionately benefit their group.[20] Then, the group inevitably pronounces that their achievement is merit based. How the ingroup views achievement is part of their identity. And ingroups greatly fear losing their identity. When the outgroup steps into our work, school, and life, we can lose our moral compass and become antisocial toward the outgroup. We can come to narrowly believe that our ingroup is morally superior and more trustworthy than the outgroup, which we hold in contempt. We come to believe that the "us" among us are simply better than the "them."

One of the human challenges to being inclusive is that we have a hard time seeing things from other people's points of view, especially those who are different from us. We tend to simplify positions that another group holds. We tend to view them as more extreme than average. Our brain is designed to have a hard time conferring benefit-of-the-doubt status to the outgroup. For these reasons, the promise of diversity, equity, and inclusion efforts comes with high uncertainty, making psychological safety critical.

When psychological safety is achieved, the culture attracts high performers, people identify issues sooner, and people learn quicker, and, as a result, competitiveness and performance are strengthened.[21]

When we feel psychologically safe, we can more easily ask questions about what the other sees that we cannot see. We can learn to harness our bitterness to build a more just, inclusive, and diverse culture. If we can feel and act with even a little bit more humanity, that is a beginning.

THE EXPLORER AND
THE ADVOCATE

The question of what it means to be a human is inextricably linked to how we live and how we treat each other. Who we will be to each other marks the difference between whether we flourish or merely survive.

This is why the great tradition of virtue is among our most powerful human inventions. When virtue is practiced well, people flourish, in part because they feel like they belong. They are not just present, and their presence is not simply tolerated. When people belong, they are part of shaping the culture. They matter and make a difference, and the benefits and results are improved engagement and performance.

We all want to come to work and feel that our boss and teammates genuinely want us to succeed. When this happens, engagement increases. When teams effectively serve customers, patients, clients, athletes, or students, the people who pay our bills probably come back because we listen to what they need and meet or exceed their expectations.

When done well, DE&I isn't a program.

Embracing diversity and being inclusive is a way to work and live. We know what works: stories that humanize differences; vulnerability, asking questions, and learning; formalized mentoring and coaching programs; integrating inclusive habits into daily operations and cultivating intrinsic motivation to help others belong, matter, and make a difference.

When it comes to DE&I, a critical insight is that the method matters as much as the content. The challenge is that while some people are committed to DE&I, others need to learn how to be advocates for others or themselves, and sometimes we need to rely on compliance with the law. The tools of commitment, advocacy, and compliance overcome different restraints. Commitment needs to overcome the restraints of evolutionary baggage. Advocacy needs to overcome the restraints of fear. Compliance needs to overcome the restraints of retribution.

The framework in Table 10.1 defines the goals, restraints, methods, and tools for commitment, advocacy, and compliance. The strategies start with commitment, then move to advocacy, and as needed, to compliance. When we cultivate commitment and advocacy, compliance is less necessary. Still, we will need compliance to define and enforce the rule of law.

Table 10.1 **Framework for Defining the Goals, Restraints, Methods, and Tools for Commitment, Advocacy, and Compliance**

Commitment Goal	Advocacy Goal	Compliance Goal
People feel that they belong, matter, and make a difference.	Advocacy: Self and others	Rule of law
Restraints: Evolutionary baggage	Restraints: Fears	Restraints: Retribution
Pull strategy: Curiosity and compassion as skills	De-escalation: Courage as a skill	Push strategy: Judgment and investigation as skills
Educational tools: Psychological safety and the power of stories	Educational tools: Bystander education and stereotype threats	Training and controls: no retribution and consistent; integrity line audits

We will detail the toolkit associated with being an explorer and an advocate because compliance with laws is more common and the tools associated with exploration and advocacy are less common. Like virtue, explorer and advocacy skills can be learned. In the process, we learn to do course corrections and pick ourselves up when—not if—we fail. As we become more skilled in using the toolkit of explorers and advocates, we start to cross boundaries that we wouldn't normally cross.

THE EXPLORER'S MINDSET

In his 1962 "We Choose to Go to the Moon" speech, John F. Kennedy condensed humanity's recorded history of 50,000 years to an equivalent time span of 50 years to help his listeners understand the rapidity of change in recent times. Using this construct, Kennedy said that we know little about the first 40 years except at that time, humans skinned animals for clothing. About 10 years ago, humans constructed shelters.

Only five years ago, humans learned to write. Christianity started less than two years ago, and the printing press came last year. Last month, electric lights, telephones, cars, and planes became available. It was only last week when penicillin, TV, and nuclear power came along. JFK went on to say, "This is a breathtaking pace, and such a pace cannot help but create new ills as it dispels old, new ignorance, new problems, new dangers."[22]

Kennedy's speech was about an external journey to the moon during a volatile time. Inclusion is an inward journey to achieve Thurman's call for dignity in the face of fear, anger, and hypocrisy. An inclusion journey starts by asking how we can get out of our bubble. Explorers are curious about what they can learn from people who are different from them. An explorer's work is fulfilling, inspiring, and sometimes perilous. The explorer pursues a productive struggle to learn, grow, and understand. Like space explorers, human explorers push humanity to move forward and make the world a better place.

Here is where things get tricky. Humans are not that great at understanding another person's experiences. As an example of this, consider what it is like to be left- versus right-handed. If you are right-handed, ask a left-handed person what it is like to live in a right-handed world. You are likely to get an earful. Door handles, most scissors, gas and brake pedals, guitars, as well as the car dashboards, just to name a few items, were all designed for right-handed people. Now this isn't to take a shot at right-handed people for being insensitive to the needs of left-handed people. Right handers don't wake up in the morning with the goal to increase inequality for left-handed people. However, the right-handed are largely unaware that that their comforts come at the expense of the left-handed.

To better understand how some of us might unknowingly benefit at the expense of others, explorers do not approach inclusion as a general perspective on virtue. Instead, explorers start with the specifics by "descending into the particulars." This is an approach called *casuistry* that was generated by theologians from the Jesuit tradition to resolve moral problems. The implications of casuistry are nonsectarian and highly generalizable to humanity. Specifically, casuistry is a method of moral reasoning used by Jesuits starting with St. Ignatius

500 years ago to understand hate. We don't abandon virtue. We start by listening and descending into the particulars before we apply virtue.[23]

Case in point: On death row, Anthony Hinton, a Black man, befriended Henry, a white supremacist. When Mr. Hinton descended into the particulars, he learned that Henry had been taught to fear and hate Black people. Henry's contempt was so deeply felt that he found, beat, stabbed, and hung a Black teenager. That may be about all most of us want to know. Casuistry applied to Henry's life: no thanks. Remarkably, Mr. Hinton said he had no anger toward Henry. On the night of his execution, Henry was asked whether he had anything to say. He said that all his life, his family taught him how to hate. On death row, he learned that the very people he was taught to hate were the ones who taught him to love. When Mr. Hinton descended into the particulars of Henry's life, he learned that we all can die slowly from our own fear. However, if we can teach people to hate, we can certainly teach people to love.[24]

We can be born to the dominant caste and still decide not to dominate. We can be born into a subordinated caste and resist the box others force us to occupy. Clearly, none of us can claim we are cured of all bias. None of us escapes the message that some groups are more able and deserving than other groups. What we can do is to put our skills of compassion, courage, and curiosity to work. Doing so loosens the grip of prejudice and bias. The more we can empathize with others, truly listen to others, and understand what they can and cannot control, the more we start to help people and stop hurting them.[25]

THE ADVOCATE'S MINDSET

When Brent Staples, a graduate student at the University of Chicago, walked near campus, he noticed that white people avoided making eye contact with him and some walked across the street to avoid him. It depressed him that strangers viewed him as a threat simply because he was a large African American man. So, he started to whistle Beatles tunes or Vivaldi when a white person walked near him to demonstrate he was not a threat. It worked. He was greeted with smiles rather than fear when he whistled Beatles tunes familiar to white strangers.

Claude Steele's research on *stereotype threats* explains two critically important insights about Brent Staples's experience. First, stereotype threats are universal. You may not have had Staples's experience, though perhaps you have been stereotyped for being old, young, gay, white, Black, male, female, politically conservative or liberal, a cancer patient, or disabled. Second, the threat of being stereotyped leads to underperformance. For example, Steele offers the example that a white sprinter faces a stereotype threat when he takes his position in the starting blocks with a group of Black competitors. The white sprinter might have to overcome pressure not experienced by Black sprinters because the stereotype threat is that white sprinters are slower than Black sprinters.

Steele and his colleagues studied how stereotype threats affect performance in a wide range of situations. One study tested how men and women of equal math ability would perform on the Graduate Record Examinations. When women were told that women usually did worse on this test than men, sure enough, they scored 15 points lower than men on the 100-point test. Even when there was no ill will against women, if they thought prejudice existed, their performance suffered. Their performance decreased when they wasted time and energy focusing on being stereotyped. But when women were told there were usually no gender differences in how people scored on this test, underperformance melted away.

In the 1950s, Gordon Allport put it this way: "One's reputation, whether false or true, cannot be hammered, hammered, hammered, into one's head without doing something to one's character."[26] Stereotype threats spring from people's having a pretty good idea how society views a group. We know what people might think about our age, being poor, being rich, or being female, no matter how inaccurate. We know that anything we do that fits a stereotype could be taken as confirmation. One false move could cause us to be reduced to the stereotype.[27]

Our challenge is to advocate for others or ourselves when—not if—stereotype threats happen. To this end, advocates practice an evidence-based skill called *bystander education* or *upstander education*. The goal is to turn bystanders into upstanders. An *upstander* is someone who stands up for and advocates actively to achieve DE&I, in contrast to a *bystander* who watches passively as inclusion is overlooked. The important point is that advocacy is a skill that can be learned by breaking down the task and practicing.

When it comes to stereotyping threats, we face a choice that isn't confusing. We know that diminishing stereotyping is right. Ideally, we de-escalate a conflict, get to a just outcome, and maintain a good working relationship. Rather than say we are powerless, we start with the premise that most people want to enact change and need help with *how* to do it. Most of us want to act ethically if given a chance, and although we are not always successful, we can tilt the odds of success in the right direction.

KEY TAKEAWAYS

What makes a person valuable? Some might conclude that valuable people are rich, talented, and well connected. Some might conclude that the work of an inner-city teacher or physician serving the rural poor defines value. Some might conclude that a valuable person is less about what they do and more about who they are. There is a reason why almost all cultures value compassion, courage, and justice and discredit exclusion, cowardice, and injustice. Virtue both clarifies our intent and creates a sense of belonging, mattering, and making a difference. The language of virtue provides a moral compass and, at the same time, readily acknowledges that we can do better.

What is earned and what is owed? When we think that our achievements are about our DNA and hard work, then we think we have earned our good fortune. We think differently about achievement when we view life as an unfair race that placed some close to the finish line while others were never coached on how the race works in the first place. When we practice virtue, we better connect than exclude people based on their station in life. When this happens, we start to create a more inclusive culture. Virtue always has and always will be the force that slowly bends the arc of the moral universe toward a more inclusive, diverse, and equitable world. And the payoff is also high performance—when you get better at who you are, you get better at what you do.

TOOLKIT

Here is a situation that calls for advocacy: an all-white male team with a chance to diversify by hiring a new teammate. The team's performance is solid, the leader and teammates work hard, and people are collaborative.

However, everyone looks, talks, and thinks the same. Everyone has the same educational and professional experience. Here is a five-step sequential scripting process to have a conversation with the leader about the team's lack of diversity. Each step ups the ante. However, step 1, 2, or 3 usually achieves the goal of a just outcome while maintaining the relationship with the leader and team.

1. **Start by asking a question.**
   - **Example:** While we have a great team, how might we better serve our customers and ourselves by becoming more diverse?

The question may be all that is needed because we've framed the issue by how it affects others rather than ourselves. Or the leader might respond that the team is great now.

2. **Seek help.**
   - **Example:** Would you be open to our talking to another person on our team about why we might want to become more diverse and how we could do this?

Draw on thoughtful allies so it's more than your idea. Or this might not work. The leader could respond that we have tried to hire qualified diverse candidates, but they aren't out there.

3. **Create a good/bad/good statement.** This means say something positive, then say something negative, and conclude with a positive statement.
   - **Good example:** Of course, we want an inclusive team-based culture.
   - **Bad example:** However, we are disadvantaged when our customers and teammates in other parts of the company are more diverse than we are.
   - **Good example:** Could we treat recruiting and retaining diverse talent as a business challenge for our team to take on?

Finally, this might result in a healthy conversation. Or the leader might respond, "The team chemistry matters. We have a good thing going."

4. **Ask again.**
   - **Example:** Is there anything that I can say to change your mind?

Perhaps this finally works. Or, the leader might respond, "I don't know if that is a good use of our team's resources."

5. **Conclude with an if-then statement.** This is your line in the sand.
   - **Example:** My concern is that if we don't actively recruit diverse talent, we will be at a competitive disadvantage and get attention that we don't want.

Now the issue is how far you want to push your point.

You could say, "The next time there's an opening on the team, I'm going to insist we consult with HR on how to diversify our talent pool."

You could decide you did your best; this time you just didn't succeed.

You could decide to leave.

———

In the vast majority of cases, steps 1, 2, and 3 offer a low-risk, high-reward likelihood. Steps 4 and 5 up the ante and increase risk. Perhaps you are in a position to tilt toward justice at the expense of a relationship. Perhaps you need the job, so you can't afford to fall on your sword.

That said, in most cases, scripting will achieve the goal to maintain the relationship and get to a good outcome, so it is well worth the effort.[28]

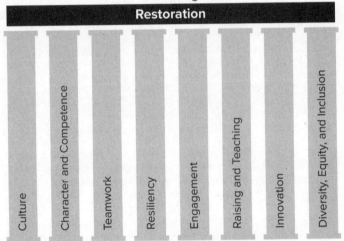

ARETÉ **Excellence**

Habits

Coaching

Restoration

Culture

Character and Competence

Teamwork

Resiliency

Engagement

Raising and Teaching

Innovation

Diversity, Equity, and Inclusion

Character

Trust · Compassion · Courage

Justice · Wisdom · Temperance · Hope

RESTORING CULTURES

Of the seven deadly sins, anger is possibly the most fun. To lick your wounds, to smack your lips over grievances long past, to roll over your tongue the prospect of bitter confrontations still to come, to savor to the last tooth-some morsel both the pain you are given and the pain you give back—in many ways it is a feast fit for a king. The chief drawback is what you are wolfing down is you. The skeleton at the feast is you.[1]
—**FREDERICK BUECHNER**

The insights of this quote become real when we notice that our best grudges follow us wherever we go. Grudges start when we didn't get something we wanted (promotion, pay raise, or recognition), or we got something we didn't want (nasty teammate, moronic boss, or a layoff). Grudges can be professional or personal, but interestingly, regardless of what or who harmed us, all grudges fester for the same three reasons:

1. We take an offense too personally.
2. We blame the offender for how we feel.
3. We create a grievance story.

At the individual level, grudges that are real gems elevate stress, increase our heart rate and blood pressure, and compromise our immune systems. At the organizational level, grudges rupture relationships, and they decrease the trust and commitment needed for performance. When people don't feel valued or respected, they quit, file claims, miss work, or disrupt teamwork. Here, the connection between grudges and leadership is obvious. Of all people, leaders need to get this right and avoid behaving in ways that are driven by grudges. Leaders' grudges can cascade a long way through an organization and cause massive egress. Despite our knowing all this, grudges and other dysfunctional behaviors still happen in every organization. The question is whether relationships will be restored.

OK, if grudges don't travel well, how about revenge? No doubt, revenge can be quite cathartic. Michael McCullough's research makes clear that anger is a moral response to solve a problem and accomplish a goal. A "Don't tread on me" philosophy keeps us safe when we can't count on police or military to protect us.[2] In other circumstances and not uncommonly, anger can be destructive. Epictetus offered an alternative to grudges and revenge, "If you do not wish to be prone to anger, do not feed the habit; give it nothing which may tend to its increase."[3]

A critical skill that repairs a ruptured relationship is forgiveness, which research suggests few people consider as a way to cope with life's blows. Dr. Frederic Luskin, who founded the Stanford Forgiveness Project, put it this way: "Holding on to a grudge really is an ineffective strategy for dealing with a life situation that you haven't been able to master. If it's bitterness, you hold it with anger. If it's hopeless, you hold it with despair."[4]

Resentment, a cousin of revenge, shifts our attention away from flourishing to ruminating on past personal affronts. Buddha cautioned that being perennially ticked off, sad, or depressed serves no constructive purpose: "Holding on to anger is like drinking poison and expecting the other person to die."[5]

Icons like Buddha and Jesus truly forgave those who caused grave harm. Remarkably, relatives of the nine victims killed in a shooting in Charleston, South Carolina, committed by white supremacist Dylann Roof offered forgiveness at his bond hearing.[6] Chris Singleton, whose mother was killed by Roof, said, "The narrative of forgiveness is submitting and it means that you're weak, or people would think that.

But I've realized that forgiving is so much tougher than holding a grudge."[7]

This amazing standard of granting grace is beyond what most of us can imagine doing under similar circumstances. However, the research on forgiveness reveals a lower standard that might be more within our reach. We don't forgive for the sake of the offender. We forgive to stop ourselves from being consumed by hate.

Those who struggle with forgiveness might have too many unenforceable rules or might try too hard to enforce the ones they have. For good reason, we get mad when a driver cuts us off. No doubt dangerous driving is wrong, but do we have the power to stop the person from weaving in and out of traffic? It is far easier to change our thinking than to get unenforceable rules obeyed, with the result that we live more peaceful lives.

Acquiring the skill of forgiveness involves taking affronts less personally, blaming the offender less, and even trying to understand the offender. The French expression *"Tout comprendre, c'est tout pardonner"* means "When you understand everything, you can forgive everything." Our goal isn't necessarily to reconcile with the offender. Our goal is to replace our toxic anger with realistic optimism.[8]

Most of the time, we forgive for reasons that are quite mundane. We give our spouses, partners, kids, and teammates a pass for minor offences, and they do the same for us. We might forgive to keep the relationship in a good place or because doing so might be good for us in the future. The cost for destroying a relationship might be too high. When we value the relationship, we tend to forgive easily and often.[9] Despite our failings, our ability to cooperate is how humans learned to go to the moon and make better light bulbs. The benefit of cooperation can only be had for the price of being tolerant about other people's mistakes because teammates, partners, and family members will sometimes let each other down.

When it comes to better performance, compassion, appreciation, and optimism work better than revenge, despair, and victimhood. At work, forgiveness helps coworkers rebuild positive relationships following conflict. In addition, when companies ask customers for forgiveness when they make mistakes, it helps rebuild customers' trust.[10] Yet, smart and capable managers often fail to lead their teams effectively because they are not skilled at forgiveness and they don't know how to repair ruptured relationships. Building forgiveness as a leadership skill isn't about being a wimp. Leaders skilled at forgiveness strengthen performance.

Embrace your "inner Edie" by asking "What's next?" rather than "Why me?" Replace victimhood with strength. A shot of gratitude combined with a reality check that life isn't always fair can dial back a 100-pound grudge to perhaps a 20-pound grudge. The grudge is still heavy, but it's no longer crippling. Instead of focusing on our wounded feelings, thereby giving power to the person who caused our pain, a life well lived is our best revenge.[11] Mahatma Gandhi gets the last word:

The weak can never forgive. Forgiveness is the attribute of the strong.[12]

RESTORATIVE JUSTICE

All cultures must respond to violation of virtues, values, or codes of conduct. The difference is how they respond when, not if, injustice happens. Our responses to injustice can go one of two ways—into retribution or into restoration. Restorative justice is an evidence-based way to limit the performance impact of grudges and other forms of dysfunctional conduct. While restorative justice originated in the criminal justice system, its core philosophies and tools contribute to an inclusive business culture founded on respect.

The purpose of retribution is to determine policies that were violated, laws that were broken, who is guilty, and the punishment the offender deserves. The purpose of restorative justice is making people better. This is achieved by the offender and offended sharing their experience of what happened, discussing the harm that occurred, and creating an agreement to repair the harm.

Restoration denounces harmful action while respecting the humanity and dignity of everyone in the process by giving them a role to repair the harm. The goal is to fix the problem, learn from the experience, and reintegrate everyone back into the culture. The practical issue is this: All teams experience relationships swinging back and forth between rupture and repair. The better teams do a better job repairing inevitable ruptures.

Restorative justice isn't about being a doormat. In fact, the process is demanding. Restoration might mean an apology, an action, or a payment. The goal is for offenders to take responsibility for their conduct, to understand the harm they caused, and to make things right. The goal for the offended is *agency*: replacing powerlessness and anxiety with having an active role in restoring justice.[13]

Restorative justice views crime or code-of-conduct violations as indicators of broken relationships. To repair the relationships, repair the harm. In schools, restorative justice offers alternatives to zero-tolerance rules (Chapter 8). An emphasis on punishment is replaced by equipping students with insights on how to avoid or confront bullying. For example, a 2007 meta-analysis of all research projects described in restorative justice conference papers published in England between 1986 and 2005 found positive results, specifically for victims. The victims were more able to work, to resume their normal life, and to sleep well. Both offender and offended gain appreciation for each person's perspective.

Restorative justice has been used to keep peace. For example, Barbara Masekela, Nelson Mandela's chief of staff, reported that South Africa's Truth and Reconciliation Commission got the country to take a step back from the brink of civil war.[14] In medicine, morbidity and mortality (M&M) conferences and root cause analyses (RCAs) are conducted to learn from errors or near misses—to determine whether death or potential injury could have been prevented. Specifically, M&M conferences and RCAs are part of healthcare's emerging commitment to developing a "just" culture, perhaps not coincidentally that the virtue of justice is explicitly named here. Ideally, a culture emerges where people are energized to reduce failure rather than fear admitting failure.

The US service academies offer interesting examples of restorative justice. At West Point, the catalyst for the adoption of restorative justice was improving the retention rate for cadets who violated the honor code. A West Point education costs taxpayers over $300,000 per student. Retaining a pipeline of bright, well-trained soldiers is important for the country. Thus, the impetus to adopt restorative justice at West Point was also partially mercenary.

Restorative justice at West Point gives cadets who have violated the honor code an opportunity to atone for their error and remain enrolled at West Point. This isn't to suggest that cadets who violate the honor code get an easy pass. Instead, the restorative justice process is rigorous. Violators enroll in a program that lasts about six months or longer to discuss where they have been, where they are now, and where they are going. They commit to creating a reflection journal focused on how to make ethical decisions under stress. They learn to link their conduct to a higher purpose, since the nation expects military leaders to behave ethically. Journal topics strive for ownership for what they did versus adopting a victim mentality.

It takes time to avoid denying responsibility, to blame others or external circumstances, and it takes time to finally own the mistake. Since this restorative justice program has been deployed, about 70 percent of cadets who violated the academy's code of conduct were retained after successfully completing the restoration process. Prior to implementing this commitment to restorative justice, the retention rate at West Point for honor code violators was virtually zero.[15]

Similarly, the Naval Academy came to grips with the question of what to do with cadets who failed. They concluded that a flawed person is not a failed person. As West Point concluded, the Naval Academy assumed that restoration takes time—six months to one year. The restorative process at the Naval Academy involves asking a senior officer to commit to the cadet's potential for redemption and the officer's commitment to helping the cadet achieve this. The senior officer puts their reputation on the line by asserting their belief that a cadet deserves another chance. The senior officer can elect to work with the cadet directly or can advise that another person is in a better position to help the cadet. In the end, an officer must affirm that the academy can take the cadet at their word, that the cadet knows what is right, and that the cadet has the courage to act ethically. If not, the cadet must resign.[16] This restorative justice process is designed to avoid continuing to beat up the offender since shame and blame do not change behavior. The process also involves mentors, journals, projects, and public speaking—none of which is mandated.

Finally, the Air Force Academy examined ethical breaches among colonels and generals. The pattern of what went wrong was clear; officers were fired for character issues, not incompetence. This raised a question about the state of honor at the academy. When leaders are people of high integrity, others also exhibit integrity. When leaders are people of low integrity, followers see themselves the same way and give themselves license to behave with low integrity. The Air Force Academy concluded that people follow leaders who care about them and who are people of character and not just competent.[17]

All organizations experience ethical breaches—some more and some less, but none can claim zero. So, the difference isn't whether an ethical breach will happen. The difference is how organizations respond to inevitable transgressions. Restorative justice is not about letting a person off the hook. It is a rigorous process to ensure that the person genuinely apologizes, acknowledges, and atones. Importantly, restoration strengthens a culture far more than retribution.[18]

RESTORATION

Given sufficient time, we can restore relationships by learning to take three steps forward: apologize, acknowledge, and atone. The first step is an apology. When done well, we examine our conduct and conclude that we need to say I'm sorry. The barriers to an apology include bruising our ego sufficiently to accept that we are not so perfect. Still, let's recognize that refusing to apologize does have a short-term upside. When we dig in and fail to apologize, we give ourselves an integrity booster shot for defending our honor. Unfortunately, over the long run, by refusing to apologize, we tick off the offended and we lock ourselves into denying responsibility and blaming others.

The second step to restoring relationships is acknowledgment. We can't restore trust until we define the harm that was committed. This involves more than a lame apology that says something to the effect that "It isn't my fault that you are hypersensitive, but since you are, I am sorry." Instead, we accept that when it came to virtue, we came up short.

The final step is to atone, or *tikkun olam*, a Jewish concept that means "repair the world." Atonement is incredibly hard to do in part because we have to give control to the person we harmed to decide whether they will forgive. In other words, we run toward rather than away from the harm we caused. It is incredibly difficult to replace dysfunctional behavior with functional behavior. Should we manage to do so, genuine remorse and restoration are signs of moral goodness and accountability. We can find the experience oddly embarrassing and liberating at the same time. We have overcome our mistake rather than allowing our mistake to define us.[19]

KEY TAKEAWAYS

Words like *restoration* and *forgiveness* can seem quaint and impractical when we operate inside cultures that view these qualities as weak and revenge as strong. The energy and strength of anger seem fantastic compared to restoration and forgiveness, which make us appear spineless.

For that reason, restorative justice might not be a good candidate for command-and-control leaders guided by a fixed mindset that people can't change. A growth mindset suggests otherwise—that is, that practicing restorative justice can reduce harm, increase empathy, and in the process, improve performance. We are all "jack-assess attached to angel wings," incapable of being perfect. So, given this reality, will retribution or restoration have a significant impact on performance?

To be clear, there are toxic relationships that should be removed rather than restored. At the same time, grave injustice isn't our normal experience. More frequently, restoration is needed to manage daily fissures caused by an annoying teammate or a cranky family member. In these cases, we might mutter under our breath the words "it's not fair." Perhaps these words suggest an injustice needs attention. At the same time, the anger that leads us to call attention to something that isn't fair doesn't need to flame our anger continually. In fact, when we keep refueling our anger, we light up the primordial parts of our brain and shut down our ability to reason.

Similar to a GPS system that sends a recalibrating message when we veer from our preplanned route, we need to recalibrate when anger and fear hijack our amygdala and move us away from the practice of virtue. Indignation is wonderfully appealing though it isn't a road that will repair ruptured relationships. Interestingly, research demonstrates that regrets have more to do with what we didn't do than what we did. The reason is this: regrets reveal what we most value, which in the case of injustice, might mean repairing a ruptured relationship. We value the kindness and courage that restore a broken relationship, so we regret when we choose inaction over action even if our effort failed.[20]

In our view, restoration of a broken relationship is a mark of excellence precisely because it is so rare and difficult to do. It is far easier to rationalize, deceive, or bury poor decisions than to come to grips with our mistakes. When we are able repair a ruptured relationship that has gone wrong, we restore ourselves. Neuroplasticity is a reminder that we can rewire our brains by where we put our attention. When we loosen the grip of a good grudge, we create space to be less distracted by fear, hatred, or anger. Doing so makes us saner and strengthens our ability to perform. Better human, better performance.

ARETÉ
Excellence

Habits

Coaching

Restoration

Culture

Character and Competence

Teamwork

Resiliency

Engagement

Raising and Teaching

Innovation

Diversity, Equity, and Inclusion

Character

Trust   Compassion   Courage

Justice   Wisdom   Temperance   Hope

COACHING

Coaches have to watch for what they don't want to see and listen to what they don't want to hear.[1]
—JOHN MADDEN

In 1875, the first Yale-Harvard football game was played. Yale hired Walter Camp, the first college football head coach. Camp created position coaches to preplan every game, develop players, and track performance. On the other side of the field, Harvard competed based on the British approach—players, not coaches, manage the team. Over the next three decades, Yale beat Harvard all but four times. After 30 years, Harvard hired a coach. About a century and half after that football game, the facts are in—coaching and deliberate practice improve performance not just in athletics but in business, the military, and healthcare.

Atul Gawande, experienced surgeon, author, and healthcare expert, wondered how people get better at what they do. Most people go to school to get better and then manage their own growth after graduation. How people get better in sports is different. Everyone needs a coach no matter how good they are. This insight led Gawande to have a coach observe one of his surgeries. Since the surgery went well, he didn't think the coach would have much to say. But the coach had a lot to say. He asked Gawande if he was aware during the surgery that the light had swung away from the wound. The coach watched him operate from reflected light for half an hour. The coach observed Gawande sometimes put his elbow in the air rather than at his side where he is more in control. His flying elbow also blocked the surgical team's view. Gawande didn't necessarily enjoy being observed. He did appreciate that coaching improved his performance as measured by a decrease in surgical complications.[2]

The purpose of coaching is to help people do their best, make better decisions, add more value, and strengthen their relationships with colleagues, customers, patients, students, and athletes.

Lots of evidence shows that when done well, coaching pays off. For example, MIT has reported that entrepreneurs who are well coached are 7 times more likely to raise funds and 3.5 times more likely to grow a business.[3] The Air Force Academy has reported that about 95 percent of cadets who were coached to develop virtue made progress on their goals; and about 95 percent of their coaches agreed they had made progress.[4] At Parker Hannifin, teams that integrated virtue into performance metrics reported they achieved their goals three months after working with a coach, and their coaches agreed.

We don't always understand the issues that hold us back, and we don't always know how to fix those issues. Research has shown that effective coaching will likely lead to moderate to large change in performance, assuming that a leader is coachable. If an organization has the will and wherewithal, coaching works for the top of the pyramid. Yet, coaching is too expensive to be scaled to middle and frontline leaders. However, as in educating our kids (Chapter 8), swim buddies can be scaled across the organization.

About 5,000 sailors apply to be a Navy SEAL, of whom 1,000 are selected. Of the 1,000 selected, 200 or fewer become SEALs. A critical part of the training is to understand that you can't become a SEAL on your own. You need help. For this reason, cadets are told on the first morning of training to get a "swim buddy" before lunch. If after lunch, the cadet didn't find a swim buddy, they are told to "get sandy." "Getting sandy" means that the cadet does pushups on the beach until they resemble a sand-caked donut. Why all the fuss over swim buddies?

Swim buddies help each other succeed. Swim buddies look out for each other.[5] Swim buddies are scalable.

Imagine an organization that encourages swim buddies and then trains them in effective coaching. This vision is worth consideration since about 70 percent of the variance in engagement is due to the direct leader. Leaders want engaged teammates, though they don't always understand the forces that restrain discretionary effort or how to fix these issues. The concept of swim buddies offers a scalable way to help leaders at all levels increase teammate engagement.

HOW DO PEOPLE LEARN BEST?

If we are going to help people grow, then we need to understand how people learn best. Some might say that constructive feedback is essential. Leaders need to give candid feedback and have difficult conversations. Well, not so fast. Rater error and neurology make clear that well-meaning advice often doesn't consider the biology of the fight-flight-freeze response and the limitation of feedback:

1. **Feedback:** "I told them. They didn't listen." So, let's assume that we think our advice is nothing short of amazing. What does the evidence have to say about feedback? Decades of research has shown that about 50 percent of your rating says far more about you than the person you rated. Too often, the giver of feedback has a higher opinion of their insights than the receiver of feedback.

2. **Fight-flight-freeze:** Criticism activates the primitive part of our brain, the amygdala—the fight, flight, or freeze part of our brain. Under conditions of fear and uncertainty, the neurological challenge is that our brain is on guard when we are judged by people we don't trust. It is useful to know that trust deactivates the primitive brain and activates the thinking brain (prefrontal cortex)—which means we are not on guard. This isn't to suggest we are victims of the primitive brain. We can still look for insights even when we disagree with

someone's feedback. We can wonder how our behavior gave someone an impression that didn't serve either of us well, even though we disagree with their reaction.

3. **Flaws:** Focusing on performance gaps doesn't enable learning. It impedes learning. Neurologically, we grow more in areas of strength because we already have thickets of synaptic connections. Of course, this doesn't mean that we should ignore weaknesses, especially a fatal flaw that continually affects our relationships negatively. It just means that we should lead with strengths, even when taking on a weakness, considering how our strengths can positively contribute.

This isn't to suggest that advice doesn't have merit, especially in predictable conditions. Pilots use checklists for good reason. There are proven ways to take off, fly, and land a plane safely. Mimicking the success in commercial aviation, surgical teams now use checklists for good reason. These are proven ways to reduce medical errors and infections. Known problem, known solution; stick with the script. However, what's the playbook for a once-in-a-century global pandemic?

WHAT COACHING IS AND IS NOT

Let's start by being clear that coaching isn't consulting, managing, mentoring, or therapy. Certainly, each of these roles could rely on coaching at times. Yet, coaching is different from all of those. Table 12.1 details how the roles and relationships of consultant, manager, mentor, and therapist differ from those of a coach.

Table 12.1 **How the Roles and Relationships of Consultant, Manager, Mentor, and Therapist Differ from Those of a Coach**

Consultant	Manager	Mentor	Therapist
Role: Consultant is an expert in leadership or functional area.	**Role:** Manager has supervisory authority and control.	**Role:** Senior leader shares insights with inexperienced leader.	**Role:** Therapist diagnoses and treats mental or behavior health.
Relationship: Consultant provides specific recommendations and advice.	**Relationship:** Manager judges performance and coaches growth.	**Relationship:** Relationship is mentored focused. Mentor sets the agenda.	**Relationship:** Therapist is a licensed professional.
Coach in the Role of Consultant: Coach helps coachees find their own way.	**Coach in the Role of Manager:** Coaching is a nonjudgmental partnership.	**Coach in the Role of Mentor:** Coaching is coachee-focused.	**Coach in the Role of Therapist:** Coach does not diagnose or treat mental or behavior health issues.
Relationship: Coach avoids or limits giving advice.	**Relationship:** Coaches do not have formal authority.	**Relationship:** Coachee sets the agenda.	**Relationship:** Coach relies on self-discovery.

CONSIDER 25/75 AS THE AIM OF COACHING

Recall the *25/75 rule* coined by Michael Matthews, professor of psychology at West Point. About 25 percent of the variance in human performance can be explained by cognitive factors, and 75 percent of the variance is explained by non-cognitive factors that can be organized by 3Cs:

1. **Character:** Virtue
2. **Challenge:** Resilience defined by bouncing back from setbacks

3. **Commitment:** Grit defined by persisting through challenges to complete a long-term goal

Think about this for a minute. The 3Cs explain about 75 percent of the variance in human performance, and all three are within our control. Yet, the 3Cs are not on the radar screen of most organizations. This is a significant lost opportunity for two reasons. First, the 3Cs are the biggest drivers of human performance and are trainable. Second, the growing influence of artificial intelligence raises an increasingly urgent question: what can we do that a computer can't? The answer is that we can become better humans by developing our 3Cs, which a computer can't do.

We live in a world with plenty to fear: global pandemics, economic volatility, despots, injustice, and climate change. Sometimes, our experiences are scary, and we fear the potential consequences that confront us with good reason. After all, it isn't paranoia when they are really after you! *What* will happen to us is not ours to decide. But *how* we respond is absolutely for us to decide. While we can't predict the future with any confidence, we can predict that virtue has served people independent of circumstances for thousands of years.

If you want to endure and perhaps even grow from adversity, start with *who*, not *what*. Our identity—*who we are*—is tied to character, challenge, and commitment, not job titles. Of course, coaching for competence has value and might be just what someone needs. In fact, improving a competency is often a safe place to start a coaching relationship. Just keep in mind that character offers a two-for-one benefit—it is a performance multiplier and a reputational protector. It is our character that is in our control and that defines us throughout our life. As Heraclitus said, "Character is destiny."[6] Better humans, better performance.

COMMON COACHING CHALLENGES

What is not always understood are the three common coaching challenges listed in Table 12.2.

Table 12.2 **Three Common Coaching Challenges**

Coaching Challenge 1	Coaching Challenge 2	Coaching Challenge 3
Strategies are unclear: • Lack clarity of the purpose of coaching • Lack clarity on best coaching practices • Lack clarity on where and when coaching would be most beneficial • Lack clear agreement between coach and coachee • Lack consistent coaching quality	Coaching effectively is harder to do than we think: • Challenging to help people find their own solution • Challenging to keep conversations positive and solution oriented • Challenging to increase our question-to-statement ratio • Challenging when relationships are too familiar or too strained (lack of trust) • Challenging to slay our ego (arrogance and self-absorbed)	Pitfalls are common: • Overreliance on our expertise • Overreliance on what we have to offer rather than what we can learn • Overreliance on pushing private thoughts and information • Overreliance on self as exemplar rather than facilitator (that is, use of the "expert" model rather than the coaching model) • Overreliance on concrete goals • Overreliance on nondirective advice when direction is needed

WHY DO INCOMPETENT PEOPLE THINK THEY ARE AMAZING?

Socrates said the principal goal in life is self-knowledge. He went on to say that self-deception is the principal barrier to self-knowledge. Our infinite capacity to self-deceive includes an area of research known as the *Dunning-Kruger effect*. This research is named after the professors who addressed the question, why do incompetent people think they are amazing? Loads of studies have revealed that we frequently over-rate our abilities even when our experience is limited. Here are some entertaining examples:

- 32 percent of software engineers in one company and 42 percent in another rated themselves in top 5 percent of all software engineers.
- 88 percent of drivers believe they have above average driving skills.
- A debate team in the bottom 20 percent in performance thought they were winning 60 percent of their debates.[7]

People with limited ability consistently overrate their expertise in fields as diverse as math, chess, ethics, and music.

When we are inexperienced, we lack the knowledge to understand what excellence looks like, and we lack the expertise to catch and correct our own errors. The good news is that once we learn what good looks like, we can recalibrate our abilities.

Experts confront a different blind spot: the curse of knowledge. They know they have expertise, but often they don't perceive how unusual their abilities are. They have been so good for so long that they have forgotten what it was like to be a beginner. Remember the discussion of the Navy SEALs and the baseball coaches (Chapter 5).

How we respond to rookie or expert mistakes depends on where we fall on the arrogance-humility spectrum. On one end of this spectrum, stubbornness + ignorance = arrogance. New insights and information flow off the arrogant like the proverbial water off a duck's back. When mistakes are made, denial, blame, and defensiveness kick in. Coaching won't easily crack the hard shell of an unreflective arrogant person.

On the other end of the spectrum is humility, which C. S. Lewis defined this way, "Humility is not thinking less of yourself; it's thinking of yourself less."[8]

Vulnerability is the close cousin of humility, defined as the courage to step into discomfort and struggle. Predictably, vulnerability isn't something that we necessarily enjoy though it leads to mental toughness and mental agility.

Importantly, vulnerability and humility are trainable skills. Both open far more options to us than arrogance does. In contrast to the arrogant person who may be headstrong when it comes to coaching,

coaching does a world of good for a humble person who is willing to seek advice, even when feedback is hard to hear.

KEYS TO EFFECTIVE COACHING

The simple skill of talking less and listening more, of telling less and asking more, is stunningly difficult to do. As if this weren't enough, let's add one more layer of complexity: the person being coached. At its core, coaching is very personal—helping people achieve what they feel is important in their life.

So, life and work are interdependent. When we support a person's desire to deepen relationships with family and friends, this effort spills over to deepen relationships with customers and colleagues. Since coaching is harder than it seems, let's focus on coaching 101—empathy, questions, and listening.

Empathy

Empathy is easy enough to understand. Put ourselves in someone else's shoes. However, it is not always easy to put the needs of another person before our own. It is especially hard to imagine our way into another person's experiences. It is doubly hard to put ourselves in someone's shoes when nothing in our background comes close to what they are experiencing.

Empathy is the front door of compassion, which demands even more of us—relieve another person's suffering. Working our way through suffering is arguably the hardest work of all and comes with no quick fixes. It takes time to both acknowledge pain and to grow from pain. We can learn to bounce back or even grow from suffering when we have at least one person who is empathic, asks appropriate questions, and listens to us.

Questions

Open-ended questions are a way to demonstrate empathy. The root word of *question* is *quest*. Questions put us on a journey to understand what good means to someone. There is certainly nothing robotic about asking good questions. That said, it is helpful to have guidelines on what good questions look like. Here are some open-ended questions adapted from Michael Stanier:

1. What is on your mind?
   - The purpose of this question is to define the issue that is important to the coachee.
2. What challenges are you facing?
   - Explore whether the issue is related to projects, people, or patterns:
     o **Projects:** Any challenges around one of your projects?
     o **People:** Any challenges with team members, customers, patients, partners?
     o **Patterns:** Any personal challenges? Patterns are potentially the greatest opportunities for growth, especially when the real challenge is strengthening one of the virtues.
3. If you had to pick one issue to focus on, which one would be the greatest challenge?
   - Often our concerns are all over the map, so confusion is to be expected. If we are clear about our challenges, we may not need a coach. When things are foggy, a coach can help. In fact, the role of the coach is to help a person clear the fog so they can focus on things that matter.
4. How important is this to you?
   - This is a diagnostic question: does the person get it, want it, or do it?
     o **Get it:** Does the person understand the issue at hand? If not, ask probing questions until they get it. If so, move to want-it questions.
     o **Want it:** Is the person motivated to change? If not, no worries; wait until they are. If they are motivated and get it, then move to do-it questions.
     o **Do it:** If the person gets it and wants it, now it's time for deliberate practice. If there is progress, then declare victory. If not, keep practicing.

5. What does good look like?
   - This is a positively framed question to get clear on what good means to someone. Once we are clear about the desired end state, then we can put deliberate practice to work.
6. What restraints limit your ability to make progress toward your goal?
   - Rather than push someone to practice virtue, assume they already want to practice virtue. Define the restraining forces that inhibit their goal, and discuss how these forces can be reduced or eliminated.
7. How would you apply deliberate practice to achieve your goal?
   - **Goal:** Define a goal that matters to you, that is specific, and that is focused.
   - **Effort:** Define the level of effort that will be needed to achieve your goal, including how to reduce or eliminate restraining forces rather than relying on willpower.
   - **Learning partner:** Identify someone who is empathetic, asks good questions, and listens well.
   - **Reflect and refine:**
     o Reflect on how well you leveraged your strengths.
     o Refine how to leverage your strengths more.
   - **Meet three to five times to review progress on your deliberate practice:**
     o At the last session, answer whether you made progress toward your goal.
     o Answer whether your learning partner thinks you made progress toward your goal.
8. What was most useful for you?
   - This question gives the coach feedback about what worked and what didn't work.[9]

Listening

It takes skill to understand rather than be understood. To listen well, we need to understand the difference between poor (level 1), average (level 2), and excellent (level 3) listening:

- **Level 1 listening:** While the other person is talking, think about what you want to say. Wait for the other person to take a breath, or better yet, talk over them, so you can speak your mind. You might be coming out of your shoes to tell the person about your experiences or your problems. It's no surprise that this level of listening isn't even within hailing distance of effective coaching.
- **Level 2 listening:** Coaches stick to *what* and *how*, not *why*. *Why* is a judgment question. While *why* is appropriate to ask in other settings, it isn't when it comes to coaching. Since the agenda is driven by the coachee, they own the *why* question. The coach toggles back and forth between probe and validate to help clarify goals and effort by asking questions such as these:
  - What would that look like for you?
  - How would you do that?
- **Level 3 listening:** Avoid tripping over the obvious by listening carefully for what isn't being said. Ask open-ended and clarifying questions to make sure you understand what the person is thinking, saying, and feeling. Rely on questions that help a person overcome adversity rather than fixate on self-esteem. Rely on questions that help leverage strengths and manage weaknesses.

Here's the thing. Programs don't change people. People who are empathic, who ask good questions, and who listen carefully change people.

WHAT DOES GOOD COACHING LOOK LIKE?

If a coach helps a leader read a balance sheet or understand project management, it is relatively easy to measure that. If the coach helps a leader by emphasizing their strengths, by learning to manage fear, by cultivating insights about their purpose and passion, how do we measure the benefits of that?

Consider that people are not fully engaged when they are frozen by fear. People step toward their potential by operating from their purpose of who they want to be and the contribution they want to make. This requires self-reflection, which is an underdeveloped capacity in many leaders who are generally action-oriented people. As shown in Table 12.3, good coaching promotes self-reflection while ineffective coaching results in unrealized potential.

Table 12.3 Features of Effective Versus Ineffective Coaching

Ineffective Coaching	Effective Coaching
Push: Your focus is on extrinsic motivators.	**Pull:** Your focus is on intrinsic motivators.
Rate person: What do you think of them?	**Support person:** How do you help them succeed?
Your focus is on pay.	Your focus is on growth and development.
You assume you are a good judge of talent.	You assume that judgment often is incorrect in assessing talent.
Talent is fixed: "You have it, or you don't" (fixed mindset).	**Talent is developed:** You adopt a growth mindset.
Deficit-based: • You add what isn't there. • You grow new branches. • You learn by improving weaknesses.	**Strength-based:** • You name and amplify strengths. • You grow new leaves on strong branches. • Focusing on weaknesses impedes learning. Instead, you focus on strengths.
Excellence is easy to define.	Excellence is hard to define.
Practicing excellence is hard to define.	Practicing excellence is easy to define.
The key to high performance is giving feedback.	The key to high performance is receiving feedback.

Effective coaching works best in organizations that view vulnerability as an act of courage. A healthy culture acknowledges that we will never be error free and we can always get better. At the same time, no matter how good someone is, they have blind spots. In contrast, a toxic culture weaponizes vulnerability. Toxic cultures hide, deny, and punish mistakes rather than own and grow from mistakes.

KEY TAKEAWAYS

A successful coach facilitates the coachee's discovery to ensure that personal goals—what matters most—align closely with the organization's goals.

As Marcel Proust said, "The real voyage of discovery consists not in seeing new sights, but in looking with new eyes."[10] People who actively get better at who they are get better at what they do.

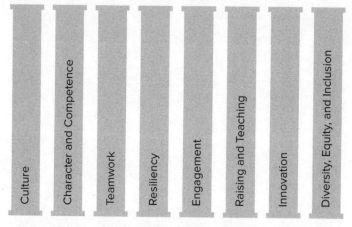

FORMING
GOOD HABITS

We are what we repeatedly do.
Excellence, then, is not an act, but a habit.[1]
—WILL DURANT

OVERVIEW OF HABITUATION

A habit is like a sled creating grooves in a hill. The more the sled slides down the same path, the deeper the grooves it cuts. Over time, the sled continues to get pulled into the same grooves. Inevitably, fresh snow fills the old grooves. We always get an opportunity to pay attention to a different route.[2]

Our habits are formed based on where we place our attention. Then, for good or for ill, we become what we practice. While we might think that habitual change is a matter of willpower, the evidence proves otherwise. The hard part isn't understanding the benefits of habits such as a good night's rest, a healthy diet, and regular exercise. The tricky part is defining and weakening the forces that restrain us from achieving healthy habits. This is why insights about restraining forces that inhibit change are so useful, as noted by Nobel Prize–winning behavioral economist Daniel Kahneman. So, the backbone of habituation is paying attention, practicing, and eliminating restraints.

Here's how that process played out when a group of production teammates at Parker Hannifin decided to pay attention to hope rather than despair after attending a virtue seminar. Parker teammates lived in a community where jobs had left, and the opioid crisis had entered. In response to the plight of their community, the Parker team wanted to replace their current groundless hope and depressing cynicism with realistic gratitude.

The Parker team produced a video that emphasized what they had, rather than what they didn't have. One teammate expressed appreciation that he was still able to raise a family on a single paycheck. He hoped Parker would be just as strong at his exit as it was on his entry.

Another teammate reported being homeless after serving in the military. After being hired for her current job at Parker, she could provide for her family as a single mom. When her grandson passed away and her teammates attended the funeral, she found out, "Wow, I'm not alone."

Another employee appreciated how Parker supported the community so she could give hope to her neighbors.

The video ends with the story of a teammate who had been diagnosed with breast cancer. Her physician suggested that she put her affairs in order. She feared losing her job. Instead, factory leaders helped her take a paid leave. She found a cancer center that offered promising treatment that she couldn't afford. Parker teammates raised the money to pay for the treatment. Her new oncologist assured her that things were not as dire as she imagined and that there was room for realistic optimism. She concluded her story with appreciation for the leaders and teammates who gave her courage and hope when it was most needed.

The production team began intentionally to act differently to navigate their circumstances. They revised and weakened old habits that paid more attention to despair by creating space for realistic hope. Revisions like these are valuable, but that doesn't mean that changing our life is easy. To make changes to the way we think and act requires the kind of discomfort and effort that many of us would rather avoid. Yet, learning to revise our habits is how we become a better spouse, partner, parent, friend, leader, teammate, and citizen. Not quickly. Not perfectly. Though progress is possible.

Each life revision is improved based on where we put our attention, what we practice, and how we define and weaken the forces that restrain us.

INTRODUCTION

Neuroscience backs up Aristotle's insight that "we are what we repeatedly do." Once upon a time, we thought that the brain stopped forming at some point. Now we know that from conception to death, neural pathways reorganize in response to our environment and experiences. This process is called *neuroplasticity*, and it enables us to learn and adapt to different experiences throughout life. We are not stuck with the brain we are born with. It is possible to convert dysfunctional ways of thinking and behaving to create productive mindsets, skills, and abilities.

Neuroplasticity comes down to this: we become what we practice. We are creatures of habit who follow predictable patterns that define who we become. So, what's a habit? Habits are automatic behaviors requiring little or no thought. Habits reduce our cognitive load because they require limited energy. This is a big deal since our brain is an energy hog: our brain uses more energy than any other human organ, accounting for up to 20 percent of our body's energy use. Habits that reduce the body's need for mental energy include showering, shaving, or brushing our teeth, actions that are 88 percent habitual.

We do these activities largely without effort and mostly automatically. Tasks at work are 55 percent habitual. Lifting weights, running, and athletics in general are 44 percent habitual. Resting, relaxing, and sitting on a couch are 48 percent habitual.[3] These percentages may or may not reflect your habitual routines. The point is that more of our life is on cruise control—that is, it is more habitual—than we might realize.

There's a catch to neuroplasticity. It is ethically neutral. Our neurons aren't weighing carefully whether our behavior is just or unjust, wise or unwise. Instead, our brain wires itself based on where we put our attention, whom we spend time with, our experiences, and what we practice. If we practice spending hours on social media, then that's who we become. If we practice virtue, then we move a step closer to this ideal.

Our risk is this: habits that are comfortable and convenient for us may not be that good for us or for others. While we need to look more deeply at our habits and ask whether we can do better, there's a catch. Habits are easy to understand and maddeningly difficult to change. Simple solutions such as "Just do it" slogans don't have the power to change habits. Every part of an adult brain is already occupied, so it doesn't have vacant lots available for a new habit. An old habit must be pruned to create space for a new habit.[4]

Knowing what to prune requires that we understand the brain is designed to help us survive. It does this by triggering a warning whenever a menace is even perceived. It also evolved a scarcity mindset. Hunter-gatherers needed to be ever vigilant to get food, clothing, and shelter. Self-gratification didn't pay off when all our attention was focused on whether we will eat today or not. But now, our hunter-gathering nature has been replaced by being shopper-gatherers, ordering food, clothes, and movies without budging off the couch. Today, we need self-control to avoid being addicted to binge-watching on-demand streaming services or polishing off a bag of chips. When it comes to our smartphone, we don't need yet one more study to prove that these devices are brilliantly addictive. Smartphone addiction won't kill us, but it surely will distract us and dictate where we put our attention.

Let's say we want teenagers to reduce the attention they pay to their smartphones and social media. All you do is point out how over-using social media contributes to loneliness, depression, and poor sleep. Then make sure the teenagers understand that private posts can backfire when they go public. Just tell teenagers what they should do, and they will listen. Right? Good luck with that!

One way that teenagers aren't much different from adults is that they desire being independent and they don't want to be told what to do. A study leveraged this insight by informing teenagers how technology companies attract funding. They jack up their stock price based on engagement metrics that measure how much time people spend on their app. They hire PhDs with expertise in addictive behavior to guide thousands of engineers skilled at leveraging technology to exploit human weaknesses. Features such as infinite scrolling enable users to endlessly swipe through content without clicking, which takes away the brain's ability to catch up to our impulses. As social animals, we compare ourselves to others. Sometimes, this can inspire us to be better people. But sometimes, comparisons lead to envy, shame, anxiety, arrogance, or anger. Algorithms learn our preferences and then put us in social bubbles with people who think like us.[5] Exploiting human vulnerabilities for commercial success has been smashingly effective as these numbers make clear:

- Daily, people check their smartphones up to 63 times; heavy users as much as 86 times.
- Daily, people spend an average of 5.4 hours on their smartphones.
- Daily, 13 percent of millennials spend over 12 hours on their smartphones and 48 minutes texting.
- Daily, baby boomers spend 5 hours on their smartphones.[6]

So, technology companies are financially incentivized to suck as much time out of your life as possible. Your attention becomes their product that they sell to advertisers. Feeling lonely? Check your phone. Feeling insecure? Check your phone.[7] While technology innovators want us hooked to their devices, they place limits on their own families' uses. Apple CEO Tim Cook would not let his nephew join social networks. Bill Gates banned his children from using smartphones until they were teenagers. Melinda Gates reported that she wished they had waited even longer. Steve Jobs would not let his young kids use iPads.[8]

Back to leveraging teenager desire for independence. When teenagers were armed with information like this, they took more control of their social media use than the control group who was told to avoid social media because it wasn't good for them.[9] To break this bad habit, we need to build friction to reduce the app's design to hijack our attention. In the moment when we reach for our phones, we can add friction by asking questions such as "What for? Why now? What else?" These questions are prompts to help interrupt the automatic reflex of looking at our phones.

AKRASIA: FAILURE OF THE WILL

Akrasia is a Greek word that means lacking command or self-control or acting against our better judgment. Sometimes, right at the moment when we want to be compassionate, just, or hopeful, we somehow aren't. When our motivation is disordered for whatever reason, we experience *akrasia*, or "failure of the will." Plato discussed *akrasia* as our tendency to do things against our better interest. So, since the days of Plato, people have not always done what would be good for them and for others.

This ancient problem takes us back to the scientific insight of homeostasis. The brain creates discomfort to effect healthful action. We get hunger pangs so we will eat. We feel cold and seek warmth. If we are bloated, the brain signals us to stop eating. These are *physiologic* responses to discomfort that in the moment are not focused on long-term healthy diets. When we are hungry, we eat what is available to us—could be a Big Mac or a Whopper instead of a salad. On a different level are the common *psychological* homeostatic triggers, including uncertainty, boredom, anxiety, and fatigue. Human response to these triggers varies. One person can respond to financial instability with crushing anxiety while another responds as if it is a nonevent.

Recall that stress is our response to an external event. It's not caused by the event itself. This is also true when it comes to failure of the will. Habitual change is governed by internal, not external, events. In the case of why we don't always practice virtue, the words *distraction* and *traction* are useful. Both words come from the Latin root *trahere*, which means "pull." Both words end in *tion*, which means "action."

So, distraction pulls us away from our intent to practice virtue, and traction pulls us toward our intent to practice virtue. Distraction is fed by self-defeating habits that rely on blame and shame. For example, we blame the external world for bad habits such as phone addiction being caused by technology companies. We feel shame for eating too much and exercising too little, so we view our failure as a character flaw. Both blame and shame become default habits that contribute to failure of the will.

In contrast, we gain traction to practice virtue by accepting responsibility for our conduct. While we can't control feeling bored, anxious, fatigued, or lonely, we can control whether we respond in healthy or unhealthy ways. For example, we can respond to boredom by starting a conversation or by staring at our smartphone.[10]

Here is an important insight about failure of the will. Willpower is overrated. Like energy, willpower is a limited resource that gets depleted with use just as muscles fatigue with heavy use. So, if willpower is an overrated aspect of self-control, who are these strong-minded people who can stroll past a bowl of ice cream? A study of 205 adults examined how people exercise self-control. People were tracked intensively for three weeks by comparing their stated goals with what they did.

The findings concluded that effortful restraint was not the key to a life well lived.[11] Those who possessed high self-control were not gifted with supercharged willpower and moral superiority. The people who most readily agreed to statements such as "I am good at resisting temptations" reported fewer temptations throughout the study. They excelled at self-control by hardly using self-control at all. They had learned that the key was controlling their environment and choices as much as possible so that they didn't have to rely on willpower that would wither as their energy was depleted.[12]

The counterintuitive insight is that it is easier to pursue healthy goals when it doesn't require much effort. The most self-disciplined among us don't view healthy habits as a chore. They have learned to enjoy healthy sleep, diet, and exercise habits.[13]

So, those who avoid gorging on the ice cream in the refrigerator don't have more self-control than the rest of us. They just don't buy ice cream in the first place.

When it comes to smartphone addiction, we don't have to abstain completely from phone use. However, rather than rely on willpower, we can weaken the forces that cause us to be distracted by our phones by taking actions such as these:

1. Turn off notifications. Apps use the color red to draw our attention.
2. Remove toxic apps that profit from addiction, polarization, and misinformation.
3. Track your screen time to reduce the attention that you give to screens.
4. Delete Facebook, Instagram, and games, and cut back to the essentials of calendar, email, contacts, and perhaps a search engine.
5. While you are at it, charge your phone someplace other than your bedroom.[14]

The purpose of pruning nonessential activities related to screens is to create space for the essentials of love, work, and play.

THE ESSENTIAL LIFE

What's essential? One answer is leading a balanced life, though what that means may not be clear. Psychologist Erik Erikson suggested that we pay attention to the three great spheres of life: love, work, and play. Erikson's research showed that people who led the fullest life managed to achieve a reasonable balance among these three spheres. At the end of life, people full of regret concluded that they had lived the wrong life or did not live life well. They paid attention to one of life's three spheres at the expense of the others. Erikson said that paying attention to all three spheres with equal dedication led not just to success but also to serenity.[15]

Erikson's love, work, and play ideal provides us with a way to audit how well we balance these three spheres of our life. For many, their audit might reveal that they work too much or play too little. This insight then slams into the immutable "168 wall." One hundred sixty-eight is the number of hours in a week. Rich or poor, educated or not, married or single, we all get the same number of hours per week. Our use of time raises the question: "What are we living for?" It is interesting that most people use the phrase "work-life balance." We flip the phrase to be "life-work balance."

First we need a life, and then we work. Pre-COVID, life-work balance was certainly an issue. As the pandemic has eased, many have hit the gas pedal with a sense of urgency to live a more balanced life. Organizations struggling to attract and retain talent have become more responsive to helping people balance life and work. The best organizations strive to offer a reasonable life and work balance all the time, not just during pandemics and talent shortages.

At the individual level, it is not possible to always live a perfectly balanced life. In the Analects, Confucius argued that true humanity was impossible for most mortals, including himself. He recognized the difficulty of living simply, modestly, and in self-control. We are all a mix of healthy and unhealthy habits that support or inhibit paying attention to Erikson's three great spheres of life. Benjamin Franklin had an impactful way to measure the quality of our habits. He defined net worth by what remains when we subtract our bad habits from our good ones. We are not going to eliminate bad habits. We just hope our good habits are greater than our bad habits.

We are not only creatures of habit in that we follow predictable patterns; we also are habit-creating creatures. We create new habits from intentionally acting in new ways. When we are ready to take on the immutable 168 wall, we define and weaken forces that restrain a balanced life.

The way to live a balanced life is often in plain sight, which takes us to our infinite capacity to delude ourselves. Our words make clear that meaningful relationships and character are more important than money and success. Our actions might suggest the opposite. Money and success are not inherently wrong. The question is, "Are we able to get the order right—meaning before money, relationships before success?"

Sometimes, our shortcomings are not due to disorder. We can also fail due to our blind spots, meaning we literally cannot see why our life is out of balance. A healthy nudge from people we know, like, and trust can reveal our behavior more clearly to us.

STRUGGLE AND SAFETY

The greatest danger of turbulent times is the temptation to deny reality. For example, turbulence requires that organizations accept the reality that command and control must be replaced by decentralization to increase agility and speed in decision-making. This is a good outcome since smaller teams enable people to make a difference rather than being a cog in a huge machine.

This also means that organizations must accept that learning is a lifelong process, so their people stay abreast of change. For this reason, an organization's most pressing task is teaching people how to learn.

Today, organizations have come to accept these facts. Or have they? The insights in the paragraphs above were written by Peter Drucker, who arguably was the greatest management thinker of the last century. In 1946, Drucker wrote about decentralization. In 1959, Drucker wrote about the risk of turbulence and the need to teach people how to learn. Drucker's insights make clear that there is nothing new about turbulence and uncertainty. The open question is whether organizations have heeded Drucker's wisdom from over 60 years ago.

What we know is that if you want to learn, you need to embrace struggling. This is the key insight of a growth mindset.

The insight of a growth mindset aligns with neuroplasticity. When we struggle, we fire up neurons to make us smarter. So, how do we get people to struggle in order to learn and to normalize discomfort associated with uncertainty? The paradox is that we need stability to embrace change. We need some stability—some constant—to undergird our ability to navigate adversity. An effective way to build stability may surprise you: step into gratitude.

DELIBERATE PRACTICE AND GRATITUDE

How do people get good at something? In a word, practice. And the best don't just practice. They *practice deliberately*. Anders Ericsson, known as the "expert on experts," learned this insight by studying world-class performers in athletics, the arts, surgeons, and even chess. Ericsson found that the best among us practiced four mutually reinforcing steps—*goal, effort, partner,* and *reflection*.[16] His findings showed that how we practice has as strong or stronger impact on our performance as ability. To illustrate how this works, we will apply deliberate practice to gratitude.

Why gratitude? Gratitude is a keystone habit that increases our ability to create other habits such as fitness, diet, sleep, or other virtues. When we strengthen healthy habits, we feel more hopeful. Gratitude primes our brain to notice when good things happen. A grateful person understands that our world cannot be held together with will and strength; we need other people. When we adopt this perspective by practicing gratitude, the benefits are impressive:

- Grateful people more readily block negative and toxic emotions such as envy, resentment, regret, or depression. We can't be resentful and grateful at the same time. One counters the other.
- Grateful people handle adversity and stress better.
- Grateful people strengthen social ties. They become clearer that we can't get through life without the support of others.

Gratitude, humility, and appreciation are like a muscle that we can exercise just as we can exercise being ungrateful, entitled, and cynical. We all know people who have everything to make them grateful and still they are miserable. We all know people who have had great tragedies and still they are grateful. So, it's not our circumstances, but how we respond to our circumstances that makes some of us grateful and others ungrateful. This doesn't mean that we are grateful for violence, exploitation, injustice, or the loss of a dear friend or family member. Sometimes, we are grateful for certain aspects of unwanted events: grateful that a loved one is no longer suffering or, grateful that an illness gave us a new perspective. We can learn something from a difficult experience. We can grow from adversity or learn how to take a stand against injustice.[17]

When we respond well with gratitude, we are more likely to give to others than to take. We become less fearful acting out of a sense of abundance rather than scarcity. At other times, we miss the value of gratitude because our habit is one of distraction rather than a habit of traction to reflect on its meaning. However, when, not if, we miss the opportunity to be grateful, we often get another chance.

So, let's apply Ericsson's model of deliberate practice with goal, effort, coaching or learning partner, and reflection to being more grateful.

Goal of Gratitude

In the case of gratitude, we choose to reduce resentment, regret, and depression. We choose to increase our ability to handle adversity and stress, and we choose to strengthen our connections with others. Gratitude is like other motivations: we move and change in the direction that we appreciate because we are more curious and open to learning. We are also more likely to create enduring habitual change when our goals are fulfilling and enjoyable.[18]

We are more likely to achieve a goal when we focus our efforts. Many people report that their awesome multitasking skills are the key to their performance. Instead, research has made it clear that the more we multitask, the less we accomplish and that those who think they are best at multitasking are often the least productive. Even briefly multitasking such as quickly checking our emails negatively affects performance. It's the switch itself that hurts, not how long we switch.

The term *attention residue* reveals our brain's struggle to switch between tasks. When we jump from task to task, our thoughts from the previous task interfere with giving the current task our full attention. It takes time for attention residue to clear out, and in the meantime, performance drops. A National Academy of Sciences study revealed that multitasking among youth correlated with poorer memory, increased impulsivity, and changes in brain function. Our brain multi-shifts rather than multitasks. For this reason, focused effort produces better results, especially when practicing a new complex habit such as gratitude. In addition, focused effort reduces errors.

To get the best performance out of our brain requires that we replace the habit of multitasking with the habit of focused effort.[19]

Still, deliberate practice involves more than goal setting. We need to define and weaken forces that restrain us from a goal like practicing gratitude.

Effort: How Can We Weaken Restraints?

People don't come to work striving to be an ingrate, so the question is, what restrains someone from practicing gratitude? Perhaps the most ungrateful among us are driven by arrogance, vanity, and an insatiable appetite for admiration. For others, being an ingrate is a result of feeling entitled, so we have no reason to feel thankful. When we believe that life owes us, grievances outnumber gifts. While few people are always hopeless ingrates, none of us is immune from narcissistic tendencies that ignore the ties that bind people and that reject the need to pay back or pay forward.

Over time, most of us grow out of our self-absorption, though few of us kick this habit altogether. There is a good reason why this is hard. Thinking of our needs comes easily. Thinking about the needs of others takes effort. Doing so requires humility, which is closely related to gratitude. Humility promotes learning by cultivating curiosity, which turns us toward our need to rely on others and acknowledge our limitations.

An especially powerful act of humility is a gratitude visit. Think of a person who had a profound impact on you. They invested in you when they didn't have to. They believed in you when you hadn't earned anything. You are a better person because of them, and they changed the trajectory of your life. However, you haven't thanked them properly, and they are still alive. Write a one-page testament to how this person changed your life for the better. In the spirit of humility, the focus of the letter is on them and their contribution, not you. Define in detail how they took an interest in you and how they helped you develop one or more of the virtues. Ideally, call the person, ask to meet with them, and read the letter out loud to them. If it is truly not possible to express your gratitude face-to-face (don't be too easy on yourself), then send the letter. This effort isn't yet a habit, but it is a good start to creating a habit of gratitude.

When it comes to restraints, consider why you are not already practicing gratitude. Perhaps restraints are the kinds of things that affect just about all habitual change—the pressure to perform, time limitations, effort needed to change, and fear of failure.

Coaching or Learning Partner

The best athletes know that to get better requires pushing through discomfort with the support of a coach who holds them accountable. Like athletes, our performance increases when we actively seek feedback and support.

Otherwise, our performance stagnates or even declines when we are afraid to ask for help. Ask someone you know, like, and trust to help your deliberate practice. The best partners are empathetic, ask good questions, and listen well. A good partner helps you determine how to reduce restraints. They are invested in helping you follow through to create a habit that you are motivated to strengthen.

Reflection

A team of Dutch researchers learned that reflection was a key factor in overcoming performance stagnation. When people assess what they have learned and integrate their insights into future actions, they push through what formerly limited their performance.[20]

We can avoid a gratitude plateau by asking, "How did expressing gratitude affect us and the person we thanked?" At least in the moment, this reflection is a reminder of what we know but don't always acknowledge—that we are not self-sufficient. Reflection can help us avoid suboptimal performance in all domains, not just gratitude.

———

To recap, the four elements of deliberate practice are goal, effort, coaching or learning partner, and reflection. We used the example of gratitude to illustrate these four steps because gratitude is a keystone habit.

The key takeaway is that deliberate practice can be applied to any domain such as practicing virtue, improving our sleep, or becoming more fit. We become what we practice, and there is no better way to practice than to do so deliberately.

KEY TAKEAWAYS

We can't get better easily or quickly, but we can make virtue a habit by practicing deliberately.

To clear space for virtue, we must get rid of emotions that block us from doing anything else—the restraining forces in our lives. Fear and anger in particular hijack the amygdala in our brain so we are unable to imagine practicing virtue.

When we let go of fears or resentments, we free space in our brain to feel, to know, to act, and to live differently.[21]

This is not easy to do in a world that seeks the external validation that can distract our attention away from practicing virtue. External validation builds our habits from the outside in rather than from the inside out. Our attention is directed to external achievements, material success, or staring at our smartphones.

Instead, when we focus on interior development, we cultivate habits that link our welfare to the welfare of others. We learn to respond to pressure by focusing on our teammates and our purpose. Our internal navigation system aims at practicing virtue, so we aren't intimidated exploring uncharted terrain. We learn to actively seek tough challenges that are important and hard. And when we fail, we recover quickly. These are the kinds of leadership qualities that replace calcification and decline with innovation and growth.

The world can be a menacing and unpredictable place. It is quite reasonable to seek predictability. However, insulation leads us to become risk averse at the very time that we need to take intelligent risks. While fear and anger spread rapidly under stress, their embers cool in a culture defined by care and trust. The so-called soft skills such as vulnerability create the psychological safety we need to handle pressure a bit better.

Ancient wisdom and the science of habituation reveal that we are shaped by what we pay attention to, by what we practice, and by how we can weaken what holds us back. This is the critical insight of Aristotle and of neuroplasticity. Excellence, then, is not an act but a habit that we repeatedly do.

HABIT TOOLKIT

To weaken restraints to building a habit of gratitude, here are three simple evidence-based strategies: *piggybacking*, *cues*, and *crisis*.[22]

247

Piggybacking

The point of piggybacking is adding a behavior to something you already do. For example, your doctor prescribed some medicine that you haven't taken before. To help you remember to take the medicine, place it next to your toothbrush, which you use every night. String habits together like a chain. Use what you already have in place to develop new habits.

Application of piggybacking to gratitude: You already have routine staff meetings. At the start of the meeting, piggyback by taking five minutes to ask: "Which teammates exhibited virtue in a way that made our team better and our results stronger?" This question helps a team understand what they did right, so they can do it again. It is also an opportunity to express gratitude to teammates for their good work. Creating a habit of gratitude as part of a regular meeting sanctions it and helps make gratitude contagious outside the meeting.

Cues

The purpose of a cue is to have already made the decision to create a habit. A disciplined author wakes up having already decided to write at least two pages of material each morning, or an athlete has already decided to work out at the same time each day. Over time, the cue creates a habit—writing or exercising become automatic.

Application of cues to gratitude: Your cue could be that each night you ask: "What happened today for which I'm grateful?" Over time, this cue becomes automatic, at least most nights.

Crisis

"A crisis is a terrible thing to waste," as many have said. A crisis is an opportunity to reinvent ourselves. Traumatic experiences are not contests to decide what was the worst thing we experienced. Nor are crises the kinds of experiences we seek. However, if we live long enough, we assuredly experience disruptive events that force us to adapt.

Potentially, these events provide an opportunity for *post-traumatic growth* (PTG), which means that we learn to live a more intrinsically motivated life governed by relationships and experiences that create a sense of purpose. The irony is that the insights that trauma might provide are already known to us.

Application of crisis to gratitude: Gratitude is inextricably linked with belonging to each other. COVID-19 separated us from family and friends who help bring out our best selves. When it was safe to be with others, some created a new habit that strengthened relationships by expressing gratitude to those who have meant the most to them.

ARETÉ

Excellence

Habits

Coaching

Restoration

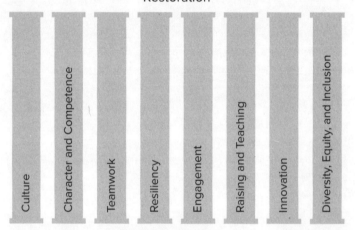

Culture

Character and Competence

Teamwork

Resiliency

Engagement

Raising and Teaching

Innovation

Diversity, Equity, and Inclusion

Character

Trust   Compassion   Courage

Justice   Wisdom   Temperance   Hope

THE VALUE OF VIRTUE

People knew there were two ways of coming at truth.
One was science, or what the Greeks called Logos,
reason, logic. And that was essential that the discourse of
science or logic related directed to the external world.
The other was mythos, *what the Greeks called* myth,
which didn't mean a fantasy story, but it was a narrative
associated with ritual and ethical practice, but it
helped us to address problems for which there were no easy
answers, like mortality, cruelty, the sorrow that overtakes
us all that's part of the human condition. And these two
were not in opposition; we needed both.[1]
—KAREN ARMSTRONG

In ancient Greece, stories and facts were recognized as two distinct ways of thinking. *Logos* sought truth, and *mythos* sought meaning. Mythos relied on narratives or stories. Logos focused on logic and facts. Mythos and logos were viewed as complementary ways to think; both were considered important.

Today, the dominant organizational language is more logos than mythos. We rely on numbers, computation, artificial intelligence, algorithms, and metrics. Recall the adage, "You can't manage what you don't measure." Fair enough, but the converse view is that "Not everything that matters can be measured." The language of logic contributes to efficiency, speed, convenience, and progress. Logos, or reason, enables people to function effectively in the world. Logos is essential to our survival. Yet, the mythos questions that often go unanswered are these: "Why are we doing this? What is all this for?" Mythos typically comes as story.

Stories have the potential to elevate us to excel by deepening meaning and unlocking potential; after all, stories inspire, and facts convince. Author and professor Joseph Campbell said that stories serve as a moral compass for each generation. Stories and lore provide guideposts of how we can live our life and educate us about how to become responsible adults. Without this insight, Campbell stated that we mistake celebrities who pursue fame and fortune for heroes. The celebrity strives to be known rather than to give or achieve for others.

A celebrity culture tends to worship youth over the elderly, which leads us to strive for appearance over wisdom. Campbell concluded that a celebrity culture produces children who act like adults and adults who act like children.[2] As we age, mythos and virtue guide us to become more responsible. Stories can teach and inspire. We learn to release ourselves from fear, desire, and malice by pursuing virtue instead. Without the guideposts of mythos and virtue, we are weakened by anxiety, stress, and adversity. We can't eliminate pressures and adversity, but the practice of virtue makes us more resilient.

Logos minus mythos contributes to what E. O. Wilson called humanity's real problem: "Paleolithic emotions, medieval institutions, and godlike technology." Our technologies are stunningly brilliant at advancing globalized trade, exploring Mars with helicopters, engineering driverless cars, and replacing chemotherapy with targeted genetic treatments to cure cancer. Technology also weaponizes worldwide terrorism, provides a megaphone for hate, and makes for an anxious future for those who lack digital skills.

An example of this divide between the wonders of technology and the incompleteness of technology alone—the logos-mythos divide—is evident in our response to the pandemic. Amazingly, scientists around the globe collaborated to develop a vaccine with unprecedented efficacy and speed. Yet sadly, our institutions and cultures struggled to put needles into enough arms to achieve herd immunity or to assure that access to the vaccine was equitable around the globe.

Albert Einstein put the limitation of science this way:

> Science has provided the possibility of liberation for human be-
> ings from hard labor, but science itself is not a liberator. It creates
> means not goals. Man should use [science] for reasonable goals.
> When the ideals of humanity are war and conquest, those tools
> become as dangerous as a razor in the hands of a child of three.
> We must not condemn man's inventiveness and patient conquest
> of the forces of nature because they are being used wrongly and
> disobediently now. The fate of humanity is entirely dependent
> upon its moral development.[3]

VALUES AND VIRTUE

Here is a simple way to understand the relationship between values
and virtues. Values express our beliefs. Virtues put our values into action. Remember that it isn't a virtue until we act. Let's say an organization valued integrity. How this value would be defined and how it
would be put into action would be unclear.

The seven virtues define what integrity means and provide insights and tools to put integrity into practice. For example, if we want
more trust, then we need to practice trustworthy acts. The virtues
come with a robust playbook to help teams put values such as trust
into action. The result will be better humans and better performance.

Now let's descend into the particulars. While values and virtues
have similarities, the differences between values and virtues are not
widely understood. Values in particular are confusing because the
word carries multiple meanings such as economic value, or valuable experiences such as customer or teammate experience, or what
people believe is important.

Values often lean against a logos wall that uses metrics for the
studs. For example, a key profit metric is total shareholder return. As
another example, customer value metrics might include "likelihood to
recommend." In the nonprofit sector such as healthcare, patient safety
relies on medical error metrics, or the patient experience includes
timeliness-of-care metrics such as "wait time to see a healthcare

professional." These are perfectly appropriate and important logos metrics.

There are also values that lean more against the mythos wall best constructed by stories. Still, logos-oriented leaders bring their measurement stick prowling for value metrics more than stories. Indeed, engagement metrics are indirect measures for how well the culture lives up to its values. However, people are not motivated by engagement scores. When data and dollars metrics matter more than community and character stories, then people feel like replaceable cogs in a machine. When that happens, there's no human reason to stay in a job or to give our all. The goal is morale—how people actually feel in the workplace—not chasing engagement scores. Remember the root word for *morale* is *moral*, which takes us back to virtue.

The impact of culture also influences value and virtue differently. Values are extensively shaped by the culture that it reflects and belongs to. For example, business wants to win, something you are not likely to hear in healthcare. Healthcare wants to treat patients and make them better. These are not words you are likely to hear in business. Even within the same industry, one culture might emphasize innovation, and another might emphasize operational excellence. So, values are principles that are considered important to a specific organization.

Whereas values are specific to a particular culture, virtues are universal and transcend organizations and cultures. An act of compassion is the same in New York as it is in Islamabad. Furthermore, acting with compassion to help the sick was the same in the 1918 to 1919 Spanish flu pandemic as it has been during the COVID-19 pandemic. Unlike values, virtues offer a multicultural framework, which is especially important to global organizations that are committed to diversity and inclusion.

Values can help an organization stand out from the crowd. Virtues do not differ from culture to culture. What does stand out and differentiate organizations and cultures is not the values they espouse but rather how well virtue is practiced. Values may or may not have a moral dimension. Virtues always have a moral dimension. Values don't speak to how someone can best live. Virtues define what it means to live life well.

The punch line is that if an organization or a leader has the opportunity to start from scratch to define their principles, it is best to go with building a virtue-based culture. If the culture is preformed, then they should work on anchoring virtues into existing values. For example, as an academic medical center, if our mission is "educating those who serve" and we value training the next generation of healthcare professionals superbly, then we should instill virtue—compassion, trust, wisdom, justice, and so on—into the educational process and the learning environment.

To be clear, we mustn't think of values *or* virtues as a dichotomous choice. They are not mutually exclusive. We should think of values *and* virtues.

Values express our beliefs. Virtues put our beliefs into action.

VIRTUE AND ORGANIZATIONAL EXCELLENCE

At their best, organizations are not personal platforms for individual careers. Instead, the best organizations shape the character of their people, enabling the institutions to fulfill their societal purpose. This means that lawmakers put the rule of law ahead of getting elected; journalists put accurate reporting ahead of social media hits; doctors fully embrace a "patients-first" philosophy before medical procedures; and business leaders put people and the planet ahead of profits.[4]

When organizations adopt the virtues as a common language of excellence, there are tangible benefits. Having a common language about what the virtues are and what they mean changes the culture by changing the conversations among people and how they practice excellence. When virtue is present, relationships and performance are strengthened. Stories about when we got the virtues right ring true, which doesn't deny that we fall short of our aspirations.

Virtues can and should force hard decisions when, not if, we fall short of our ideals. The virtues unify us because most of us want to do something that is not purely selfish and we want to be part of something larger than ourselves. In contrast to having a set of self-proclaimed values, there are thousands of years of human experience that define what virtue means and decades of empirically validated activities surrounding the ways in which virtue is practiced well.

The ancient Greeks understood that humans had a natural desire to pursue moral excellence. This pursuit to "aim at the good" included practicing virtue even in a world that could sometimes be harsh and cruel. This is exactly why a group of high school students decided to use the virtues to better understand organizations and themselves. After studying virtue, they reached several conclusions about what happened when the virtues were absent, including these:

- Egomaniac leaders who lacked virtue created dysfunctional cultures.
- Self-centered leaders created close-minded, toxic cultures where people distrusted each other and their customers.
- When team members lacked faith in each other, there was no shared purpose. People hid mistakes and lied to superiors. When this happened, people worked for a paycheck, not the company. They were less likely to perform at their best or stay in the organization.
- In contrast, when the virtues were present, the students noted real benefits: teams were more productive, creative, and collaborative, and they worked harder. When that happened, virtue became a reality that people could see and feel.

This all got started when a high school junior heard what his father learned at work about the virtues in a seminar on the subject of embracing and teaching the virtues as the foundation for performance. His son became intrigued and read our earlier book about virtue-based performance, *Exception to the Rule*.[5] He then asked his father to introduce him to an author of the book, one of us, to learn how to launch a club where students could study and practice virtue.

Imagine this. As the ancient Greeks suggested, high school students wanted to learn how to practice virtue because it was intrinsically meaningful to them. Rather than limit their education to extrinsic goals such as grades, advanced placement classes, and college applications, they wanted to become better humans. Students wanted an education about virtue because these ideas were missing in their curriculum. Their school's mission was to "inspire and empower learners," but the school—in its compliance mindset—nevertheless required the new club to find a teacher because the school's rule was that every club had to have a teacher overseeing it. In addition, the school's mission was silent on the value of character.

Finding a teacher who would empower students to learn and practice virtue turned out to be a challenge. Students called their initiative an "innovative leadership club" so that the request wouldn't be rejected because of the word "virtue." It seems curious to imagine that the word *virtue* would be a liability rather than an asset, but this serves as a reminder that the virtues—though time-honored—are still foreign and perhaps even threatening in many organizations, including many high schools.

In the end, these students reported that they learned how internal changes to their character yielded external results. They found a teacher who was willing to endorse the group but who stepped aside so they could self-manage their club. These empowered students adjusted to COVID-19 by delivering content online. They designed activities like this one:

- Think about the people who are closest to you in life.
- Use the "trust-to-distrust" spectrum, and consider this question: "Where would your closest family and friends place you?"
- Reflect on your strengths and where you want to get better.

The purpose of this story is not to disparage high schools. Rather, the purpose is to demonstrate that students want to learn and practice virtue in ways traditional curricula don't support. Sadly, schools must comply with legislative mandates to test students on what they know using curricula that are silent on the issue of building character.

While universities don't face the same kind of testing mandates as K–12 schools, they also tend to teach logos more than mythos. We can learn from Plato's Academy's concern for leaders who lacked the moral strength required to act according to the common good. Since Plato's concern applies equally well today, organizations would be wise to teach virtue to fill the void left by schools and universities.

A holistic investment in virtue, beyond making it a simple mandate or a platitude, protects the organization's reputation by helping people do the right thing, for the right reasons, in the right way. At the individual level, investing in embracing and teaching virtue helps people replace fear and angst with courage and purpose. Better humans, better performance.

This story about high school students reflects a much broader human hunger to apply ancient wisdom to contemporary problems.

The virtues are available to all of us, but they are often hidden in plain sight, as they seemed to be in the high school.

The ancients also clearly suggested that virtue is best pulled, not pushed. In other words, the virtues are attractors because they have intrinsic and universal appeal, not because they have been disseminated or mandated as organizational propaganda. About 2,500 years ago, Confucius counseled leaders to practice virtue because people willingly follow a ruler of good character governed by acts of compassion and generosity (a *pull*), making coercion (a *push*) unnecessary. Mencius, a follower of Confucian philosophy, believed that even though humans tend toward benevolence and wisdom, virtue needs to be cultivated.[6] In the case of the high school students, they didn't study and practice virtue because they had to. They did so because they wanted to.

PRIORITY MATTERS: VIRTUES FIRST AND PERFORMANCE FOLLOWS

In our professional lives, we need to do well in our jobs. After all, we need to make a living. While individual success is a good thing, supporting teammates and customers is a better thing. While a comfortable life is a pleasant thing, using our skills to lift up others even when it makes us uncomfortable is a better thing. Fortunately, success and significance are not mutually exclusive. We can do good and be good. Our individual priorities are not necessarily wrong or wacky. The challenge is getting the order right.

In our personal lives, self-care can include activities such as yoga, mindfulness, and a kale diet. Good health is something to be respected, though pursuing good health to an extreme can become a narcissistic project. It is important to take care of ourselves; yet we become disordered when self-care slips into self-absorption. A "selfie" culture flies in the face of research that makes it clear that what truly fortifies us are meaningful connections and other-oriented actions.

In business, the folly of blindly and exclusively focusing on logos and numbers applies even to economic value. If you add the value of tangible assets such as buildings, land, and merchandise, that would be less than 10 percent of the Standard and Poor's (S&P) Index's $28 trillion market value. Stated differently, intangible assets, such as customer relationships, and intellectual property, as well as human talent and culture, account for 90 percent of the index's total assets.[7] Stated personally, 90 percent of your 401(k) plan has no hard assets to back up your retirement savings! Risk associated with your 401(k) is mitigated if the stocks you own are managed by character-based leaders. Hard-to-measure factors such as leadership, teamwork, and culture have a huge influence on whether wealth is created or destroyed.

Even when we manage to pursue something meaningful, we will do so with a group of imperfect people who get cranky with one another and the people they serve. That doesn't mean that virtue is absent. It just means that practicing virtue is a high bar, an aspiration.

Consider the example of healthcare providers—physicians, nurses, and heath science professionals like respiratory therapists and physical therapists. All are evidence-based people using science in service of patients' well-being. So, imagine the disappointment and the pain of an ICU nurse or doctor who loses an unvaccinated patient to COVID-19. Understandably, preventable deaths and health risks to others make caregivers discouraged and perhaps even angry. Despite these emotions, caregivers serve in accordance with the virtues— compassion is at the center of their work, whether caring for those vaccinated or not.

Rising above negative emotions to serve competently and compassionately is at the center of practicing medicine excellently.

The better the doctor, nurse, or healthcare professional, the better the patient outcomes.

DEFAULT TO OUR TRAINING

Under pressure, we default to our training. This insight is understood by soldiers, athletes, and astronauts. In the military, volunteers sign up to be put in harm's way. In boot camp, a drill sergeant makes it clear that the military plans to take you up on your offer. Similarly, at NASA, astronauts volunteer to explore space in a life-threatening, zero-oxygen atmosphere. In both cases, people are trained to remain resilient in the face of adversity. Although professional sports are not about life-or-death experiences, the pressure to win is intense. So, athletes are trained to perform despite the pressure of screaming fans in stadiums and critical sports commentators who are ready to pounce on their mistakes.

There is much to learn from elite performers though even in their case, there is a glaringly missed opportunity. The better performer part is taken with great seriousness and rigor. The better human part is often not as well developed. Too often, organizations committed to elite performance revert to ethics defined as compliance to protect the organization's reputation. I reward you for what you do well, and I punish you for when you mess up—the carrots-and-sticks approach.

Expanding the definition of *ethics* to mean "practicing virtue" is an important and inexpensive investment in optimizing the organization's performance and protecting its reputation. Yet, when it comes to elite performance, the real head scratcher is this: character defined as virtue is a performance amplifier. *Virtue* means "excellence," it is malleable, and when practiced well, it strengthens performance. Plenty of organizations are unaware of this research, so it should come as no surprise that this would be true even for organizations committed to elite performance. That said, when organizations are silent about putting ancient wisdom into practice, they are leaving performance potential on the table.[8]

While elite performers are not necessarily better humans, they do differ from the rest of us in at least two ways. First, they volunteered to work in adverse conditions. Second, they have been trained to handle uncertainty. The rest of us didn't sign up for adversity or uncertainty. In fact, most of us would be quite pleased with stability. Our normal response to a crisis is that if we can just get to the other side of this mess, then we will be OK. We aim for stable and fulfilling careers, good health, happy families, and a comfortable life. All natural enough and quite understandable. But, when these goals come under threat, which they inevitably do, we often find ourselves fearful, anxious, and pessimistic.

And then there is the reality of life. Adversity finds us. Consider the pandemic. Who among us wanted it? But who among us could ignore it without the risk of peril to ourselves, loved ones, or society? Healthcare workers caring for COVID-19 infected patients were in a battle, just as if they were in the military—long, dangerous deployments. This was also true for frontline workers—truck drivers, people who worked in meatpacking plants, production workers, and other essential workers, all of whom put their personal health at risk to keep others safe. Most frontline workers didn't sign up for that kind of risk, and they didn't receive the kind of training offered to soldiers, astronauts, or athletes.

Most of us may lack physical and psychological tools to regulate our energy to manage fatigue. We may lack tools such as after action reviews to learn how to adapt rapidly to new circumstances. We may not have been aware of just how looking out for teammates strengthens performance and resilience. Lack of this training about character and about how to practice virtue in trying circumstances may well explain the high degrees of burnout we are presently seeing, as people are leaving these occupations that have been made stressful by external circumstances.[9] This is why we wrote this book.

As the pandemic has taught us, a world of certainty and safety, free from danger, risk, and harm, just isn't an option. Just as elite performers learn how to perform under pressure, so too do the rest of us need to be taught to move away from fear and toward hope.

Individually, we can learn to respond effectively to stress, pressure, and adversity.

Collectively, we can cocreate resilient cultures that are agile and adaptive. And once we learn to perform well under uncertain conditions, we are never the same. We become better humans and better performers.[10]

But how do we learn to excel in uncertain conditions? *Areté* in Greek refers to excellence of any kind, including moral virtue. An excellent person becomes highly effective by using courage, compassion, wisdom, and other virtues to achieve results when, not if, things go awry. By relying on *areté* as a principle for living, we can become what we practice. Aristotle said this. Neuroplasticity has proven this.

And how do we become an excellent team under uncertain conditions? Teammates best adapt to changing circumstances when they feel like they belong, matter, and make a difference. When people feel valued, they step up to add value.

The best predictor of team performance is how people treat each other, even more than who is on the team.[11] Psychological safety comes first. Motivation and accountability for results come second— and the order matters. Teams perform well when vulnerability, asking questions, and learning are practiced intentionally. Teams perform poorly when humiliation, blame, and ignoring each other distract people from performance.[12] The best teams don't surrender to disagreements and bickering; they presume goodwill. If goodwill can't be presumed, then they rethink their cause and their approach or whether they are on the right team.

How do cultures become resilient? Cultures are like gardens; they will grow whether or not leaders tend to them. Language, stories, and practice create resilient cultures. Leaders can tend a culture and enhance it by adopting the language of virtue and integrating its practice into daily operations. In addition, cultures are well tended through stories. Effective stories accept the facts of their situation. These narratives are realistically optimistic, inclusive, and resilient.

Here's a narrative (paraphrased) from the CEO of a healthcare organization that successfully combatted the scourge of COVID-19: "Yes, there is a pandemic. It poses an existential threat to all of us and to our world. But we can navigate it. We can rely on each other. We can exercise compassion, trust, and justice in the face of adversity. We will make mistakes because we are fallible and because the situation is changing very quickly, but we will adjust, be nimble, and we will communicate with each other. Acting in these ways, we will prevail." These are winning words that will harness the energy and high performance in the organization. Leaders play a key role in shaping stories to tend the garden of culture.

In contrast, ineffective stories deny the brutal facts or are full of toxic positivity: "The pandemic will just go away—don't worry." Such alternative narratives are exclusive, negative, and fragile. Leaders need to acknowledge people's worries about the future. At the same time, they need to be clear that there is no option to go backward.

KEY TAKEAWAYS

We all confront the question, "How will we face uncertainty?" We can't always control what happens to us, though we can always control how we respond and whether we respond with virtue. One of the ways that the Stoics cultivated virtue was to use the phrase *memento mori*, which means "Remember that you must die." Interestingly, we knew this before the pandemic. What the pandemic did was remind us of this reality.

However long we live, all life on Earth relies on resilience. We can more readily face an uncertain future when we face it together rather than alone. When we focus on others, we become less anxious, less fearful, and more able to handle uncertainty. Virtues such as trust and compassion release the grip of anxiety and fear.

In addition, choosing to practice virtue has the potential to reset our priorities to live more intrinsically and to deepen our relationships. Practicing virtue offers proven lessons in how to lead, how to work together as teams, and how to build cultures.

Thousands of years of research makes clear that virtues make better humans and better humans perform better.

Epilogue

It has been my experience that folks who
have no vices have very few virtues.[1]
—Abraham Lincoln

I f ever there were a time in our world, in our nation, in our organizations, in our communities, and in our families to call for more trust, compassion, courage, justice, wisdom, temperance, and hope, this is that time. If ever there were a time when we need less narcissism, distrust, cowardice, injustice, intolerance, and despair, this is that time. Here are four calls to action to cultivate better people and better performance.

1. RELATIONSHIPS ARE FIRST, RESULTS SECOND

Relationships are the best buffer against stress, the best predictor of resilience, and the best predictor of post-traumatic growth. When it comes to teamwork, how people treat each other is a better predictor of performance than who is on the team.[2] Teams that are accountable and motivated to perform help their members feel psychologically safe.[3]

Relationships also have an outsized impact on how well we live and how long we will live. An ongoing study that began in 1938 has followed the economically affluent (Harvard graduates) and economically impoverished (people born in Boston's inner city). The findings have shown that having close relationships better predicts who will live life long and well than having more money and fame, higher social class and IQ, or even better genes. Humans are built for connection, and our best relationships are defined by trust, compassion, courage, justice, wisdom, temperance, and hope.

2. WITHOUT A STRONG CULTURE, STRATEGY CANNOT SUCCEED

Our second call to action is to recommend that leaders adopt virtue as the common language of an excellent culture. Just as accounting is the language of business, virtue is the language of excellent individuals, teams, and cultures. Furthermore, without a common language of virtue, we are morally inarticulate.

The sport of culture building is not something at which most people excel since culture is more abstract than strategy. Yet who would dispute that culture is more powerful than strategy, process, or structure? Until you can define a culture, you can't affect it. And there is no better way to define an excellent culture than to use the language of virtue. Leaders need to continually relight the practice of virtue for people to feel like they belong, matter, and make a difference. This all might feel fluffy until we understand that belonging, mattering, and making a difference increases organizational engagement and performance by releasing people's discretionary effort.

3. PRACTICE DELIBERATELY

Our third call to action is to practice virtue with intentionality. We become what we practice. This simple statement was emphasized by Aristotle almost 2,500 years ago and is now reinforced by neuroscience. We understand that we can't get fit by working out for a week.

Physical fitness takes deliberate practice over time. So is the case for excellence of all kinds, whether it's competence or character.

It's through deliberate practice, for example, that a chief financial officer builds her financial acumen and her moral backbone to be a good steward of an organization's resources. Excellence becomes a habit through deliberate practice. Once we invest in the effort and become more skilled, what used to be effortful becomes automatic.

Where to Start

Clearly, habits don't change when we do too little. Habits also don't change when we try to do too much, too fast. Individuals and teams can start changing by creating micro-habits. You don't suddenly jump off the couch deciding to run a marathon. You might just start with a run around the block. Here are some habits that are the equivalent of a short run around the block.

Trust and Compassion
Ask your own kids or other kids you care about these three questions:

1. Were you brave?
2. Were you kind?
3. Did you learn from your mistakes?

In addition, take these steps:

- *Virtue moments:* Take five minutes at the start of a meeting to ask for examples of times when a teammate made your team stronger and your team's results better by practicing virtue.
- Compile a list of people who bring out the best in you, and put together a plan to spend more time with them.

Courage and Hope
When you are fearful, ask three questions:

1. What is the worst that could happen?
2. What is the likelihood that the worst will happen?
3. If the worst happened, could I handle it?

In addition, take these steps:

- Define virtues you practiced well to attack results that were not going well.
- Practice some form of gratitude.

Justice
Review your calendar for the week to determine whom you will be working with. Ask yourself how you want to show up and what people need from you.

Wisdom and Temperance
When someone is upset, can you remain curious for 120 seconds to learn what is upsetting them and how you can best respond?

Ask four questions weekly:

1. Did I reflect on the virtues?
2. In what acts of compassion was I involved?
3. In what acts of social justice was I involved?
4. Did I learn from my mistakes?

In addition, take these steps:

- Start your day asking, what good can I do today?
- End your day asking, what good did I do today?

Our tools shape how we see the world. The way we see the world can shape our tools. When we use mythos tools like those in the preceding list, we can enrich how we use logos tools. Select one mythos micro-habit that matters to you. Start now. Start over. Start again.

4. PULL, DON'T PUSH

Our fourth call to action is to pull, not push. In many organizations, the word *ethics* has come to mean "compliance with a set of rules" or "compliance with the law" rather than its ancient meaning of *areté*— "excellence" of any kind. Compliance defines the moral bottom or floor, whereas virtue defines us at our best. If you want compliance, then rely on sharper sticks and sweeter carrots. However, carrots and sticks will take us only so far. If you want commitment to excellence, then you have no choice but to rely on a pull strategy. Exceptional leadership and teams understand that a virtue-based culture is more powerful than a rule-based culture.

A *pull strategy* leverages strengths rather than focusing on weaknesses. Appreciative inquiry research makes it clear that a strengths-based approach changes behavior far better than a deficit-based approach. Focus on strengths by asking questions such as, "What do we look like at our best? What barriers restrain us from being our best?"

Cultures will grow whether or not leaders tend to them. The best cultures are tended by leaders who follow these four calls to action:

1. Relationships are first, results second.
2. Without a strong culture, strategy cannot succeed.
3. Practice deliberately.
4. Pull, don't push.

KEY TAKEAWAYS

The practice of virtue is so important that it is a must-have, not a nice-to-have. Good leaders, teams, cultures, and families can't flourish without virtue. Virtues are capabilities that have been shaped by evolution and that are universally seen as good across the globe. The practice of virtue is an imperative, calling for us to step more robustly into our capacity to affect our lives, the lives of others, and our performance. Virtue is a constant, practical force that enables us to bounce back from setbacks. However, we don't always think of virtue as the key ingredient enabling humans to endure hard times. It can be missed or be taken for granted, even when needed most.

We can learn to listen generously by asking more and talking less. We can learn to appreciate our strengths and the strengths in others. We can cultivate inclusion and engagement by increasing the number of people who belong, who matter, and who make a difference. When we do so, it becomes clear that the soft stuff is hard and that practicing the soft stuff delivers hard results.

We don't always practice virtue, of course, though virtues are available to us anytime we are ready to become better humans and better performers. Neuroplasticity is one of the great discoveries of our lifetime. We know that our brain keeps forming across our lifespan and that we can shape who we become based on where we put our attention and what we practice.

Yet knowing the value of virtue doesn't mean we will put our ideals into practice. For that matter, even the best among us won't practice virtue all the time. That certainly takes some of the pressure off. But virtue can sharpen our focus when things go sideways and can provide extra energy to take on tasks that are important and hard. At least we know that virtue is an option, and that is no small thing.

We end where we started, with Plutarch: "What we achieve inwardly will change [our] outer reality."[4] Better humans, better performance.

NOTES

Preface

1. U.S. Army Heritage and Education Center, "Who First Originated the Term VUCA (Volatility, Uncertainty, Complexity and Ambiguity)?," accessed March 19, 2022, https://usawc.libanswers.com/ faq/84869.
2. David Brooks, "The Moral Bucket List," *New York Times*, April 11, 2015, accessed March 1, 2022, https://www.nytimes.com/2015/04/12/opinion/sunday/david -brooks-the-moral-bucket-list.html.
3. Plutarch, "Plutarch Quotes," BrainyQuote, accessed February 12, 2022, https:// www.brainyquote.com/authors/plutarch-quotes.

Chapter 1

1. Anthony Ray Hinton, personal interviews with Peter Rea on January 21, 2019, in Cleveland, Ohio, and March 8, 2019, in Birmingham, Alabama.
2. Anthony Ray Hinton, *The Sun Does Shine: How I Found Life, Freedom, and Justice* (New York: St. Martin's Griffin, 2019).
3. Bryan Stevenson, "Just Mercy Quotes," Goodreads, https://www.goodreads.com /work/quotes/28323940-just-mercy-a-story-of-justice-and-redemption.
4. Jen Picciano, "Edwins Leadership and Restaurant Institute Sees Huge Enroll- ment Increase, Expands with Prison Tablets," *Cleveland 19 News*, June 11, 2021, accessed February 13, 2022, https://www.cleveland19.com/2021/06/12 /edwins-leadership-restaurant-institute-sees-huge-enrollment-increase -expands-with-prison-tablets/#:~:text=Their%20investment%20is%20 working.,it's%20at%20around%20 30%20percent.
5. Ibid.
6. Tony Cenicola, "52 Places for a Changed World," *New York Times*, accessed Feb- ruary 22, 2022, https://www.nytimes.com/interactive/2022/travel/52-places -travel-2022.html.
7. Hinton, personal interviews; and Hinton, *The Sun Does Shine*.
8. Edith Eger, personal interview with Peter Rea in February 2019, in San Diego.
9. Edith Eger, *The Choice: Embrace the Possible* (New York: Simon & Schuster, 2017).

10. Bret Stephens, "Can We Really Picture Auschwitz?," *New York Times*, April 4, 2021.

11. Eger, personal interview.

12. Ibid.

13. John Lewis, "Together, You Can Redeem the Soul of Our Nation," *New York Times*, July 30, 2020.

14. Omid Safi, "The Problematic Idea of Success," *On Being*, May 19, 2026, https://onbeing.org/blog/the-problematic-idea-of-success/.

15. Jigoro Kano, "Jigoro Kano Quotes," QuoteFancy, accessed February 12, 2022, https://quotefancy.com/kano-jigoro-quotes.

16. Reinhold Niebuhr, "Reinhold Niebuhr Quotes," QuoteFancy, accessed February 12, 2022, https://quotefancy.com/reinhold-niebuhr-quotes.

17. Richard Feynman, "Richard Feynman Quotes," BrainyQuote, accessed February 12, 2022, https://www.brainyquote.com/authors/richard-p-feynman-quotes.

18. Mike Tyson, "Mike Tyson Quotes," LibQuotes, accessed February 12, 2022, https://libquotes.com/mike-tyson.

19. Sean DeLaney, "The Distillation of Jonny Kim: What Got You There," WGYT, n.d., accessed February 12, 2022, https://whatgotyouthere.com/the-https-whatgotyouthere-com-the-distillation-of-nasa-astronaut-jonny-of-jonny-kim/.

20. David Sloan Wilson, "Evolving a City," *On Being with Krista Tippett*, podcast, October 17, 2013, accessed February 17, 2022, https://onbeing.org/programs/david-sloan-wilson-evolving-a-city/.

21. Coleman Ruiz and Preston Cline, "After Action Reviews," Mission Critical Team Institute, podcast, October 1, 2018, accessed February 12, 2022, https://missioncti.com/wp-content/ uploads/2020/05/AAR-v.1.-10-02-2018.pdf.

22. Robert Yerkes and John Dodson, "The Relation of Strength of Stimulus to Rapidity of Habit Formation," *Journal of Comparative Neurology and Psychology*, vol. 18, no. 5 (1908), pp. 459–482.

23. Sebastian Junger, "Sebastian Junger Quotes," QuoteFancy, accessed February 12, 2022, https://quotefancy.com/sebastian-junger-quotes.

24. Dorothy Day, "Dorothy Day Quotes," Goodreads, https://www.goodreads.com/author/quotes/119043.Dorothy_Day?page=3.

25. Ceri Evans, *Perform Under Pressure* (New York: HarperCollins, 2019).

26. Yerkes and Dodson, "The Relation of Strength of Stimulus to Rapidity of Habit Formation."

27. Andy Walshe, CEO, personal interview with Peter Rea, Liminal Collective, 2019.

Chapter 2

1. "The Grounding Virtues of The On Being Project," *The On Being Project*, accessed February 13, 2022, https://onbeing.org/social-healing-at-on-being/the-six-grounding-virtues-of-the-on-being-project/.

2. Nicholas A. Christakis, *Blueprint: The Evolutionary Origins of a Good Society* (New York: Little, Brown Spark, 2020).

3. David Sloan Wilson, "Evolving a City," *On Being with Krista Tippett*, podcast, October 17, 2013, accessed February 17, 2022, https://onbeing.org/programs/david-sloan-wilson-evolving-a-city/.

4. William James, "Top William James Quotes," QuoteFancy, accessed February 12, 2022, https://quotefancy.com/william-james-quotes.

5. Christopher Peterson and Martin Seligman, *Character Strengths and Virtues: A Handbook and Classification*, vol. 1 (New York: Oxford University Press, 2004).

6. David S. Moore, *The Developing Genome: An Introduction to Behavioral Epigenetics* (New York: Oxford University Press, 2017).

7. Ernest Hemingway, "Ernest Hemingway Quotes," BrainyQuote, accessed February 12, 2022, https://www.brainyquote.com/authors/ernest-hemingway-quotes.

8. Alex Edmans, *The Business Case for a High Trust Culture*, Great Place to Work Report, https://www.greatplacetowork.ca/images/reports/Business_Case_for_High_Trust_Culture.pdf.

9. Leslie McKenzie, personal interview with Peter Rea on January 28, 2022.

10. Adapted from a remote course taught by Tal Ben-Shahar, Harvard Whole Mind Institute, 2013.

11. Hippocrates, "Hippocrates Quotes," BrainyQuote, accessed February 13, 2022, https://www.brainyquote.com/authors/hippocrates-quotes.

12. Unpublished research conducted by Parker Hannifin in 2019.

13. Winston Churchill, "Winston Churchill Quotes," BrainyQuote, accessed February 13, 2022, https://www.brainyquote.com/authors/winston-churchill-quotes.

14. Ernest Hemingway, "Ernest Hemingway Quotes."

15. Desmond Tutu, "Desmond Tuto Quotes," BrainyQuote, accessed February 13, 2022, https://www.brainyquote.com/authors/desmond-tutu-quotes.

16. Epictetus, "Epictetus Quotes," Goodreads, accessed February 13, 2022, https://www.goodreads.com/author/quotes/13852.Epictetus.

17. Mahatma Gandhi, "Mahatma Gandhi Quotes," BrainyQuote, accessed February 13, 2022, https://www.brainyquote.com/authors/mahatma-gandhi-quotes.

18. Epictetus, "Epictetus Quotes."

19. Roark Denver, personal interview with Peter Rea in Phoenix, Arizona, on February 20, 2015.

20. Martin Luther King, Jr., "Martin Luther King, Jr., Quotes," BrainyQuote, accessed February 13, 2022, https://www.brainyquote.com/authors/martin-luther-king-jr-quotes.

21. Maya Angelou, *Maya Angelou: The Complete Poetry* (New York: Random House, 2015).

22. William F. Lynch, *Images of Hope: Imagination as Healer of the Hopeless* (Notre Dame, IN: University of Notre Dame Press, 1974).

23. Viktor E. Frankl, *Man's Search for Meaning* (New York: Simon & Schuster, 1985).

Chapter 3

1. Ryan Lilly, "Ryan Lilly Quotes," Goodreads, https://www.goodreads.com/quotes/5101112-growing-a-culture-requires-a-good-storyteller-changing-a-culture.

2. Walter Isaacson, *The Code Breaker: Jennifer Doudna, Gene Editing, and the Future of the Human Race* (New York: Simon & Schuster, 2021).

3. Kurt Lewin, *Resolving Social Conflicts: Selected Papers on Group Dynamics [1935 to 1946]* (New York: Harper & Row, 1948).

4. David Brooks, "America Is Having a Moral Convulsion," *Atlantic*, October 5, 2020, accessed February 13, 2022, https://www.theatlantic.com/ideas/archive/2020/10/collapsing-levels-trust-are-devastating-america/616581/.

5. Mary Crossan, Daina Mazutis, Mark Reno, and Peter Rea, "Leadership Virtues and Character: A Perspective in Practice." In Alejo Sison, Gregory Beabout, and Ignacio Ferrero, eds., *Handbook of Virtue Ethics in Business and Management* (New York: Springer, 2017), pp. 509–519.

Chapter 4

1. Bruce Weinstein, *The Good Ones: Ten Crucial Qualities of High-Character Employees* (Novato, CA: New World Library, 2019).
2. Jim Collins, "Good to Great," *Fast Company*, September 30, 2001, accessed March 19, 2022, https://www.fastcompany.com/43811/good-great.
3. William Harms, "Heckman's Research Shows Non-cognitive Skills Promote Achievement," *University of Chicago Chronicle*, vol. 23, no. 7, January 8, 2004, http://chronicle.uchicago.edu/040108/heckman.shtml.
4. Adapted from Adam Grant, *Give and Take: A Revolutionary Approach to Success* (New York: Penguin, 2013).
5. Ibid.
6. Marcus Tullius Cicero, "Marcus Tullius Cicero Quotes," BrainyQuote, accessed February 13, https://www.brainyquote.com/authors/marcus-tullius-cicero-quotes.
7. David Sturt and Todd Nordstrum, "10 Shocking Workplace Stats You Need to Know," *Forbes*, March 8, 2018, accessed February 13, 2022, https://www.forbes.com/sites/davidsturt/2018/03/08/10-shocking-workplace-stats-you-need-to-know/?sh=377009af3afe.
8. Robert Emmons, *Thanks: How Practicing Gratitude Can Make You Happier* (Boston: Houghton Mifflin, 2007).
9. Carol Dweck, "What Having a 'Growth Mindset' Actually Means," *Harvard Business Review*, January 13, 2016, pp. 213–226, https://hbr.org/2016/01/what-having-a-growth-mindset-actually-means.
10. Ibid.
11. Carol Dweck, "The Power of Believing That You Can Improve," TED, November 2014, accessed February 13, 2022, https://www.ted.com/talks/carol_dweck_the_power_of_believing_that_you_can_improve?language=en.
12. Angela Duckworth, *Grit: The Power of Passion and Perseverance* (New York: Scribner, 2018).
13. Giraffe Heroes Project, https://www.giraffe.org/.

Chapter 5

1. Charles Darwin, *On the Origin of Species: A Facsimile of the First Edition* (Cambridge: Harvard University Press, 1964).
2. Jody H. Gittell, *High Performance Healthcare: Using the Power of Relationships to Achieve Quality, Efficiency and Resilience* (New York: McGraw Hill Professional, 2009).
3. Ibid.
4. Terry P. Clemmer, Vicki J. Spuhler, Donald M. Berwick, and Thomas W. Nolan, "Cooperation: The foundation of improvement," *Annals of Internal Medicine*, vol. 128, no. 12, June 15, 1998, pp. 1004–1009, doi:10.7326/0003-4819-128-12_part_1-199806150-00008.
5. Peter Cappelli and Anna Tavis, "The Performance Management Revolution," *Harvard Business Review*, vol. 94, no. 10, October 2016, pp. 58–67; and Marcus Buckingham and Ashley Goodall, "Reinventing Performance Management," *Harvard Business Review*, vol. 93, no. 4, April 2015, pp. 40–50.
6. Cappelli and Tavis, "The Performance Management Revolution"; and Buckingham and Goodall, "Reinventing Performance Management."
7. Marcus Buckingham and Ashley Goodall, "The Feedback Fallacy," *Harvard Business Review*, vol. 97, no. 2, March 2019, pp. 92–101.
8. Charles Duhigg, *Smarter, Faster, Better* (New York: Penguin Press, 2016), p. 61.

9. Carol Dweck, "What Having a 'Growth Mindset' Actually Means," *Harvard Business Review*, January 13, 2016, pp. 213–226.

10. Coleman Ruiz, Illumina, personal interview with Peter Rea, December 2019.

11. Adapted from Liminal Collective, *Transformative Teams: User Manual*, 2019, which was inspired by David Politis, CEO of BetterCloud, on "The CEO User Manual," https://www.youtube.com/watch?v=F9OBNiEuXMk.

12. Amy Edmondson, "Psychological Safety and Learning Behavior in Work Teams," *Administrative Science Quarterly*, vol. 44, no. 2, 1999, pp. 350–383.

13. Amy Edmondson and Per Hugander, "Four Steps to Boost Psychological Safety at Your Workplace," *Harvard Business Review*, June 22, 2021, accessed February 13, 2022, https://hbr.org/2021/06/4-steps-to-boost-psychological-safety-at-your-workplace.

14. Thomas L. Friedman, "It's a 401(k) World," *New York Times*, April 30, 2013, p. A25.

Chapter 6

1. Tim Ferriss, "How to Develop Mental Toughness: Lessons from 8 Titans," *The Tim Ferriss Show* blog, 2016, accessed February 13, 2022, https://tim.blog/2016/12/14/mental-toughness/.

2. Walter Cannon, *The Wisdom of the Body* (New York: Norton, 1967; originally copyrighted 1932 by Walter Cannon).

3. Lisa F. Barrett, *Seven and a Half Lessons About the Brain* (Boston: Houghton Mifflin, 2020).

4. Jay Belsky, Avshalom Caspi, Terrie E. Moffitt, and Richie Poulton R, *The Origins of You: How Childhood Shapes Later Life* (Cambridge: Harvard University Press, 2020).

5. Bessel van der Kolk, *The Body Keeps the Score: Brain, Mind, and Body in the Healing of Trauma* (New York: Penguin Books, 2015).

6. Barrett, *Seven and a Half Lessons About the Brain.*

7. James Doty, "The Magic Shop of the Brain," *On Being with Krista Tippett*, podcast, November 8, 2018, accessed February 13, 2022, https://onbeing.org/programs/james-doty-the-magic-shop-of-the-brain-nov2018.

8. Ibid.

9. Robert Waldinger, "What Makes a Good Life? Lessons from the Longest Study on Happiness," TED, November 2015, accessed February 13, 2022, https://www.ted.com/talks/robert_waldinger_what_makes_a_ good_life_lessons_from_the_longest_study_on_happiness/ transcript?language=en.

10. Doty, *The Magic Shop of the Brain.*

11. James B. Stockdale, *Thoughts of a Philosophical Fighter Pilot* (Stanford, CA: Hoover Institution Press, 1995).

12. Brent Gleeson, *Embrace the Suck: The Navy SEAL Way to an Extraordinary Life* (New York: Hachette, 2020).

13. Michel de Montaigne, "Michel de Montaigne Quotes," BrainyQuote, accessed July 22, 2022, https://www.brainyquote.com/quotes/michel_de_montaigne_108601.

14. Don Joseph Goewey, "85 Percent of What We Worry About Never Happens," *Huffington Post*, August 25, 2015, accessed February 13, 2022, https://www.huffpost.com/entry/85-of-what-we-worry-about_b_8028368.

15. Christine Runyan, "What's Happening in Our Nervous Systems?," *On Being with Krista Tippett*, podcast, March 18, 2021, accessed February 13, 2022, https://onbeing.org/programs/christine-runyan-whats-happening-in-our-nervous-systems/.

16. Winston Churchill, "Winston Churchill Quotes," BrainyQuote, accessed February 13, 2022, https://www.brainyquote.com/authors/winston-churchill-quotes.

17. Kelly McGonigal, "How to Make Stress Your Friend," TED, June 2013, accessed February 13, 2022. https://www.ted.com/talks/kelly_mcgonigal_how_to_make _stress_your_friend?language=en.

18. American Psychiatric Association, "What Is Posttraumatic Stress Disorder (PTSD)?," updated August 2020, accessed February 13, 2022, https://www.psychiatry .org/patients-families/ptsd/what-is-ptsd.

19. Steven M. Southwick and Dennis S. Charney, *Resilience: The Science of Mastering Life's Greatest Challenges* (Cambridge, UK: Cambridge University Press, 2018).

20. Linda A. King, Daniel W. King, John Fairbank, Terence M. Keane, and Gary Adams, "Resilience Recovery Factors in Post-traumatic Stress Disorder Among Female and Male Vietnam Veterans: Hardiness, Postwar Social Support, and Additional Stressful Life Events," *Journal of Personality and Social Psychology*, vol. 74, no. 2, March 1998, pp. 420–434, doi:10.1037//0022-3514.74.2.420.

21. Daniela Montalto as quoted in "Understanding the Difference Between a Difficult Moment & a Trauma," NYU Langone Health, accessed February 13, 2022, https://nyulangone.org/news/understanding-difference-between-difficult -moment-trauma.

22. George A. Bonanno, *The End of Trauma: How the New Science of Resilience is Changing How We Understand PTSD* (New York: Basic Books, 2021).

23. Lorna Collier, "Growth After Trauma," *Monitor on Psychology.* vol. 47, no. 10, November 2016, pp. 48–52, https://www.apa.org/monitor/2016/11/growth -trauma#:~:text=Post%2Dtraumatic%20growth%20(PTG),often%20see%20 positive%20growth%20afterward.

24. Friedrich Nietzsche, "Friedrich Nietzsche Quotes," BrainyQuote, accessed February 2022, https://www.brainyquote.com/authors/friedrich-nietzsche-quotes.

25. Stephen Joseph, *What Doesn't Kill Us Makes Us Stronger: The New Psychology of Posttraumatic Growth* (New York: Basic Books, 2011).

26. Van der Kolk, *The Body Keeps the Score.*

27. Viktor E. Frankl, *Man's Search for Meaning* (New York: Simon & Schuster, 1985).

28. Gregory Boyle, *The Whole Language: The Power of Extravagant Tenderness* (New York: Avid Reader Press, 2021).

29. Rebecca Solnit, *A Paradise Built in Hell: The Extraordinary Communities That Arise in Disaster* (New York: Penguin, 2010).

30. Ibid.

31. Salvatore R. Maddi and Deborah M. Khoshaba, *Resilience at Work: How to Succeed No Matter What Life Throws at You* (New York: AMACOM, 2005).

32. Ibid.

33. Marcus Buckingham, "What Really Makes Us Resilient?," *Harvard Business Review*, September 29, 2020, accessed February 13, 2022, https://hbr.org/2020/09 /what-really-makes-us-resilient.

34. Lisa Zigarmi and Davia Larson, "An Exercise to Help Your Team Overcome the Trauma of the Pandemic," *Harvard Business Review*, September 1, 2020.

35. Brendan Caldwell, Baldwin Wallace University conductor, personal interview with Peter Rea on January 2020.

36. Winston Churchill, "Winston Churchill Quotes."

37. "7 Profound Quotes from Nelson Mandela," *All Women's Talk*, accessed March 19, 2022, https://inspiration.allwomenstalk.com/profound-quotes-from-nelson- mandela/.

38. Billie Jean King, *Pressure Is a Privilege: Lessons I've Learned from Life and the Battle of the Sexes* (New York: LifeTime Media, 2009).

39. Ceri Evans, personal interview with Peter Rea on September 20, 2020.

40. Socrates, "Socrates Quotes," QuoteFancy, accessed February 15, 2022, https://quotefancy.com/socrates-quotes.
41. Thomas Aquinas, "Thomas Aquinas Quotes," QuoteFancy, accessed February 15, 2022, https://quotefancy.com/thomas-aquinas-quotes.
42. T. S. Eliot, "T. S. Eliot Quotes," QuoteFancy, accessed February 15, 2022, https://quotefancy.com/t-s-eliot-quotes.
43. Yasha Wallin, "'What Good Shall I Do This Day?' Asked Benjamin Franklin Every Single Morning," Good, March 6, 2013, accessed March 19, 2022, https://www.good.is/articles/what-good-shall-i-do-this-day-asked-benjamin-franklin-every-singlemorning.
44. Lindsey Monger, "Hunting the Good Stuff During Resiliency Training," January 5, 2015, https://www.army.mil/article/140671/hunting_the_good_stuff_during_resiliency_training.
45. Ira Byock, The Four Things That Matter Most (New York: Atria Books, 2014), p. 7.

Chapter 7
1. Douglas Conant, "Douglas Conant Quotes," QuoteFancy, accessed March 19, 2022, https://quotefancy.com/douglas-conant-quotes.
2. Tomas Chamorro-Premuzic, "Does Money Really Affect Motivation? A Review of the Research," Harvard Business Review, April 10, 2013, accessed February 15, 2022, https://hbr.org/2013/04/does-money-really-affect-motiv#:~:text=When%20rewards%20are%20tangible%20andlike%20money%20%E2%80%94%20actually%20increase%20motivation.
3. Timothy A. Judge, Ronald F. Piccolo, Nathan P. Podsakoff, John C. Shaw, and Bruce L. Rich, "The Relationship Between Pay and Job Satisfaction: A Meta-Analysis of the Literature," Journal of Vocational Behavior, vol. 77, no. 2, October 2010, pp. 157–167.
4. Annamarie Mann, "Why We Need Best Friends at Work," Gallup at Work blog, updated January 15, 2018, accessed February 18, 2022, https://www.gallup.com/workplace/236213/why-need-best-friends-work.aspx#:~:text=Our%20research%20has%20repeatedly%20shown,who%20say%20otherwise%20(29%25).
5. Michael Housman and Dylan Minor, Toxic Workers, working paper 16-057, Harvard Business School, November 2015, accessed February 15, 2022, https://www.hbs.edu/ris/Publication%20Files/16-057_d45c0b4f-fa19-49de-8f1b-4b12fe054fea.pdf.
6. Gallup, "What Is Employee Engagement and How Do You Improve It?," Gallup Workplace, blog, accessed March 19, 2022, https://www.gallup.com/workplace/285674/improve-employee-engagement-workplace.aspx.
7. Bill Aulet, personal interview with Peter Rea, Entrepreneurship and Innovation at MIT, Cambridge, December 2015.
8. Gallup, "What Is Employee Engagement and How Do You Improve It?"
9. BlessingWhite, Employee Engagement Report 2006, BlessingWhite, 2006; and Towers Perrin, "Working Today: Understanding What Drives Employee Engagement," The 2003 Towers Perrin Talent Report, Towers Perrin, 2003.
10. David Sturt and Todd Nordstrom, "10 Shocking Workplace Stats You Need to Know," Forbes, March 8, 2018, accessed February 13, 2022, https://www.forbes.com/sites/davidsturt/2018/03/08/10-shocking-workplace-stats-you-need-toknow/?sh=377009af3afe.
11. Susan Sorenson, "How Employees' Strengths Make Your Company Stronger," Business Journal, Gallup, February, 20, 2014, https://news.gallup.com/businessjournal/167462/employees-strengths-company-stronger.aspx.

12. Archana Ramesh, "Why Belonging Is Important at Work: Employee Engagement and Diversity," *Glint* blog, 2020, accessed February 18, 2022, https://www.glint inc.com/blog/why-belonging-is-important-at-work-employee-engagement-and -diversity/.

13. David DeSteno, *Emotional Success: The Power of Gratitude, Compassion, and Pride* (Boston: Houghton Mifflin Harcourt, 2018).

14. Nicole F. Roberts, "Emotional & Physical Pain Are Almost the Same—to Your Brain," *Forbes*, February 14, 2020, accessed February 17, 2022, https://www.forbes .com/sites/nicolefisher/2020/02/14/emotional--physical-pain-are-almost-the -sameto-your-brain/?sh=c422f8b46c1d.

15. Brian J. Brim, "Strengths-Based Leadership: The 4 Things Followers Need," *Gallup: Clifton Strengths*, October 9, 2015, accessed February 17, 2022, https://www.gallup .com/cliftonstrengths/en/251003/strengthsbased-leadership-things-followers -need.aspx.

16. Albert Einstein, "Albert Einstein Quotes," BrainyQuote, accessed February 17, 2022, https://www.brainyquote.com/authors/albert-einstein-quotes.

17. Stephen Dubner, "How to Launch a Behavior-Change Revolution," *Freakonomics Radio*, podcast, October 25, 2017, accessed February 17, 2022, https://freakonomics .com/podcast/how-to-launch-a-behavior-change-revolution.

18. Peter F. Drucker, "Peter F. Drucker Quotes," QuoteFancy, accessed February 17, 2022, https://quotefancy.com/peter-f-drucker-quotes.

19. Brian Brim and Jim Asplund, "Driving Engagement by Focusing on Strengths," *Business Journal*, Gallup, November 12, 2009, accessed February 18, 2022. https://news.gallup.com/businessjournal/124214/driving-engagement-focusing -strengths.aspx.

20. Edward O. Wilson, "Edward O. Wilson Quotes," QuoteFancy, accessed February 18, 2022, https://quotefancy.com/e-o-wilson-quotes

21. Lisa Rotenstein, Matthew Torre, Marco Ramos, et al., "Prevalence of Burnout Among Physicians: A Systematic Review," *JAMA*, vol. 320, no. 11, September 18, 2018, pp. 1131–1150, doi:10.1001/jama.2018.12777.

22. Robert A. Karasek, Jr., "Job Demands, Job Decision Latitude, and Mental Strain: Implications for Job Redesign," *Administrative Science Quarterly*, vol. 24, no. 2, June 1979, pp. 285–308.

23. Adam Grant, "Burnout Isn't Just in Your Head. It's in Your Circumstances," *New York Times*, March 19, 2020, accessed February 18, 2022, https://www.nytimes .com/2020/03/19/smarter-living/coronavirus-emotional-support.html.

24. Patti Neighmond, "People Who Feel They Have a Purpose in Life Live Longer," *Shots: Health News from NPR*, July 28, 2014, accessed February 18, 2022, https:// www.npr.org/sections/healthshots/2014/07/28/334447274/people-who-feel -they-have-a-purpose-in-life-live-longer.

25. Dominic O. Vachon, *The New Science of Compassion and Its Practical Application to Medical Education and Clinical Practice*, University of Notre Dame, July 2020.

26. David Zax, "Want to Be Happier at Work? Learn How from These 'Job Crafters,'" *Fast Company*, June 3, 2013, accessed March 19, 2022, https://www.fastcompany .com/3011081/want-to-be-happier-at-work-learn-how-from-these-job-crafters.

Chapter 8
1. "Intelligence Plus Character: The Purpose of Education," Character Lab, updated June 16, 2019, accessed March 20, 2022, https://characterlab.org/tips-of-the -week/intelligence-plus-character/.

2. Carl Bowman, Jeffrey Dill, James Hunter, and Megan Juelfs-Swanson, *Culture of American Families Executive Report*, Institute for Advanced Studies in Culture, December 2012, accessed February 18, 2022, https://iasculture.org/research/publications/culture-american-families-executive-report; and Marie-Anne Suizzo, "Parents' Goals and Values for Children: Dimensions of Independence and Interdependence Across Four U.S. Ethnic Groups," *Journal of Cross-Cultural Psychology*, vol. 38, no. 4, July 2007, pp. 506–530.

3. *Making Caring Common Executive Summary*, Harvard Graduate School of Education, accessed March 20, 2022, https://static1.squarespace.com/static/5b7c56e255b02c683659fe43/t/5bae774424a694b5feb2b05f/1538160453604/report-children-raise.pdf.

4. Adam Grant and Allison Sweet Grant, "Stop Trying to Raise Successful Kids, and Start Raising Kind Ones," *Atlantic*, December 2019, accessed February 17, 2022, https://www.theatlantic.com/magazine/archive/2019/12/stop-trying-to-raise-successful-kids/600751.

5. Madeline Levine, *Ready or Not: Preparing Our Kids to Thrive in an Uncertain and Rapidly Changing World* (New York: HarperCollins, 2021).

6. Carol Dweck, *Self-Theories: Their Role in Motivation, Personality, and Development* (London and New York: Routledge, 2016).

7. *8 Things to Remember About Child Development*, Center on the Developing Child at Harvard University, updated 2016, accessed February 18, 2022, https://developingchild.harvard.edu/resources/8-things-remember-child-development/.

8. Lisa F. Barrett, *Seven and a Half Lessons About the Brain* (Boston: Houghton Mifflin, 2020).

9. Paul Tough, *How Children Succeed: Grit, Curiosity, and the Hidden Power of Character* (Boston: Houghton Mifflin Harcourt, 2012).

10. John W. Bailie, *A Science of Human Dignity: Belonging Voice and Agency as Universal Human Need*, presented at the International Institute for Restorative Practices (IIRP) Conference, October 24–26, 2018, Detroit, MI, accessed February 18, 2022, https://www.iirp.edu/images/pdf/IIRP_Paper_Series_2019-03-27_V07_D.pdf.

11. Danielle Sered, *Accounting for Violence: How to Increase Safety and Break Our Failed Reliance on Mass Incarceration* (New York: Vera Institute of Justice, 2017), https://d3n8a8pro7vhmx.cloudfront.net/commonjustice/pages/82/attachments/original/1506608259/accounting-for-violence.pdf?1506608259.

12. Philip Brown and John W. Bailie, "Restorative Justice and Restorative Practices." In Philip Brown, ed., *Student Discipline: A Prosocial Perspective*. (Lanham, MD: Rowman & Littlefield, 2016), pp. 44–52.

13. Adapted from Bob Costello, Joshua Wachtel, and Ted Wachtel, *The Restorative Practices Handbook: For Teachers, Disciplinarians and Administrators*, 2d ed. (Bethlehem, PA: International Institute for Restorative Practices, 2019).

14. Ibid.

15. Ibid.

16. Adapted from Francesca Trianni and Carlos H. Martinelli, "Bryan Stevenson": Believe Things You Haven't Seen," *Time*, accessed March 20, 2022, https://time.com/collection-post/3928285/bryan-stevenson-interview-time-100.

Chapter 9

1. Peter F. Drucker, "Peter F. Drucker Quotes," QuoteFancy, accessed February 17, 2022, https://quotefancy.com/peter-f-drucker-quotes.

2. Charles Darwin, *On the Origin of Species: A Facsimile of the First Edition* (Cambridge: Harvard University Press, 1964).
3. Dacher Keltner, "The Compassionate Species," *Greater Good Magazine*, July 31, 2012, accessed February 18, 2022, https://greatergood.berkeley.edu/article/item/the_compassionate_species.
4. Paul Zak, *Trust Factor: The Science of Creating High-Performance Companies* (New York: AMACOM, 2017).
5. Peter F. Drucker, "Peter F. Drucker Quotes."
6. Robert D. Hare, *Without Conscience: The Disturbing World of the Psychopaths Among Us* (New York: Guilford Press, 1999).
7. Tomas Chamorro-Premuzic, "Why Bad Guys Win at Work," *Harvard Business Review*, November 2, 2015, accessed February 18, 2022, https://hbr. org/2015/11/why-bad-guys-win-at-work.
8. Edward O. Wilson, "E. O. Wilson Quotes," QuoteFancy, accessed February 18, 2022, https://quotefancy.com/e-o-wilson-quotes.
9. Jeff Dyer, Hal Gregersen, and Clayton Christensen, *The Innovator's DNA* (Boston: Harvard Business Review Press, 2011).
10. Amy Azzarito, "From Babylon to Brooklyn: The History of Rooftop Gardens," *Food52*, blog, March 2, 2015, https://food52.com/blog/12407-from-babylon-to-brooklyn-the-history-of-rooftop-gardens.
11. BBC, "Case Study of Sustainable Transport: The BRT in Curitiba, Brazil," Sustainable Living, *BBC Bite Size*, https://www.bbc.co.uk/bitesize/guides/zqvxdmn/revision/5.
12. Blake Morgan, "20 Fresh Examples of Customer Experience Innovation," *Forbes*, October 21, 2019, accessed February 22, 2022, https://www.forbes.com/sites/blakemorgan/2019/10/21/20-fresh-examples-of-customer-experience-innovation/?sh=5ad3bf427c41.
13. Bill Murphy, "A Stanford Economist Who Studies Remote Work Says Half of All Workers Will Make This Big Change in 2022," *Inc.*, January 2022, https://www.inc.com/bill-murphy-jr/a-stanford-economist-whostudiesremote-work-says-half-of-allworkers-will-make-thisbigchange-in2022.html.
14. Peter Cappelli, "What's the Future of the Office?," *Knowledge at Wharton*, September 21, 2021, https://knowledge.wharton.upenn.edu/article/whats-the-future-of-the-office/.
15. Dyer, Gregersen, and Christensen, *The Innovator's DNA*.
16. Ibid.
17. Adam Smith, *The Wealth of Nations*, Books 1–3 (Lexington, KY: Seven Treasures Publications, 2009).
18. Milton Friedman, "A Friedman Doctrine: The Social Responsibility of Business," *New York Times*, September 13, 1970.
19. Maggie Schear, "You Read BlackRock's Letter on Purpose: Now What Should You Do?," *BrightHouse*, blog, 2018, accessed February 22, 2022, https://www.thinkbrighthouse.com/2018/03/you-read-blackrocks-letter-on-purpose-now-what-should-you-do/#:~:text=It%20will%20ultimately%20lose%20the,necessary%20for%20long%2Dterm%20growth.
20. Cappelli, "What's the Future of the Office?"
21. Adam Smith, *The Theory of Moral Sentiments to which is Added a Dissertation on the Origin of Languages* (London: George Bell and Sons, 1767).
22. Royal Household, "The Royal Family Thank the National Health Service," The Royal Household, updated July 5, 2021, accessed March 20, 2022, https://www.royal.uk/royal-family-thank-national-health-service.

23. Brian Donley, CEO, Cleveland Clinic London, Cleveland Learning Alliance, March 3, 2022.

24. Cleveland Leadership Alliance, May 19, 2021.

25. Information conveyed to Peter Rea during a personal tour of Intuit in Mountain View, California, on March 2015.

26. Charles Kiefer, personal interview with Peter Rea in March 2015.

27. David Kelley, founder of IDEO, "Why You Talk Less and Do More," *Design Thinking*, IDEO blog, https://designthinking.ideo.com/blog/why-you-should-talk-less -and-do-more.

28. Marc Emmer, "95 Percent of New Products Fail. Here Are 6 Steps to Make Sure Yours Don't," *Inc.*, accessed March 20, 2022, https://www.inc.com/marc-emmer/95-percent-of-new-products-fail-here-are-6-steps-to-make-sure-yours -dont.html#:~:text=According%20to%20Harvard%20Business%20School,is%20 70%20to%2080%20percent.

Chapter 10

1. Maya Angelou, *Maya Angelou: The Complete Poetry* (New York: Random House, 2015).

2. Voltaire (François-Marie Arouet), *Candide* [Optimism] (London: Penguin, 2013).

3. Christo Brand and Vusumzi McGongo, personal interview with Peter Rea at Robben Island, Cape Town, South Africa, on July 18, 2016.

4. Gordon W. Allport, Kenneth Clark, and Thomas Pettigrew, *The Nature of Human Prejudice* (Reading, MA: Addison-Wesley, 1979).

5. United States Census Bureau, "Quick Facts: United States," accessed February 22, 2022, https://www.census.gov/quickfacts/fact/table/US/PST045221.

6. McKinsey & Company, *Focusing on What Works for Workplace Diversity*, April 2017, accessed February 22, 2022, https://www.mckinsey.com/~/media/McKinsey /Featured%20Insights/Women%20matter/Focusing%20on%20what%20 works%20for%20workplace%20diversity/Focusing-on-what-works-for-work place-diversity.pdf.

7. Mahatma Gandhi, "Mahatma Gandhi Quotes," QuoteFancy, accessed February 22, 2022, https://quotefancy.com/mahatma-gandhi-quotes.

8. Martin Luther King, Jr., Remaining Awake Through a Great Revolution, speech presented at the National Cathedral, March 31, 1968, Washington, DC.

9. Stephen Scott and Amy Edmondson, "Unlocking Diversity's Promise: Psychological Safety, Trust and Inclusion," Reuters Financial Regulatory Forum, April 13, 2021, accessed February 22, 2022, https://www.reuters.com/article/bc-finreg -unlocking-diversity-inclusion/unlocking-diversitys-promise-psychological -safety-trust-and-inclusion-idUSKBN2C01N2.

10. McKinsey & Company, *Focusing on What Works for Workplace Diversity*.

11. Julie Coffman, Elyse Rosenbloom, Andrea D'Arcy, and Laura Thompson Love, *10 Proven Actions to Advance: Diversity, Equity, and Inclusion*, Grads of Life and Bain & Company, https://gradsoflife.org/wp-content/uploads/2021/08/BAIN_ GRADS_OF_LIFE_REPORT_10_proven_actions_to_advance_DEI.pdf.

12. Ibid.

13. Scott and Edmondson, "Unlocking Diversity's Promise."

14. Alexandra Kalev and Frank Dobbin, "Companies Need to Think Bigger Than Diversity Training," *Harvard Business Review*, October 20, 2020, accessed February 22, 2022, https://hbr.org/2020/10/companies-need-to-think-bigger-than-diversity -training.

15. Howard Thurman, *Jesus and the Disinherited* (Boston: Beacon Press, 2022).

16. Thomas F. Pettigrew and Linda R. Tropp, "Does Intergroup Contact Reduce Prejudice? Recent Meta-Analytic Findings." In Stuart Oskamp, ed., *Reducing Prejudice and Discrimination* (New York: Psychology Press, 2013), pp. 103–124.
17. Abraham Joshua Heschel, "Abraham Joshua Heschel Quotes," BrainyQuote, accessed March 20, 2022, https://www.brainyquote.com/authors/abraham-joshua -heschel-quotes.
18. Allport, Clark, and Pettigrew, *The Nature of Human Prejudice.*
19. Kim Elsesser, "Rethinking Diversity and Inclusion by Focusing on Employees' Needs," *Forbes,* May 26, 2021, accessed February 22, 2022, https://www.forbes .com/sites/kimelsesser/2021/05/26/rethinking-diversity-and-inclusion-by -focusing-on-employees-needs/?sh=6e0c3fed3a1d.
20. Nicholas A. Christakis, *Blueprint: The Evolutionary Origins of a Good Society* (New York: Little, Brown Spark, 2020).
21. Scott and Edmondson, "Unlocking Diversity's Promise."
22. John F. Kennedy, Moon Speech, Rice Stadium on September 12, 1962, accessed February 22, 2022, https://www.rev.com/blog/transcripts/john-f-kennedy -jfk-moon-speech-transcript-we-choose-to-go-to-the-moon#:~:text=We%20 chose%20to%20go%20to,we're%20willing%20to%20accept.
23. Kevin Jackson, "Malcolm Gladwell Talks Casuistry and Catholicism with the Hosts of *Jesuitical*," podcast, *America, Jesuit Review,* September 27, 2019, accessed February 22, 2022, https://www.americamagazine.org/faith/2019/09/27 /malcolm-gladwell-talks-casuistry-and-catholicism-hosts-jesuitical.
24. Anthony Ray Hinton, *The Sun Does Shine: How I Found Life, Freedom, and Justice* (New York: St. Martin's Griffin, 2019).
25. Isabel Wilkerson, *Caste: The Origins of Our Discontents* (New York: Random House, 2020).
26. Gordon Allport as quoted in Claude M. Steele, *Whistling Vivaldi: How Stereotypes Affect Us and What We Can Do* (New York: Norton, 2011).
27. Scott and Edmondson, "Unlocking Diversity's Promise."
28. Daniel Arce and Mary Gentile, "Giving Voice to Values as a Leverage Point in Business Ethics Education," *Journal of Business Ethics,* vol. 131, no. 3, 2015, pp. 535–542.

Chapter 11
1. Frederick Buechner, *Wishful Thinking: A Theological ABC* (New York: Collins, 1973).
2. Michael McCullough, *Beyond Revenge: The Evolution of the Forgiveness Instinct* (New York: Wiley, 2008).
3. Epictetus, "Epictetus Quotes," Goodreads, accessed February 13, 2022, https:// www.goodreads.com/author/quotes/13852.Epictetus.
4. Frederic Luskin as quoted in Amy Blaschka, "Here's What Science Says About Grudges—and Two Ways to Stop Them from Forming in the First Place," *Forbes,* May 21, 2019, accessed March 20, 2022, https://www.forbes.com/sites/amy blaschka/2019/05/21/heres-what-science-says-about-grudges-and-two-ways-to -stop-them-from-forming-in-the-first-place/?sh=3ac97caf6c7a.
5. Buddha, "Buddha Quotes," BrainyQuote, accessed February 22, 2022, https:// www.brainyquote.com/authors/buddha-quotes.
6. Mark Berman, "Gunman Shot Each Charleston Church Victim Multiple Times, Police Say," *Washington Post,* June 19, 2015, accessed February 22, 2022, https:// www.washingtonpost.com/news/post-nation/wp/2015/06/19/gunman-shot -each-charleston-church-victim-multiple-times-police-say.

7. Rasha Ali, "Five Years After Charleston Church Massacre: How 'Emanuel' Reveals the Power of Forgiveness," *USA Today*, June 17, 2019, accessed February 22, 2022, https://www.usatoday.com/story/life/movies/2019/06/17/emanuel-explores-power-forgiveness-after-charleston-church-massacre/1478473001.

8. Alex Harris, Frederic Luskin, Sonya Norman, et al., "Effects of a Group Forgiveness Intervention on Forgiveness, Perceived Stress, and Trait-Anger," *Journal of Clinical Psychology*, vol. 62, no. 6, June 2006, pp. 715–733.

9. McCullough, *Beyond Revenge*.

10. Harris, Luskin, Norman, et al., "Effects of a Group Forgiveness Intervention."

11. Tim Herrera, "Let Go of Your Grudges. They're Doing You No Good," *New York Times*, May 19, 2019, accessed February 22, 2022, https://www.nytimes.com/2019/05/19/smarter-living/let-go-of-your-grudgestheyre-doing-you-no-good.html.

12. Mahatma Gandhi, "Mahatma Gandhi Quotes," BrainyQuote, accessed February 13, 2022, https://www.brainyquote.com/authors/mahatma-gandhi-quotes.

13. John Braithwaite, "Restorative Justice and De-professionalization," *The Good Society*, vol. 13, no. 1, 2004, pp. 28–31.

14. Barbara Masekela, Nelson Mandela's chief of staff, Baldwin Wallace, Fall 2003 Kamm Lecture.

15. Personal interview with Peter Rea at West Point in December 2012.

16. Personal interview with Peter Rea at the Naval Academy in 2014.

17. Personal interview with Peter Rea at the Air Force Academy on April 4, 2013.

18. "The Power of Apologies," *Hidden Brain*, podcast, June 21 2021, accessed February 23, 2022, https://hiddenbrain.org/podcast/the-power-of-apologies.

19. Louis Newman, "The Refreshing Practice of Repentance," *On Being with Krista Tippett*, podcast, September 17, 2014, accessed February 23, 2022, https://onbeing.org/programs/louis-newman-the-refreshing-practice-of-repentance.

20. Daniel H. Pink, *The Power of Regret* (New York: Penguin, 2022).

Chapter 12

1. John Madden, "John Madden Quotes," BrainyQuote, accessed March 20, 2022, https://www.brainyquote.com/quotes/john_madden_158608.

2. Atul Gawande, "Want to Get Great at Something? Get a Coach," TED, April 2017, accessed February 23, 2022, https://www.ted.com/talks/ atul_gawande_want_to_get_great_at_something_get_a_coach.

3. MIT innovation program, January 2017.

4. Personal interview by Peter Rea at the Air Force Academy on April 4, 2013.

5. Information conveyed to Peter Rea during a personal tour of the Naval Base Coronado in California in March 2019.

6. Heraclitus, "Heraclitus Quotes," BrainyQuote, accessed March 20, 2022, https://www.brainyquote.com/authors/heraclitus-quotes.

7. David Dunning, "Why Incompetent People Think They're Amazing," TED, November 2017, accessed February 23, 2022, https://www.ted.com/talks/david_dunning_why_incompetent_people_think_they_re_amazing/transcript?language=en.

8. C. S. Lewis, "C. S. Lewis Quotes," Goodreads, accessed February 23, 2022, https://www.goodreads.com/quotes/7288468-humility-is-not-thinking-less-of-yourself-it-s-thinking-of.

9. Adapted from Michael B. Stanier, *The Coaching Habit: Say Less, Ask More & Change the Way You Lead Forever* (Toronto, ON: Box of Crayons Press, 2016).

10. Marcel Proust, "Marcel Proust Quotes," BrainyQuote, accessed February 23, 2022, https://www.brainyquote.com/authors/marcel-proust-quotes.

Chapter 13

1. Will Durant, "William Durant Quotes," BrainyQuote, accessed March 20, 2022, https://www.brainyquote.com/quotes/will_durant_145967.
2. Michael Pollan and Katherine May, "The Future of Hope," *On Being with Krista Tippett*, podcast, January 20, 2022.
3. Wendy Wood, *Good Habits, Bad Habits: The Science of Making Positive Changes That Stick* (London: Pan Macmillan, 2019).
4. Will Storr, "The Brain's Miracle Superpowers of Self-Improvement," *BBC Future*, November 24, 2015, accessed February 23, 2022, https://www.bbc.com/future/article/20151123-the-brains-miracle-superpowers-of-self-improvement.
5. Center for Humane Technology, *The Dark Side of Social Media*, infographic, https://www.humanetech.com/infographic-dark-side-social-media.
6. Deyan Georgiev, "How Much Time Does the Average American Spend on Their Phone in 2022?," *Techjury* blog, 2022, accessed February 23, 2022, https://techjury.net/blog/how-much-time-does-the-average-american-spend-on-their-phone.
7. Hilary Andersson, "Social Media Apps Are 'Deliberately' Addictive to Users," *BBC News*, July 4, 2018, accessed February 23, 2022, https://www.bbc.com/news/technology-44640959.
8. Nellie Bowles, "A Dark Consensus About Screens and Kids Begins to Emerge in Silicon Valley," *New York Times*, October 26, 2018, accessed February 23, 2022, https://www.nytimes.com/2018/10/26/style/phones-children-silicon-valley.html.
9. Angela Duckworth, "Need an Instagram Intervention," Character Lab, October 3, 2021.
10. Nir Eyal, *Indistractable: How to Control Your Attention and Choose Your Life* (Dallas, TX: BenBella Books, 2019).
11. Brian Resnick, "Why Willpower Is Overrated," *Vox*, January 2, 2020, accessed February 23, 2022. https://www.vox.com/science-and-health/2018/1/15/16863374/willpower-overrated-self-control-psychology.
12. Wilhelm Hofmann, Roy F. Baumeister, Georg Förster, and Kathleen D.Vohs, "Everyday Temptations: An Experience Sampling Study of Desire, Conflict, and Self-Control," *Journal of Personality and Social Psychology*, vol. 102, no. 6, June 2012, pp. 1318–1335, doi:10.1037/ a0026545.
13. Brian M. Galla and Angela L. Duckworth, "More Than Resisting Temptation: Beneficial Habits Mediate the Relationship Between Self-Control and Positive Life Outcomes," *Journal of Personality and Social Psychology*, vol. 109, no. 3, September 2015, pp. 508–525, doi:10.1037/ pspp0000026.
14. Kevin Roose, "Do Not Disturb: How I Ditched My Phone and Unbroke My Brain," *New York Times*, February 23, 2019, accessed February 23, 2022, https://www.nytimes.com/2019/02/23/business/cell-phone-addiction.html.
15. Doris Kearns Goodwin, "Lessons from Past Presidents," TED, February 2008, accessed February 23, 2022, https://www.ted.com/talks/doris_kearns_goodwin_lessons_from_past_presidents?language=en.
16. Anders Ericsson and Robert Pool, *Peak: Secrets from the New Science of Expertise* (Boston: Houghton Mifflin Harcourt, 2016); and personal interviews with by Peter Rea in 2017.
17. David Steindl-Rast, "Want to Be Happy? Be Grateful," TED, June 2013, accessed February 23, 2022, https://www.ted.com/talks/david_ steindl_rast_want_to_be _happy_be_grateful/transcript? language=en.

18. Nik Kinley and Shlomo Ben-Hur, "The Missing Piece in Employee Development," *MIT Sloan Management Review*, May 25, 2017, accessed February 23, 2022, https://sloanreview.mit.edu/article/the-missing-piece-in-employee-develop ment/.
19. Sophie Leroy, "Dr. Leroy's Words About Her Research on Attention Residue," University of Washington Bothell School of Business, accessed February 23, 2022, https://www.uwb.edu/business/faculty/sophie-leroy/attention-residue.
20. Laura Jonker, Marije T. Elferink-Gemser, Ilse M. de Roos, and Chris Visscher, "The Role of Reflection in Sport Expertise," *Sport Psychologist*, vol. 26, no. 2, 2012, pp. 224–242.
21. Stephen Batchelor, "Finding Ease in Aloneness," *On Being with Krista Tippett*, April 23, 2020, accessed February 23, 2022, https://onbeing.org/programs /stephen-batchelor-finding-ease-in-aloneness.
22. Wood, *Good Habits, Bad Habits*.

Chapter 14

1. Karen Armstrong, "Karen Armstrong Quotes," AZ Quotes, https://www .azquotes.com/quote/1332711.
2. Joseph Campbell with Bill Moyers, *The Power of Myth* (New York: Anchor Books, 1991).
3. Albert Einstein, "Albert Einstein Quotes," Goodreads, accessed February 27, 2022, https://www.goodreads.com/quotes/9109639-science-has-provided-the -possibility-of-liberation-for-human-beings.
4. Yuval Levin, *A Time to Build: From Family and Community to Congress and the Campus: How Recommitting to Our Institutions Can Revive the American Dream* (New York: Basic Books, 2020).
5. Peter J. Rea, James K. Stoller, and Alan Kolp, *Exception to the Rule: The Surprising Science of Character-Based Culture, Engagement, and Performance* (New York: McGraw Hill Professional, 2017).
6. Confucius, *Stanford Encyclopedia of Philosophy*, updated March 31, 2020, accessed February 27, 2022, https://plato.stanford.edu/entries/confucius.
7. Aran Ali, "The Soaring Value of Intangible Assets in the S&P 500," *Visual Capitalists*, November 12, 2020, accessed February 27, 2022, https://www.visualcapitalist .com/the-soaring-value-of-intangible-assets-in-the-sp-500.
8. Andy Walshe, CEO of Liminal Collective, personal interview with Peter Rea on December 6, 2021.
9. Coleman Ruiz, *What It's ACTUALLY Like on Deployment*, Mission Critical Team Institute, https://colemanruiz.com/2020/04/13/what-its-actually-like-on -deployment.
10. Preston Cline, Mission Critical Teams, Cleveland Learning Alliance, January 5, 2022.
11. Google, "Project Aristotle," *Re:Work*, Google blog, https://rework.withgoogle .com/print/guides/5721312655835136.
12. Amy C. Edmondson, *The Fearless Organization: Creating Psychological Safety in the Workplace for Learning, Innovation, and Growth* (Hoboken, NJ: Wiley, 2018).

Epilogue

1. Abraham Lincoln, "Abraham Lincoln Quotes," BrainyQuote, https://www .brainyquote.com/quotes/abraham_lincoln_161243.

2. Google, "Project Aristotle," *Re:Work*, Google blog, https://rework.withgoogle
.com/print/guides/5721312655835136.
3. Amy C. Edmondson, *The Fearless Organization: Creating Psychological Safety in the Workplace for Learning, Innovation, and Growth* (Hoboken, NJ: Wiley, 2018).
4. Plutarch, "Plutarch Quotes," BrainyQuote, accessed February 12, 2022, https://
www.brainyquote.com/authors/plutarch-quotes.

Index

A

AAR. *See* After action review
Adversity and crisis. *See also* Trauma
  benefit-finding exercise after, 119
  character building nature of, x, 1–6,
    8, 10–11, 37, 248–249, 261–262
  gratitude role in handling, 248
  hiring interview questions on, 69
  hope in face of, 40–41, 42
  as noncognitive factor of success, 12
  organization decentralization
    during, 242
  resilience in face of, 103–104, 108,
    111, 114–117
  service to others during, 114–115
  teamwork under, 10–11, 77
  virtue practiced during, x–xi, 17,
    52–53
Affluence, 8, 203, 266
African Americans. *See* Black people
After action review (AAR), 92, 97,
  98–100
Allport, Gordon, 186, 194–195, 201
Anger, 2, 35–36, 109, 200, 207–209,
  214–215, 247
Anxiety, 15–16, 96–97, 146–147
Apartheid, 40–41, 185–186
Areté (excellence), ix, 22, 262, 268
Aristotle, 7, 22, 23, 49–50, 235, 247,
  262, 266
Arrogance, 42, 97, 166, 223–225, 245
Asian Americans, 190–191

B

Barrett, Lisa Feldman, 150–151
Belonging, sense of, 131–134, 139–142,
  187, 192–197

Bias, 22, 67–69, 118, 187–190, 200
Black people, 3, 187, 190–193, 200–201.
  See also Apartheid
Bonanno, George, 112
Brain function. *See* Neurology

C

Calmness. *See* Temperance
Cannon, Walter, 105
Character, xii
  adversity building, x, 1–6, 8, 10–11,
    37, 248–249, 261–262
  affluence obstacle in building, 8
  coaching goal of, 221–222
  competence valued after, ix, 7, 60–62,
    166
  hiring consideration of, 60–64, 166
  kids taught to value, over
    achievement, 145–147
  noncognitive skills relation to, 11–12,
    63–64
  in teamwork and organizational
    culture, 10–11, 62–63
  wisdom around growth of, 37–38
Children and parenting. *See also*
  Schools
  character emphasis over achievement
    in, 145–147
  growth mindset and, 148–150
  learning patterns, recognition and
    reworking of, 150–153
  mistakes and failure acceptance for,
    148–149, 153, 159
  restorative practices around,
    156–158, 159
  swim buddy and trusted-advisor
    system for, 153–155

Children and parenting *(cont'd)*
  technology habits and, 236–238
  virtue self-assessment questions and, 121, 149–150, 267–268
Christakis, Nicholas, 21
Christensen, Clayton, 170, 183
Cleveland Clinic, 125–126, 138, 141, 143, 163, 173–174
Coaching
  arrogance-humility spectrum relation to, 223–225
  benefits of, 217–219
  challenges and obstacles, 219–220, 222–223
  defining role of, 220–221
  DE&I, 190–191
  empathy and, 77, 225
  features of effective, 84, 228–230
  goals of, 221–222
  habits creation with, 246
  military, 75–77, 218–219, 224
  noncognitive skills and, 221–222
  skills, 77, 225–228
  sports, 75–77, 217–218, 224, 246
Comfort, 13–14, 104, 105, 163, 238. *See also* Discomfort
Commitment. *See* Grit
Compassion
  catch phrase for, 55
  COVID-19 pandemic and, 29, 254
  engagement impacted by, 28, 29, 55, 127–128
  evolutionary theories and, 162–163
  innovation and, 164, 170, 172, 173–174, 183
  neurology of, 28, 107
  organizational culture and, 28, 234
  service to others over self with, 27–28, 43, 259
  trauma transformed with, 3–4
Competence, character over, ix, 7, 60–62, 166
Confucius, 22, 241, 258
Courage, 267
  catch phrase for, 55
  conditions for virtuous, 30
  of forgiveness, 36, 210
  grit relation to, 67
  hope relation to, 42, 44
  innovation and, 164, 167, 175, 178, 183
  lack of, demonstrations of, 44

  medical professional example of, 31–32
  neurology and hormones role in, 30–31
  under pressure, 33
  as relative to each person, 29, 43
  vulnerability role in, 32, 43, 230
COVID-19 pandemic, x, 169, 249
  compassion during, 29, 254
  human folly and successes during, 138–139, 252, 259
  job loss protection during, 125–126
  leaders response to, 116, 262–263
  medical professionals during, 125–126, 163, 173–174, 259, 261, 262–263
  resilience and, 103–104, 114–117
  virtue-based organizational culture during, 52–53
Crisis. *See* Adversity and crisis
Criticism, 130, 219–220
Culture. *See* Organizational culture

D

Darwin, Charles, 75, 162, 176
Day, Dorothy, 14, 115
Deci, Edward, 126
DE&I. *See* Diversity, equity, and inclusion
Discomfort, normalizing, x, 13–19
Diversity, equity, and inclusion (DE&I)
  advocate mindset in, 200–202
  anti-bias training around, 189–190
  contact hypothesis and, 186, 194–195
  cultural groupings and, 195–196
  empathy role in, 199–200
  explorer mindset in, 198–199
  in hiring, 192
  incarceration story about creating, 185–186
  psychological safety role in, 191, 196
  in schools, 200–201
  shared stories creating, 194–195
  short-term programs impact on, 188–189
  statistics on, 186–187
  stereotypes and, 186–187, 194, 201–202
  tools and trainings for, 189–192, 197–198, 203–205
Dodson, John, 15

Doudna, Jennifer, 49
Drucker, Peter, 91, 134–135, 161, 164, 242
Dweck, Carol, 66, 90, 147–149

E
Edmans, Alex, 25
Edmondson, Amy, 94
EDWINS, 1–3
Eger, Edith "Edie," 1, 3–6, 36–38, 110, 113, 116, 210
Einstein, Albert, 133, 253
Empathy
  as coaching skill, 77, 225
  DE&I and, 199–200
  impacts of practicing, 50, 117, 172
  incarceration stories and, 3–4, 185–186, 200
  PTG cultivation and, 113
Engagement
  compassion impact on, 28, 29, 55, 127–128
  deficit-based thinking obstacle for, 136–137
  definition and facts of, 128–131
  drivers of, 55, 65–66, 127–128, 132–133
  financial reward relation to, 126–127, 137–138
  job crafting and, 137–138, 140–143
  job loss protection example and, 125–126
  making a difference role in, 137–138, 140–143
  purpose clarity impacting, 78, 81, 86–89, 91, 127, 143, 171–175
  relevance and strengths-based approach in, 130–131, 134–137, 142
  remote-based work, 174
  sense of belonging and, 131–134, 139–140, 141–142, 187
  tools and conversation for increasing, 139–143
  in virtue-based organizational culture, 7, 8, 9, 55–56, 122, 138
Entitlement, 8, 115, 166, 200, 243, 245
Equity. See Diversity, equity, and inclusion
Ericsson, Anders, 242–243, 244
Erikson, Erik, 240–241

Ethics, 38–39, 260, 268
Excellence (areté), ix, 22, 262, 268

F
Failure. See Mistakes and failure
Fear, 2, 18, 19, 29–31
  of failure, 32–33, 76, 183
  innovation relation to, 32–33, 178–182, 183
  neurology of, 108–109, 247
  reality compared future imaginings, 84, 108–109, 110, 118
  selfishness reaction in, 114–115
  "worst case" questions in dealing with, 84, 118–119
Feedback, 69–70, 219
Financial success, 91, 172
  engagement relation to, 126–127, 137–138
  innovation and, 166–167, 181–182
  virtue-based organizational culture impact on, 28, 52–53
Fink, Laurence, 171–172
Force field analysis model, 50–51
Forgiveness, 122
  in face of injustice, 3–4, 35–36, 200, 208–209
  leaders skills in, 209–210
  neurology of, 214–215
  relationship restoration and, 36, 209–210, 213–214
  teamwork and, 209–211, 214
Frankl, Viktor, 5, 19, 42–43, 113
Friedman, Thomas, 101
Friedman Doctrine, 171

G
Gandhi, Mahatma, 36, 187, 193, 210
Gawande, Atul, 217–218
Genetics, 23, 49, 106
Gittell, Jody, 79–80
Giving nature and practice, 64–65, 71
Grant, Adam, 64, 146
Gratitude, 42, 65–66, 72, 242–249
Greeks, ancient, xiii, 222, 251, 270
  Aristotle, 7, 22, 23, 49–50, 235, 247, 262, 266
  on failure of will, 238
  on gratitude, 65
  virtues according to, ix, 22, 24, 103, 256–257

Grit, 67, 72, 132, 222
Growth mindset
  children taught to develop, 148–150
  goals viewed with, 90
  intelligence malleability and,
    147–148
  neuroplasticity relation to, 242
  "not yet" thinking with, 66, 91, 149
  research and example of, 56, 66–67
  resiliency and, 112, 114–115
  self-assessment of, 71–72
  wisdom relation to, 37–38
Grudges, 119, 207–210, 215, 245

H

Habits
  balanced life and, 240–241
  coaches role in creating, 246
  failure of will role in, 238–240
  forming, overview of, 233–235
  gratitude practice impact on, 65,
    242–249
  of innovation, 167–170
  multitasking, 39, 244
  neurology and, 23, 90, 105, 235–238,
    266–267
  self-reflection on, 246, 267–268
  technology-related, 39, 236–240, 244
  toolkit, 247–249
  virtue cultivated through, 6, 22–24,
    49–50, 167, 234, 236, 238–239,
    262, 266–268
Heckman, James, 11, 63
Hinton, Anthony Ray, 1, 3–4, 6, 19, 200
Hiring
  4Gs performance virtues
    consideration in, 63–67
  combating bias in, 67–69
  credentials and priorities, 59, 60–67,
    166
  DE&I considerations in, 192
  interview question examples, 68–69
Hispanic Americans, 187, 190–191
Hoban, Jack, 34
Holocaust, 1, 4–5, 19, 42, 113
Homeostasis, 104, 105, 163, 238
Ho'oponopono, 122
Hope, 267–268
  in adversity and crisis, 40–41, 42
  catch phrase for, 55
  courage relation to, 42, 44
  as engagement driver, 132–133
  gratitude relation to, 42
  innovation and, 164, 167
  lack of, impacts, 45
  learning and choosing, 41–43
  resilience and, 118
Humility, 7, 42, 97, 116, 139, 223–225,
  243, 245
Humphrey, Robert, 34–35

I

Incarcerated adults, 1–4, 156–157,
  185–186, 200
Inclusion. See Diversity, equity, and
  inclusion
Injustices, reaction to, 3–4, 8, 35–36,
  200, 208–209
Innovation
  compassion role in, 164, 170, 172,
    173–174, 183
  courage necessary for, 164, 167, 175,
    178, 183
  discovery characteristics and habits
    of, 167–170
  fear role in, 32–33, 178–182, 183
  financial ends and, 166–167, 181–182
  growth contrasted with operational
    structure for, 175–178
  hope and, 164, 167
  justice and, 164, 169, 172
  organizational culture and, 161–162,
    170–175
  restraints to, 162, 178–182
  risk consideration in, 164–166,
    178–182, 183
  social capital impact for, 170
  teamwork and, 162–163, 180–181
  temperance and, 164, 169
  training, 166–167
  trust role in, 163–164, 168, 169, 170
  VOCs and, 168, 179–180
  wisdom and, 164, 169
Intelligence, 37, 63–64, 145, 147–148, 155
Isaacson, Walter, 49

J

James, William, 22
Job crafting, 137–138, 140–143
Job loss, 115, 125–126
Job satisfaction, 126–127. See also
  Engagement

Judgment of others, 9, 10, 50
Justice, 44, 268
    catch phrase for, 55
    ego obstacles in, 33
    injustices response and, 3–4, 8,
        35–36, 200, 208–209
    innovation and, 164, 169, 172
    military approach to, 34–35,
        211–214
    restorative, 156–158, 159, 210–214

K

Kahneman, Daniel, 50, 133, 233–234
Kennedy, John F., 198–199
Kids. *See* Children and parenting;
    Schools
Kim, Jonny, 10–11
King, Martin Luther, Jr., 40, 145, 187,
    193

L

Leaders, 7, 29, 35
    COVID-19 response from, 116,
        262–263
    dark-triangle, 165–166
    feedback sought by, 69–70, 219
    forgiveness skills of, 209–210
    listening and inquiry skills for,
        86–87, 134
    Plato's Academy approach to, 24
    poll on qualities desired of, 132
    strengths-based approach of, 83–85,
        130–131, 134–136, 269
    trust in, 25–26, 97
    virtuous, xiii, 27, 53–54, 256–257
Lewin, Kurt, 50
Listening skills, 86–87, 134, 141,
    227–228
Logos-mythos thinking and tools,
    251–254, 257, 259, 268

M

Mandela, Nelson, 119, 185, 194, 211
Maslow, Abraham, 22
McKenzie, Lesley, 25–26
Medical professionals
    Cleveland Clinic, 125–126, 138, 141,
        143, 163, 173–174
    courage example, 31–32
    COVID-19 and, 125–126, 163,
        173–174, 259, 261, 262–263

deficit-based thinking obstacle for,
    136–137
engagement example with, 138
job crafting example of, 141, 143
listening skills of, 134, 141
teamwork approach and training for,
    80–82
Military, x, xi, 4, 7, 70, 91
    coaching, 75–77, 218–219, 224
    conflict deescalation training and,
        34–35
    justice approach in, 34–35, 211–214
    PTSD experience for, 111–112
    training approach for, 10–11, 34–35,
        38, 75–78
Mistakes and failure
    arrogance and, 224
    children taught to handle, 148–149,
        153, 159
    failure of will with habits and,
        238–240
    innovation and fear of, 32–33, 183
    learning from, 7, 65, 76, 105–106, 121
    "not yet" thinking about, 66, 91, 149
Motivation, 12, 39–40, 56, 94, 96–97,
    132
Multitasking, 39, 244
Mythos-logos thinking and tools,
    251–254, 257, 259, 268

N

Narcissism, x, 9, 127, 135, 165, 245, 259
NASA, 11, 38, 53, 260
Navy SEALs, 4, 10–11, 38, 75–77, 91
Neurology
    of anger and forgiveness, 214–215
    compassion and, 28, 107
    courage and, 30–31
    of criticism, 219–220
    of fear, 108–109, 247
    habits and, 23, 90, 105, 235–238,
        267–288
    of homeostasis, 104, 105, 163, 238
    hope and, 41
    of multitasking, 39, 244
    neuroplasticity, 23, 215, 233,
        235–238, 270
    of resilience, 105–106
    stress and, 106
Noncognitive skills, 11–12, 19, 63–64,
    221–222

O

Organizational culture
  assessment of, 47–48
  change obstacles and drivers in,
    50–52
  character impact on, 10–11, 62–63
  compassion and, 28, 234
  innovation and, 161–162, 170–175
  psychological safety in, 92, 94–97,
    99, 100
  pull rather than push strategy in, 51,
    54, 146, 258, 268–269
  purpose clarity and action role in, 78,
    81, 88–89, 91, 127, 143, 171–175
  trust role in, 49, 52, 54, 55
  virtue as metric in assessment of, 28,
    47–48, 53–54
  virtue-based, cultivation of, 7–8,
    48–49, 52–55, 57, 268–269
  virtue-based, engagement in, 7, 8, 9,
    55–56, 122, 138
  virtue-based, language around,
    54–55, 255–256, 262–263, 266

P

Parenting. *See* Children and parenting
Parker Hannifin, 8, 28, 128, 163, 234
Performance. *See specific topics*
Plato, 24, 238, 257
Post-traumatic growth (PTG), 19,
  112–113, 248
Post-traumatic stress disorder (PTSD),
  19, 110–111, 113
Pressure
  anxiety declining benefits of, 15–16
  courage under, 33
  default to training under, 38, 75–78,
    103, 120, 260
  leaning into discomfort of, 14–16
  resilience under, 106, 120
  self-discovery question on virtue in, 45
  sports, performing under, 14, 75–76,
    260
  temperance under, 38–39
  tools for dealing with, 17–18
Prisons. *See* Incarcerated adults
Pro-social behaviors, 17, 19, 21–22, 88,
  104, 118, 131
Psychological safety. *See* Safety
PTG. *See* Post-traumatic growth
PTSD. *See* Post-traumatic stress disorder

Purpose
  clarity and engagement around, 78,
    81, 88–89, 91, 127, 143, 171–175
  financial success and sense of, 91
  PTG cultivation and, 113

R

Relationships
  constructive over destructive
    communication in, 120
  focus on empowering, 121
  forgiveness in restoration of, 36,
    209–210, 213–214
  loneliness and lack of strong, 14
  priority, over performance, 265–266
  PTG cultivation and, 113
  resilience and role of, 104, 106,
    107–108, 118
  self-discovery question on virtue in, 45
  sports performance and, 12–13
  teamwork focus on building, 78,
    79–82, 88, 92, 94, 97, 101
  trauma survival relation to, 19, 111
  trust role in strong, 26, 43
  virtue cultivation impact on, 7–8
  well-being impacted by, 107, 266
Resilience
  benefit-finding exercise for, 119
  as coaching goal, 221–222
  during crisis and adversity, 103–104,
    108, 111, 114–117
  fear and, 108–109
  growth mindset role in, 112, 114–115
  neurology behind, 105–106
  under pressure, 106, 120
  reason factor in, 104, 109–110, 118
  regulation/feelings of safety role in,
    104, 105–106, 118
  relationships factor in, 104, 106,
    107–108, 118
  service to others role in, 110–111, 119
  stress, 110
  studies on human, 19
  tools for building, 118–122
  training, 103–104
  trauma and, 1–6, 19, 110–117, 118
Restorative practices, 156–158, 159,
  210–214
Risk, 18, 30, 32–33, 67, 164–166,
  178–182, 183
Robben Island prison, 185–186

Roof, Dylann, 208–209
Rumi, 9, 112–113

S
Safety, 242
  DE&I and psychological, 191, 196
  evolution and, 163
  neurology of fear and, 108–109, 247
  resilience relation to feelings of, 104,
    105–106, 118
  teamwork and psychological, 92,
    94–97, 99, 100, 262
Schools
  DE&I in, 200–201
  growth mindset in, 148
  kindness over metrics in, 22, 257–258
  restorative practices in, 156–158, 159
  student patterns in, 150–153
  virtues taught and studied in,
    145–147, 256–258
Self-discovery and self-assessments
  of 4Gs performance virtues, 71–73,
    149–150
  coaching promoting, 229
  on gratitude, 72
  on habits, 246, 267–268
  narcissism obstacle to, 9
  questions, 45, 121–122, 267–268
  teamwork and, 45, 93–96
  virtues, 23–24, 45, 71–73, 121–122,
    149–150, 267–268
Selfishness, 114–115, 162, 165–166
Seligman, Martin, 23, 41
Selye, Hans, 16
Service to others
  compassion and, 27–28, 43, 259
  crisis response and, 114–115
  obstacles to, 9–10, 13–14
  resilience relation to, 110–111, 119
  self-interest, x, 14, 171
  teamwork purpose clarity and, 88, 91
Singleton, Chris, 208–209
Smith, Adam, 171, 172
South African apartheid, 40–41,
    185–186
Spiegel, Elizabeth, 153
Sports
  coaching in, 75–77, 217–218, 224, 246
  performing under pressure in, 14,
    75–76, 260
  relationships role in success in, 12–13

  teamwork in, 12–13, 75–78
  trust cultivation in, 25–26
Stanier, Michael, 226
Staples, Brent, 200–201
Steele, Claude, 201
Stephenson, Bryan, 2, 4, 19
Stereotypes, 186–187, 194, 201–202
Stockdale, James, 108, 111
Strengths, leveraging, 78, 83–85, 94,
    130–131, 134–137, 142, 269
Stress, 16–19, 45, 106, 109–111, 113

T
Teachers. *See* Coaching; Schools;
  Training
Teamwork, 234
  AAR for, 92, 97, 98–100
  adversity experience and, 10–11, 77
  assessment tools, 82, 85, 87, 89, 92,
    95–96
  character role in, 10–11, 62–63
  chartering role in, 86
  DE&I example in, 203–205
  forgiveness skills and, 209–211, 214
  hiring interview questions on, 68
  innovation and, 162–163, 180–181
  job crafting applied in, 142–143
  medical professionals approach to,
    80–82
  Navy SEALs approach to, 10–11,
    75–78
  negotiation training for, 81
  psychological safety and, 92, 94–97,
    99, 100, 262
  purpose clarity and engagement for,
    78, 81, 86–89, 91, 173–175
  relationship building in, 78, 79–82,
    88, 92, 94, 97, 101
  results delivery in, 78, 90–92
  self-assessments around, 45, 93–96
  selfishness overcome by virtuous,
    165–166
  in sports, 12–13, 75–78
  strengths-based focus for, 78, 83–85,
    94, 130–131, 135–136
  survival relation to, 21
  team user manual, 92–94, 99
  trust building for, 76–79, 92–95, 97,
    99–100
Technology, 39, 49, 77, 138–139,
    236–240, 244, 251–253

Temperance, 268
  catch phrase for, 55
  innovation and, 164, 169
  lack of, impacts, 44
  in pressure response, 38–39
  remote-based work and, 169
  self-assessment of, 72
  with technology, 39, 236–240
  tools for practicing, 39–40
  training for, 38
Training
  anti-bias, 187, 188, 189–190, 200
  default to, under pressure, 38, 75–78,
    103, 120, 260
  DE&I, 189–192, 197–198, 203–205
  innovation, 166–167
  military, 10–11, 34–35, 38, 75–78
  NASA, 11, 38, 53, 260
  Navy SEALs teamwork, 10–11, 75–77
  negotiation, 81
  resilience, 103–104
  virtue, example of, 53–54
Trauma
  big *T* or small *t*, understanding,
    114–117
  compassion transforming, 3–4
  PTG and, 19, 112–113, 248
  PTSD, 19, 110–111, 113
  relationships role in dealing with,
    19, 111
  resiliency and, 1–6, 19, 110–117, 118
  self-discovery question on virtue in,
    45
Trust, 257, 267
  building and restoring, 26–27, 76–79,
    92–95, 97, 99–100, 157–158
  Edelman's Trust Barometer for
    measuring, 49
  as engagement driver, 55, 132
  innovation and, 163–164, 168, 169, 170
  in leaders, importance, 25–26, 97
  organizational culture and, 49, 52,
    54, 55
  performance relation to, evidence on,
    25–26
  relationship strength and, 26, 43

V
Values, 253–255
Victimhood, 5–6, 110, 210

Virtues, seven classical, xii, 8
  compassion as, 27–29, 43
  courage as, 29–33, 43–44
  history of, ix, 24
  hope as, 40–43, 44–45
  justice as, 33–36, 44
  temperance as, 38–40, 44
  trust as, 25–27, 43
  wisdom as, 36–38, 44
Virtue/virtues. *See also specific virtues
    and topics*
  4Gs performance, defining and
    recognizing, 63–67, 71–73,
    149–150
  ancient Greeks on, ix, 22, 24, 103,
    256–257
  deliberate practice of, x–xi, 17, 52–53,
    118, 266–268, 270
  habits role in cultivating, 6, 22–24,
    49–50, 167, 234, 236, 238–239,
    266–268
  imperfections mixed with, 9–10, 48,
    91, 128, 214, 259
  obstacles to practicing, 8, 9–10, 33
  in poll on qualities desired of leaders,
    132
  as priority before performance, x, 7,
    53, 60–61, 258–259
  self-assessment work on, 23–24,
    45, 71–73, 121–122, 149–150,
    267–268
  universal/cross-cultural nature of,
    8–9, 56, 203
  values relationship to,
    253–255
Voice of the customer (VOC), 53, 168,
  179–180, 181
Vulnerability, 26, 32, 43, 113, 224–225,
  230

W
White supremacy, 4, 200, 208–209
Wilson, E. O., 138, 162, 165–166,
  252
Wisdom, 36–38, 44, 55, 72, 164, 169,
  268

Y
Yerkes, Robert, 15

ABOUT THE AUTHORS

Peter Rea, PhD, is vice president of integrity and ethics at the Parker Hannifin Corporation. In 2012, Peter joined Parker in a newly established position with the purpose of preserving Parker's reputation and protecting its financial strength. Previously, Peter was the founding Burton D. Morgan Chair for Entrepreneurial Studies and the founding director of the Center for Innovation and Growth at Baldwin Wallace University. He chairs Ohio University Medical School's Advisory Board. He has lectured and consulted internationally in the areas of strategy, leadership, culture, and ethics defined as virtue.

———

James K. Stoller, MD, MS, is professor and chair of the Education Institute at Cleveland Clinic and a pulmonary and critical care physician in the Respiratory Institute there. He holds the Jean Wall Bennett Professorship in Emphysema Research and the Samson Global Leadership Academy Endowed Chair at Cleveland Clinic. He designed and has codirected the Cleveland Clinic Leading in Health Care course and the Samson Global Leadership Academy for Healthcare Executives at Cleveland Clinic. He also directs the American College of Chest Physicians Post-Graduate Course on Leadership, and he has directed the American Thoracic Society's Emerging Leadership Program. He has presented and consulted internationally regarding developing physician leaders at medical schools, business schools, and healthcare organizations.

———

Alan Kolp, PhD, is Faculty in Residence and previous holder of the Chair in Faith and Life at Baldwin Wallace University. Alan was the cofounder of the Center for Innovation and Growth at Baldwin Wallace University. Before coming to Baldwin Wallace, Alan was dean and professor at Earlham College and Earlham School of Religion in Richmond, Indiana. He spent a year in Germany on a Fulbright Fellowship and has taught in England. He has been a visiting scholar at the Graduate Theological Union, University of California at Berkeley, and at Kellogg College, Oxford University.

ALSO FROM THESE AUTHORS

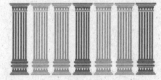

TITLE: EXCEPTION TO THE RULE
ISBN: 1260026833